SIGNS FROM
THE FUTURE

SIGNS FROM THE FUTURE

A PHILOSOPHY OF WARNINGS

SANTIAGO ZABALA

Columbia University Press   *New York*

Columbia University Press
Publishers Since 1893
New York   Chichester, West Sussex

Copyright © 2025 Columbia University Press
All rights reserved

Library of Congress Cataloging-in-Publication Data
Names: Zabala, Santiago, 1975– author
Title: Signs from the future : a philosophy of warnings / Santiago Zabala.
Description: New York : Columbia University Press, [2025] |
Includes bibliographical references and index.
Identifiers: LCCN 2025021617 (print) | LCCN 2025021618 (ebook) |
ISBN 9780231221726 hardback | ISBN 9780231221733 trade paperback |
ISBN 9780231563871 ebook
Subjects: LCSH: Warnings—Philosophy | Warnings—Political aspects |
Philosophy—Forecasting
Classification: LCC BD460.W37 Z33 2025 (print) | LCC BD460.W37 (ebook)

Cover design: Chang Jae Lee
Cover image: Graham Caldwell, *Compound Eye*

GPSR Authorized Representative: Easy Access System Europe,
Mustamäe tee 50, 10621 Tallinn, Estonia, gpsr.requests@easproject.com

CONTENTS

Preface vii

Introduction 1

I PHILOSOPHICAL WARNINGS 15

1 We Have Murdered God 19
2 Science Does Not Think 29
3 One Becomes a Woman 39
4 The Banality of Evil 51

II IGNORING WARNINGS 61

5 I'm Not a Keyboard Jihadi 85
6 There Is No Rush to Regulate AI 97
7 The "Don't Say Gay" Law 105
8 We Kill People Based on Metadata 113

III BEING WARNED 121

9 Compound Eye 125
10 Radical Listening 139
11 The Battle of Interpretation 151
12 Truth Is Not Enough 161

Afterword 171

Acknowledgments 177
Notes 179
Bibliography 221
Index 233

PREFACE

The image I have chosen as the cover image for this book is *Compound Eye*, a sculpture by the American artist Graham Caldwell; it's a fitting illustration of what warnings are as well as what constitutes them. The sculpture is composed of mirrors, similar to rearview mirrors in cars. As one walks toward *Compound Eye*, the horizon of what one sees through the mirrors widens, giving a feeling of pressure that calls for a response. The different sizes of the mirrors demand that we interpret what they reflect, as they reveal that they are never objective representations of reality. In this horizon, signals become signs, history turns into the past, and the future becomes what, in French, is meant by *avenir*, what is coming toward us. Caldwell's sculpture stresses these necessary differences to reveal warnings, and it works as a model we can use to think them through and become involved in them.

This book aims to think of philosophy as a warning, and its goal is to outline a "philosophy of warnings." Although no one has ever written a "philosophy of warnings," many philosophers have warned us about God, science, and many other concepts. But contrary to the philosophy of religion or the philosophy of science—which have become distinct subdisciplines—my philosophy of warnings does not pretend to expertise in the applications of the field, such as providing "warning studies" or "trigger warnings" with any particular skill or insight. Also, my interest is not to put forward a comprehensive warning philosophy—this would inevitably repeat the monological pattern of philosophical discourse; a single "philosophy of warning" would be a contradiction. Being warned is always an integral part of thinking. Philosophy is not meant to clarify other sciences' conceptual queries or ethical impasses using ontology or logic but rather to disclose fundamental queries and impasses—that is, to articulate the challenging questions that animate history. This is why the central question of this book is: Why don't we listen to warnings?

An invitation from the University of Turin to deliver a series of lectures in 2021 and several conferences in Europe, China, and the United States in the following years are at the origin of this book. In these lectures and seminars, I realized that my previous book's central idea—"the greatest emergency is the absence of emergency"—could also be referred to as a warning and an indication of a philosophy of warnings. While readers will judge whether I have achieved my goal of interpreting philosophy as a warning and disclosing its philosophical import, I hope the book will provide some insights into the meaning of warnings, especially since we rarely listen to them.

SIGNS FROM
THE FUTURE

INTRODUCTION

Signs from the future are not constitutive but regulative in the Kantian sense; their status is subjectively mediated; that is, they are not discernible from any neutral "objective" study of history, but only from an engaged position—following them involves an existential wager in Pascal's sense.

—Slavoj Žižek, *The Year of Dreaming Dangerously*

Greta Thunberg once told *Time* magazine that "it is possible to treat a crisis like a crisis, it is possible to put people's health above economic interests, and it is possible to listen to the science." With these statements the environmental activist was inviting us not simply to change but also to acknowledge that we have ceased to imagine these possibilities—that is, to interpret the events around us. This is particularly evident in the last example: listening to science. Why are we unable to listen to science when it warns us of climate change, biodiversity loss, and coming pandemics? The movie *Don't Look Up*—where two astronomers attempt to warn humanity about an approaching comet that will destroy human civilization—is an excellent example of our inability to listen to warnings. This inability is linked to our indifference toward warnings, those signs from the future that we have ceased to consider. What Thunberg demands from us is an "engaged position," an existential involvement with our future, as Slavoj Žižek suggests.[1]

The goal of this book is to outline a philosophy of warnings for the twenty-first century.[2] The ongoing global return to order through realism in philosophy, politics, and the increasingly narrow focus of experts has prevented us from taking warnings seriously. Too often these are disregarded as useless or insignificant—much like environmentalists, artists, and philosophers are discarded as—when in fact, they are vital to understanding our spiritual predicament. Although philosophers can't solve the ongoing emergencies—philosophy was never meant to solve anything—we can interpret their signs. "A sign," as Umberto Eco points out, "is not only something which stands for something else; it is also something that can and must be interpreted."[3]

Warnings—not to be confused with predictions—are not meant to convince anyone but instead invite us to reevaluate our priorities for the future. Unlike recent philosophies of animals, plants, or insects, my philosophy of warnings is more than a philosophical elucidation of a global environmental emergency. It is the ontology within which these issues exist. Phenomenologically, we could say that these reacting philosophies are regional ontologies whereas mine is the fundamental philosophy that encompasses all of them. Warnings allow us to think transcendentally without losing sight of actual politically, socially, and technologically urgent matters.

Although the COVID-19 pandemic triggered this new fundamental stance, the philosophy of warnings is not limited to this pandemic or other specific, ongoing global emergencies. Nor is it completely new. Like animals, plants, and insects, warnings have been a topic of philosophical investigation for centuries.[4] The difference lies in the meaning they have acquired now. As Richard Rorty would say, we once had prophets to tell us to be alert to the warnings of the gods, but we secularized that office into that of the philosopher, who, as one among equals, advised us to use our imagination, to interpret signs, because those are all we get. The pandemic has shown how little prepared we were for a global emergency, even one whose coming had been announced for decades by scientists and urban theorists, among others. But why haven't we been able to take these warnings seriously, and how can we begin to address them adequately in the future?

The three parts that constitute this book are not simply meant to respond to these questions by articulating the philosophical meaning of warnings in the twenty-first century. They also show that *philosophy is a warning*. The ontological approach that distinguishes philosophy from other disciplines both addresses problems from a global perspective and also warns us of other disciplines' narrow focus. "This word Being," as Martin Heidegger once said, "serves as a warning to us," a warning that reality is not made merely of beings and that its truth is not exclusively what can be measured or verified. This is also the meaning behind the theses of Michel Foucault ("our society is one not of spectacle, but of surveillance"), Judith Butler ("gender is performative"), and Donna Haraway ("technology is not neutral").[5] These philosophers invite us to think beyond traditional paradigms of politics, nature, and science but also warn us of what might happen if we do not or cannot. It should not come as a surprise that warnings can be traced back to Greek mythology, Confucianism, and Plato's *Apology*.

Apollo, for example, provided Cassandra with the gift of prophecy even though she could not convince others of the validity of her predictions. Parmenides warned against following the path of nonbeing, for nonbeing, he said, cannot even be thought. And Socrates warned the Athenians—after he was sentenced to death—that their inequity and mendacity undermined the democracy they claimed to honor. Augustine, in *De doctrina Christiana*, warned that some expressions in the Bible had to be taken figuratively and not literally. Confucian thinkers have warned that positive emotions like freedom, joy, and happiness can turn into distortions of the world and the self. Tung Chung-shu interpreted natural disasters as warning signs that rulers must avoid abusing their powers and cultivate virtues; Francis Bacon warned that "nature [cannot] be commanded except by being obeyed"; and Thomas Hobbes warned that *"auctoritas non veritas facit legem,"* "authority, not truth, makes the law." Immanuel Kant warned that ideas of reason should not be used dogmatically to speculate about the intelligible world but regulatively to systematize our experience of the phenomenal world as nature is "the text of our interpretation."[6]

More than a century ago, Nietzsche warned us how the "scope and tower-building of the sciences has grown to be enormous, and with this also the probability that the philosopher grows weary while still learning or allows himself to be detained somewhere to become a 'specialist'—so he never attains his proper level, the height for a comprehensive look, for looking around, for looking *down*." Against Gaston Bachelard, who coined the term "Cassandra complex" to refer to the idea that events could be known in advance, Theodore Adorno warned that any claim to know the future should be avoided, as Hegel had already anticipated. Against the dangers of reifying and objectifying the mathematical models that operate at the heart of our physical theories, Edmund Husserl warned that a crisis was threatening the European tradition of reason and philosophical inquiry. It is probably in this spirit that Walter Benjamin warned we should pull the brake on the "storm of progress" and Herbert Marcuse of the dehumanizing effects of mass society, consumerism, and technology as they were stacking disaster upon disaster.[7]

After Frantz Fanon warned that colonialism infects history, wounding the colonized and colonizer, and after Edward Said told us to be suspicious of "false universals," Zygmunt Bauman recalled that every time the modernist dream embraces power, "genocide follows." This is probably why Alain Badiou warned of the totalitarian danger of enforcing a truth on a situation as it ignores the nameless, which resists being subsumed under a truth-procedure. This is the spirit that probably led Manfred Stanley in the 1970s to warn against the rise of "technicism" in interpreting human actions and motivations and, in 1974, Francoise d'Eaubonne to coin the term "ecofeminism" to warn us that humanity will not survive the ecological consequences of patriarchy as overpopulation and the destruction of resources will inevitably create an unsustainable condition. This condition—as the philosopher Kyle Whyte explained—is particularly evident among Indigenous communities, which are more vulnerable to climate change because of colonialism. "It may be too late, he warned, to achieve environmental justice for some Indigenous peoples, and other groups, in terms of avoiding dangerous climate change." When Michel Foucault was asked whether "the role of philosophy is to warn of the dangers of power," his response was upfront: "This has always been an important function of philosophy. In its critical aspect—and I mean critical in a broad sense—philosophy is that which calls into question domination at every level and in every form in which it exists, whether political, economic, sexual, institutional, or what have you."[8]

This call is evident in John Dewey, who warned of the political consequences of funding narrow vocational education "for the few economically able to enjoy it, and would give to the masses a narrow technical trade education for specialized callings, carried on under the control of others," and also in the work of sociologists and economists such as Max Weber and Thomas Piketty. Weber warned that the outstanding achievements of contractual freedom create opportunities to exploit property ownership as a means to "the achievement of power over others," and Piketty believes that "market economy . . . if left to itself . . . contains powerful forces of divergence, which are potentially threatening to democratic societies and to the values of social justice on which they are based." More recently, the philosopher Justin E. H. Smith warned that too many people ignore the fact that the internet "is essentially a privately owned point-scoring video game," treating it "as if it were the public sphere. This has led to an absurd predicament for the good-faith actors and a luscious opportunity for the bad-faith ones."[9] Giorgio Agamben began his controversial book on the COVID-19 pandemic—*Where Are We Now: The Epidemic as Politics*—with "A Warning": Biosecurity will now serve the overwhelming power of governments through a new form of tyranny called "technological-sanitary" despotism. As he specifies:

> We can use the term "biosecurity" to describe the government apparatus that consists of this new religion of health, conjoined with the state power and its state of exception—an apparatus that is probably the most efficient of this kind that Western history has ever known. Experience has in fact shown that, once a health threat is in place, people are willing to accept limitations on their freedom that they would never theretofore have considered

enduring—not even during the two world wars, nor under totalitarian dictatorships.[10]

Several philosophers critically responded to Agamben: Jean-Luc Nancy, for example, believes attacking governments during the pandemic was more like a "diversionary manoeuvre than a political reflection." Žižek, who also dismissed a reading of the pandemic in the lines of a biopolitical state of exception, preferred to warn us of the "new forms of class struggle" that will be intensified by the lockdowns, and Bruno Latour directly interpreted the pandemic as a warning: "It would be a mistake to believe that the pandemic is a crisis that will end, instead of the perfect warning for what is coming, what I call the new climatic regime."[11] Despite Agamben's polemical thesis, what is important for my argument is that his book points out our inability to listen to warnings.

The translator or publisher of Agamben's book translated the heading of a piece of the front matter, *"Avvertenza,"* as the "Foreword" instead of as "Warning," which would be the literal translation. The same translation appeared in the second updated edition. Given that Italian uses the same word—*prefazione*—for both "preface" and "foreword," there could be three reasons for this change: the translator's interpretation, the publisher's style, or even an error in the Italian original. This last reason is quite unlikely, considering the book aimed to warn of a "great transformation" of "governance" that "operates through the introduction of a sanitation terror and a religion of health." Also, given that *Homo Sacer* and *State of Exception*, two of Agamben's most celebrated books, are meant to warn us against the effects of sovereign power on life, namely, that they function by integrating bare life as the focal point of the legal order and create a permanent state of exception, warnings have been a constant in his oeuvre. Regardless of the reasons for this change or error on the part of the translator and publisher, it must be interpreted as a symptom of what my book claims: that we don't listen to warnings.[12]

These examples and the works of the four philosophers that I examine in part 1—Nietzsche, Heidegger, Simone de Beauvoir, and Hannah Arendt—not only reveal that philosophy can be intended as a warning but also illustrate the difference between warnings and predictions. Predictions call out what will take place regardless of our actions, a future as the only possible continuation of the present. Warnings instead point toward what is to come and are meant to involve us in the possibility of a radical break, a discontinuity with the present signaled by alarming signs that we are asked to confront.

Whereas predictions belong to the domain of futurology—where the future is forecast from the present trends in society—warnings are hermeneutical; that is, they strive to change the future by reinterpreting the past. This is why in order to "change our future," as Žižek explains, "we should first (not 'understand' but) change our past, reinterpret it in such a way that it opens up toward a different future from the one implied by the predominant vision of the past."[13] Warnings are sustained by signs that request our involvement for a different future. A "warning," as Jane Anna Gordon and Lewis R. Gordon point out, suggests "that there is something one could do";[14] that is, that there is always an alternative to the present. The problem is not only whether we accept the involvement that warnings request from us but also whether we are willing to confront them at all. Our inability to accept this involvement was particularly evident with the COVID-19 pandemic.

Although the origin of the pandemic is rooted in our industrial and economic system (growth at all costs, especially at the expense of the environment, and extractive, wealth-concentrating capitalism draped in the robes of globalization), its spread can be laid at the feet of those who failed to acknowledge the gravity of the emergency. Another way to say this is that they are the ones who were incapable of accepting the involvement that years of warnings sought to ready us for. If emergencies come about when warnings are ignored, then it is necessary to take a step back and question the hierarchy of emergencies at a time when crisis follows crisis but none unsettles the grip of oppressive power over the people of the world.

Our "greatest emergency" has become the "absence of emergency." This does not entail, for example, that the coronavirus was not a fundamental emergency that we should have confronted at all levels. It simply suggests that the greatest emergencies are the ones we do not confront—the suppressed crises that led to the pandemic but also the ones still concealed in and by the globally dominant governments' and corporations' responses to the pandemic, the volume of vital warnings that we still ignore in terms of climate change, biodiversity loss, and coming wars. But why aren't we listening? How can we prevent the warnings we ignore from becoming emergencies that we have to confront abruptly? The answer to this question does not rest only in governments' inability to confront those absent emergencies or complicity in absenting them but most of all in our inability to heed these absent emergencies. At this point, it becomes clear that another term for "absent emergencies" is "warnings."

As I will show in part 2, contemporary indifference toward warnings is rooted in the ongoing global return to order through realism in the twenty-first century. This return is not only political, as demonstrated by the various right-wing populist forces that have taken office worldwide, but also cultural, as shown by the return of some intellectuals to Eurocentric Cartesian realism. The idea that we can still claim access to truth without being dependent upon interpretation presupposes that knowledge of objective facts is enough to guide our lives. Within this transparent realism, warnings are cast off as unfounded, contingent, and subjective, even though philosophers and historians of science such as Bruno Latour and Naomi Oreskes continue to remind us that no "attested knowledge can stand on its own" because only "the social character of scientific knowledge makes it trustworthy."[15] What "realism offers as a modality," as Amanda Boetzkes points out, "is a sphere of *experience without authority*":

> Otherwise put, realism proffers a sensation of what cannot be subsumed into disciplinary thinking, even philosophy. It is a mediation of what is unmediated about reality. . . . Realism without authority suggests the possibility that there is an alternative play of the senses with reality than that which is put into action by both the scientific method and the political sphere. It recuperates a (perhaps) utopian version of Kant's Sensus Communis insofar as it seeks recourse to the collective deliberation over the interpretation of the sense of reality. It also presumes that such sense can be retrieved "freely." Such a challenge discloses what is "unrealistic" about realism.[16]

The internet and, in particular, social media, as Stanley Fish points out, have intensified this realism without authority, further discrediting traditional vectors of legitimation (international agencies, major newspapers, credentialed academics) and rendering any social media platform or tweet by an anonymous blogger credible because it presents itself as transparent, direct, and genuine. This rejection of interpretation is weaponized by forces of capital and power in the increased demand for "referendums" or "direct democracy" in the West. Antivaccine movements, the Brexit referendum, and the lies about the outcomes of presidential elections that led to the storming of the US Capitol and Brazilian Congress all grow out of a manipulation of realism to reject collaborative, communal facts arrived at through interpretation. Judith Butler is right when she affirms that "we are living in anti-intellectual times, and . . . this is evident across the political spectrum. The quickness of social media allows for forms of vitriol that do not exactly support thoughtful debate."[17] Transparent realism, divorced from communal authority, not only promotes fake news through antiestablishment and anti-intellectual stances but also discredits the existential involvement that warnings request from us.

As I explain in part 3, the central argument in favor of a philosophy of warnings is not that what it warns of comes to pass but rather the intensity and pressure it exercises against those emergencies hidden and subsumed under the global call to order through realism. This pressure demands that our environmental, social, and political priorities be reconsidered, revealing the alarming signs of climate crisis, democratic backsliding, and the commodification of our lives by surveillance capitalism. These warnings are also why we should oppose any demand to "return to normalcy" after an emergency, which signals primarily a desire to ignore what caused the emergency in the first place. A philosophy of warnings seeks to alter and interrupt the reality we've become accustomed to through an alternative horizon of understanding (where listening and interpretation play a crucial role) that is respondent to warnings. This response is not conditioned by the evidence of truth as much as by the intensity and pressure it exercises, in other words, by the effects it has.

Thunberg's environmental activism will be interpreted as a sign from the future that we must listen to and interpret, that is, engage existentially. The primary justification for choosing this example is not simply linked to the environmental issues it raises but to show that truth is not enough for "Being warned."[18] The consequences of scientific, economic, or political warnings or predictions upon the population will depend on their intensity, not their truth. The difference, for example, between Banksy's *Devolved Parliament*—where British MPs in the House of Commons are depicted as chimpanzees—and the latest editorial on British political deadlock is not one of kind but rather of degree, intensity, and depth. Editorials by respected political analysts can be truthful, but they are rarely as powerful as a painting by Banksy. Although this power is more common in art, it also occurs in activism, as Thunberg has demonstrated.[19] How is it possible that her activism mobilizes more people than the words of the climate scientist James Hansen or the investigative journalist Naomi Klein? It is because truth is not exclusively a matter of knowledge and information but also involves senses and feelings vital to accepting the intensity and pressure of warnings.

As an ontological interpretation of those "signs from the future" that we constantly ignore, the philosophy of warnings will not prevent future emergencies but will resist the continued absencing of emergencies by thrusting us into crises hidden and subsumed under the global call to order through realism. Interpreting these warnings from the future—that is, giving voice to the warnings that are drowned out by "the real" and "the normal"—challenges our framed global order and its advocates in order to allow us to ponder signs and the future at large. In sum, the philosophy of warning is not meant to rescue us from emergencies but rather to rescue us into emergencies by interpreting, listening, and pressuring. Similar to Bernard Stiegler's "epoch of the absence of epoch,"[20] the absence of emergency has become the greatest danger we face today, signaling the abandonment of the interpretative nature of existence in favor of the return to order, realism, and right-wing populism—a move that supports only the status quo and the ability of global power to maintain its grip. Against this grip, this book's afterword will attempt to envision a politics of warnings.

I

PHILOSOPHICAL WARNINGS

Warning is a form of preserving us from something. There speaks in the warning a call to be careful, to have a care for something.
—Martin Heidegger, *What Is Called Thinking?*

P hilosophy is a warning, a warning meant to respond to threatening signs from the future. But this response also demands that we care for something; heeding a warning implies a relation of care. This is why warnings, unlike predictions, are also calls to take a stance for an alteration that could improve the future. The future of predictions is different from that of warnings, as demonstrated by the different meanings of *future* and *avenir* in French. The former refers to what will take place after the present, as something programmable, but *avenir* points toward what is to-come (*a venir*), an alteration or disturbance that is unpredictable. A similar distinction is found in German between history as *vergangen* and as *gewesen*. Whereas in the former the past becomes an irrevocable necessity we must submit to, the latter means accepting history as open to the future, as a having-been that still offers the possibility of freely deciding our lives without being encapsulated in a true knowledge. Warnings imply the possibility of alteration. But there is no need for us to change anything in the face of predictions because the inevitable outcome they anticipate demands only our submission. This is why predictions can't take into account such historical events as revolts, emergencies, or tragedies, which can only be interpreted once they occur. Warnings are meant to involve us in these events through care.

If through the history of their discipline philosophers have often been suspicious of the future of predictions, it's not because they had an alternative to propose but rather because of the absence of inquiry or dialogue that prediction presupposed. This is probably why from philosophy's inception in Greece dialogue has always been central among philosophers. In order to care for something, there must be a relation where warnings—as in the Socratic inquires and dialogues—prevail over truth, predictions, and answers. This relation elevates the difference between warnings and predictions from a theoretical to an existential affair because the salvation of those we care about is at stake.

As many readers must have noticed, chapters in this first part are titled after famous statements by philosophers—namely, Friedrich Nietzsche, Martin Heidegger, Simone de Beauvoir, and Hannah Arendt—regarding the meaning of God, science, gender, and evil. My goal is not only to interpret them as philosophical warnings but also to show that their theses were calls to alter the future. The prophetic nature of these authors' thought, as in that of the prophets of scripture, consists primarily in showing the meaning of the past and the present in relation to what will come. It is interesting to note that this prophetic feature is common to many thinkers after Hegel: Kierkegaard imagined a new era where philosophy would be destroyed by religion; Feuerbach, where it will resolve in politics; and Heidegger, where it will be replaced by technological calculation. These prophecies and warnings, as we will see, were meant to distance us from a future founded on knowledge, rationality, and progress. But how can we distinguish between philosophers who predict and those who warn us?

The difference parallels the divide between foundational and nonfoundational philosophical stances. The former relies on the future's inevitability through a determinist planning, where subject, object, and language are rigidly separated from one another. The latter hopes to alter the future by interpreting its signs independently of this separation. This metaphysical separation—as exemplified by Descartes's clear and distinct ideas or Kant's a priori truths—are attempts to escape the existence, difference, and the contingency of the subject that Herbert Marcuse, Cornelius Castoriadis, and Catherine Malabou, for example, consider vital. Contemporary versions of transcendentalism, materialism, and new realism are attempts to salvage a relation with a metaphysical realm that has been abandoned by post-Kantian thinkers. The problem with foundational stances such as these is not only that they tend to predict the future from a position independent from our lives, society, and tradition but also that they narrow philosophy's global approach. This is particularly evident in the excessive departmentalization, specialization, and fragmentation of philosophy when it submits to science and its methods. The global approach, also referred to as the "big picture," is vital for warnings to emerge because they rely on engaged interpretations.

It is important to remember that warnings, unlike predictions, are weak, vague, and subtle statements in the form of announcements that are often ignored. This is why they can only be understood through interpretation, that is, an involvement that concerns our existence rather than an objective representation in the mind. Referring to them as *signs from the future* is a way of recalling such weakness, in other words, their nonfoundationalism. Although warnings are more manifest among nonfoundational or postmetaphysical philosophers, they can also be found in foundational thinkers: They have always been a central feature of philosophy. Exploring the warnings of Nietzsche, Heidegger, de Beauvoir, and Arendt reveals a weak glimpse of the future (as *avenir*) that is coming. This future demands our involvement because this is an existential affair; that is, our salvation is at stake.

1

WE HAVE MURDERED GOD

Friedrich Nietzsche is the paradigmatic example of a philosopher linked to a single pronouncement. References to his statement that "God is dead, and we have killed him" can be found in novels, movies, and TV series. For example, his philosophy is present throughout the third season of *The Sinner* and in an episode of *The Sopranos*, where young AJ corrects Tony Soprano over the wording of the formulation: "It's not 'no God,' but 'God is dead.'"[1] Nietzsche has been presented as a "philosopher of life," the "last metaphysician," and as an "anti-transcendental thinker." This is a consequence of his revolutionary ideas and style.

It is also fair to refer to him as one of the first "philosophers of warnings." This is particularly evident in his pronouncement that "God is dead, and we have killed him," made in the third book of *The Gay Science*, published in 1882. Before venturing into the meaning of Nietzsche's warning, it is necessary to briefly recall that the death of God had already been put forward by other thinkers before him.

Although the exact formulation "God is dead" or "God has died" does not appear in Luther's published hymns, as Hegel believed, it did arise in the context of Lutheran theology as an adaptation of a Catholic chorale that can be traced back to 1628. Later Pascal, in his *Pensées* of 1670, cites Plutarch's "Le grand Pan est mort." From a philosophical point of view, according to Heinrich Heine, it is Immanuel Kant who first thought of God death's when he dismissed him from the domain of knowledge through the sharp division between things as they appear to us and things as they are in themselves. If, as he explained in the *Critique of Pure Reason*, we can have knowledge only of what is given to us in the former, that is, through experience, then God can only be a regulative idea as it isn't part of our sense of experience. The specific phrase "God is dead" in philosophy was first used by Hegel. In the *Phenomenology of Sprit* he refers to "the grief which expresses itself in the hard saying that 'God is dead,'" and in an earlier essay, "Faith and Knowledge," he designates this grief as the feeling "upon which the religion of more recent times rests." The fact that Nietzsche, in a note from 1870, stated that "I believe in the ancient German saying: all gods must die" is an indication he was probably familiar with God's mortality as expressed by these thinkers.

And so "God is dead" is not Nietzsche's finding but rather a metaphor that has its roots in Lutheran theology and European philosophy.[2] This tradition can also be described as hermeneutical, that is, belonging to the interpretation of sacred, juridical, and literary texts, whose origins can be traced back to Plato. It is this tradition that equipped Nietzsche to suggest that the "same text allows of countless interpretations" and that "there are no facts, but only interpretations." Events, as he explained, are only "a group of phenomena selected and synthesized by an interpreting being." In order to understand the "death of God" as a warning, it is important to properly situate the German thinker within the hermeneutic tradition, given the variety of interpretations his writings generated. This will enable us not only to contextualize his warning but also to begin to unravel the origins of our "philosophy of warnings" and its postmetaphysical nature.

Nietzsche, along with Karl Marx and Sigmund Freud, belongs to a group of late modern thinkers who advanced a "hermeneutics of suspicion" against traditional values. Their work inspired a number of movements, from poststructuralism to critical theory, among others. Their overall goal was to disclose the false consciousness beneath conventional philosophical ideas, religious beliefs, and political ideals associated with the modern metaphysical tradition inaugurated by Descartes. In this tradition, subjectivity was considered as a simple self-evident "given" that allowed us to doubt how things appeared. But if things are not as they appear, what about consciousness? Is consciousness also as it appears to itself? As Paul Ricoeur explained, the problem with this approach is that "meaning" and "consciousness of meaning" coincide, rending the subject undoubtable. Against this false consciousness Marx suspected that meanings were a manifestation of a subterranean class interest; Freud, of the unconscious; and Nietzsche, of the will to power.

In order to disclose these manifestations, Marx, Nietzsche, and Freud practiced a radical demythification through interpretation. This is an intellectual stance that brings to light the hidden significance of a phenomenon but that also aims toward an emancipation of knowledge. In Marx the practice of demythification aimed at reestablishing communication in real life so that authentic communication and emancipation could coincide. Freud instead pointed toward the acceptance of the anthropological limitations of an individual's will to know, in other words, that knowledge never comes to a complete reflective transparency. Both viewed tradition and knowledge as vested with ideologies and interests that had to be demythified in order for emancipation to occur. Nietzsche went further.

As the titles of some of his books reveal—*Human, All Too Human* (1878), *Twilight of the Idols* (1889), and *On the Genealogy of Morals* (1887) among others—his intention was to uncover the "instinctive" roots not only of ethics but also of religion, science, and philosophy. He believed that the "greater part of conscious thinking must still be included among instinctive activities, and that goes even for philosophical thinking." And science, which at first appears as the most neutral activity, operates in part voluntarily and in part involuntarily "because, being alive, it loves life." However, demythification for Nietzsche was meant to unravel not only a sort of unchanging natural force upon which these activities operate through systems but also the same notions of "real world," "facts," and "truth" that could justify them.

"To shake 'belief' in truth" ought to be our goal since religion, science, and philosophy do not "tell the truth," in the sense of informing us of how the "real world" is. Although philosophy has always advanced by suggesting new ways to understand reality, Nietzsche believes this was done only to provide a reassuring foundation to confront the uncertainty and mutability of the physical world. The various contrapositions of the "true" or "supersensory" world (Platonic Ideals, the Christian afterlife, or Enlightenment rationalism) to the sensory or apparent world (chairs, mountains, or the material world in general) end up revealing that truth was always only a fiction or fable generated to help us withstand determinate existential conditions. And for Nietzsche, not only does the real world of traditional metaphysics and its truth become fable but the distinction between truth and falsehood itself is also only a belief in evidentness. But why must one prefer evidentness to nonevidentness? Why is it better not to be deceived than to be deceived?

Descartes and the Western metaphysical tradition did not inquire into these matters out of a "moral prejudice," not because it lacked "objective import." The fact that scientists and philosophers find certain "truths" evident does not depend on nature, instincts, or truth but rather on their belonging to a certain epoch and community. Within these communities, "certain evident truths" have become essential for the maintenance of a certain type of life. Truth, therefore, as Nietzsche explains in *The Will to Power* (1901), "does not necessarily denote the antithesis of error, but in the most fundamental cases only the posture of various errors in relation to one another. Perhaps one is older, more profound than another, even ineradicable, in so far as an organic entity of our species could not live without it."[3] God is another word for truth.

As a warning, the death of God is meant to involve us in an event that has already occurred but that we are unprepared to understand and accept. This event is the advent of nihilism, where the "highest values devalue themselves" and where "the goal is missing; the answer to 'why' is missing." These highest values—ideals, foundational precepts, and, in particular, the supersensory world as the world that truly is, that is, God—are devalued once we understand that they were never going to be realized within the real world. Nihilism, as a historical movement, dominated previous centuries, but it is determinant of the current one. In order to proclaim this warning, Nietzsche envisaged a madman who lights a lantern in broad daylight and runs to the marketplace crying persistently, "I'm looking for God! I'm looking for God!"

> Since many of who did not believe in God were standing around together just then, he caused great laughter. Has he been lost, then? asked one. Did he lose his way like a child? asked

another. . . . Thus they shouted and laughed, one interrupting the other. The madman jumped into their midst and pierced them with his eyes. "Where is God?" he cried; "I'll tell you! We have killed him—you and I! We are all his murderers. But how did we do this? . . . Do we still hear nothing of the noise of the gravediggers who are burying God? . . . *God remains dead! And we have killed him!* How can we console ourselves, the murders of all murderers! . . . Here the madman fell silent and looked again at his listeners; they too were silent and looked at him disconcertedly. Finally he threw his lantern on the ground so that it broke into pieces and went out. "I come too early," he then said; "my time is not yet. This tremendous event is still on its way, wandering; it has not yet reached the ears of men."[4]

In this famous passage there are several indications that "the death of God" can be interpreted as a warning. Among the most evident ones is the laughter the madman causes among the crowd at the market. His warning is not taken seriously. They ask whether he has lost "his way like a child." But warnings are not objective descriptions that we can clearly represent in the mind; they are subtle, vague, and weak announcements that are often dismissed or ignored. Thus "God is dead, and we have killed him!" is not a prediction that calls out what will take place regardless of our involvement but instead is meant to implicate us in the possibility of a radical break with the present, signaled by alarming signs that we are asked to confront. These alarming signs are both the "death of God," which clearly we are still unable to understand, and also the fact that we are responsible for this death, that is, "the murderers of all murderers!" Also, the fact that the madman is trying to involve the crowd in an event that seems threatening—the fact that they killed God—shows how he cares for them.

Nietzsche's pronouncement was not meant to proclaim, as many believe, a naïve atheism meant to underline the process of secularization, in the sociological meaning of the word, or point out that we have finally perceived with clarity that "objectively" God does not exist. These would not be consistent with Nietzsche's project of hermeneutical demystification.[5] His goal was to warn us about a course of events in which we are not only involved but also responsible. If humanity started to believe in God to protect itself against the dangers of natural life, then the secure world of science and technology we have constructed render him obsolete. His reassurances are no longer necessary now that we can live without the terror felt by primitive mankind. This anthropological interpretation reveals how the death of God is a warning directed in particular to those who continue to believe in God, that is, in those radical principles of stabilization and reassurance that are no longer necessary. But if warnings are calls to alter, to take a stance for an alteration that could improve the future, what is the alteration that Nietzsche is calling for?

Although the acceptance of God's death implies that order can no longer be traced back to an intelligent designer, it does not preclude the possibility that many gods might be born. Just as Nietzsche's nihilist warning was meant to invite us to reevaluate all values, it is also an invitation to create new values because it "is the moral God who is denied," that is, the Christian God of the church and its claim to power within Western culture. Nietzsche believes we ought to "feel illuminated" by this death rather than "sad and gloomy." But where is God in this "new dawn"? The problem, as Nietzsche states, is that some of us still live under his shadow. "After Buddha was dead," he says in aphorism 108 of *The Gay Science* (1882), "they still showed his shadow in a cave for centuries—a tremendous, gruesome shadow.

God is dead; but given the way people are, there may still for millennia be caves in which they show his shadow.—and we—we must still defeat his shadow as well!"⁶

The creation of new gods is the alteration that Nietzsche's warning requests from us, but the shadows remaining after God's death are the threat, that is, what is preventing us from overcoming "our entire European morality." A morality under the authority of a God that has been murdered cannot determine values. In order to accept or acknowledge Nietzsche's warning, it is necessary to take a risk, to become involved in the creation not only of new values but also of a new humanity that can leave behind the shadows of God's death. It should not come as a surprise that the announcement of the death of God in the prologue to *Thus Spoke Zarathustra* (1892) is accompanied by the arrival of the *Übermensch*. With the death of God, the firm "grounding" upon which humanity has walked disappears: "Mankind is a rope fastened between animal and overman [*Übermensch*]—a rope over an abyss. A dangerous crossing, a dangerous on-the-way, a dangerous looking back, a dangerous shuddering and standing still."⁷

The *Übermensch* is probably the most manipulated notion of Nietzsche's philosophy. Avant-garde artists, religious fanatics, and, among many others, Nazis have adopted the term to justify their ideas, implicating Nietzsche in their works. His own sister distorted his writings to highlight fascist and racist themes close to National Socialism, rendering the *Übermensch* an ideal for Hitler's soldiers. At the origin of these manipulations is the translation of the prefix *Über-* as "super-" instead of "over-." Whereas the "superman" refers to a magnified individual who reaches a dialectic reconciliation and takes God's place, the "overman" instead simply acknowledges the death of God, that is, the illusion that reconciliation can eventually occur. Instead of a peaceful reconciliation, this acknowledgment implies an intensification of all vital activity, rendering the "subject" unthinkable as a subject. The "subject," as Nietzsche explained, "is not something given, it is something added and invented and projected behind what there is."[8]

The *Übermensch* is called on to assume the responsibility that God has died, the intensification of all vital activities, and accept the "eternal return of the same" (where "everything goes, everything returns, the wheel of being eternally turns"), but it is also capable of listening to warnings. These warnings are weak and contingent announcements that can only be understood through interpretation. But in order to interpret, one must have some of the qualities that Nietzsche attributes to the overman, such as moderation and contingency. As he explains in the long fragment "European Nihilism," written in the summer of 1887, the "strongest" will be "the most moderate, those who have no *need* of extreme articles of faith, who not only concede but even love a good deal of contingency and nonsense."[9] Nietzsche is "the prophet of the contemporary world," as Gianni Vattimo suggested,[10] because he described a humanity open to the contingency of the world after the death of God and, moreover, the death of its own "articles of faith." Heeding warnings requires these virtues.

2

SCIENCE DOES NOT THINK

At one point in Woody Allen's *Irrational Man*—a movie named after the famous book by William Barrett that introduced existentialism to the English-speaking world—Professor Abe Lucas (played by Joaquin Phoenix) asks during a dinner party whether the world needs "another book on Heidegger and fascism."[1] This statement reflects the staggering number of books dedicated to the problem of the German thinker's affiliations with Nazism. Recent publications confirm once again not only his sympathies for National Socialism but also that all the attempts to link his antisemitism and his philosophy are, as Jürgen Habermas pointed out, absurd. These are bad-faith attempts to manipulate the most important German philosopher since Hegel in order to avoid accepting the consequences that his destruction of Western metaphysics entails for liberal societies, democracies, and culture at large.[2]

Although Heidegger is not the only philosopher with racist or sexist views—David Hume considered Black people to be naturally inferior to whites, Immanuel Kant saw women as being innately morally deficient, and Gottlob Frege also sympathized with fascism and antisemitism—some continue to refer to him as "Hitler's spiritual guide" even though his writings have virtually nothing to say about politics or ethics conventionally understood. Accusations such as these might be more appropriately leveled at Nietzsche, whom Hitler praised (he gifted Mussolini the complete works of Nietzsche for his birthday), whereas he ignored Heidegger. Also, the fact that progressive writers and artists such as Hannah Arendt, Terrence Malick, and Jon Fosse, among many others, have been profoundly influenced by Heidegger's philosophy shows that it is possible to distinguish between his philosophical contributions and his racist or political views. While warnings about Heidegger's antisemitism are legitimate and abundant, what warnings does Heidegger offer us?

Contrary to Nietzsche, whose writing is filled with warnings concerning God, society, and values, Heidegger's philosophy is fundamentally a warning about the future and fate of thought in an age when science is prevailing over all domains of human knowledge. His most important book, *Being and Time* (1927), was more than just an attempt to overturn 2,500 years of Western thought by retrieving and elucidating the meaning of Being as philosophy's central question. Confronting this question would allow us not only to recognize how partial all previous responses have been but also to identify the dominant and oppressive role that science and technology plays in our lives. But what does the question of Being have to do with our technological world? Why, as he warned, does science "not think in the way thinkers think"?

To respond to these questions it is first necessary to understand why and how Heidegger retrieved the question of Being. A good place to start is his lecture courses on Heraclitus from 1943 and 1944, recently translated into English. The goal of these lectures—as well as others from the 1940s on fragments of early Greek thinkers—was to interpret the manifold terms for "*Seinselbst* [Being itself]," such as *physis*, *alētheia*, *zoē*, and so forth.

Heidegger believed these Greek words named the original, purest, and most fundamental Western understanding of Being, that is, existence as the unitary temporal disclosure of all things. Although this original understanding of Being was later forgotten (as Western philosophy began describing Being in terms of timeless and changeless entities such as *eidos*, *idea*, and *essentia*), recalling the many original terms invites us to pay attention to our relation with Being and why it is vital. "For we who have come later," Heidegger writes, "this is a warning to be aware that, also and already for the first thinkers, the saying of Being was full of enigmas."[3]

For the earliest thinkers of Being, it was a concept full of enigmas, which should not be interpreted as a problem but rather as a warning that our abilities to question what it means to "be" or "exist" should not be taken for granted. This happens every time we ignore or forget Being's temporal disclosure and the original terms used to name it. Platonism, also referred to as metaphysics, is responsible for the later approach, where things are understood as eternal entities (whether ideas, God, or the laws of modern physics) and (objectively) present references. When Plato first asked what something "actually is," such as a rock or a courageous act, his answer was never "this gray rock" or "that courageous act," because those are simply temporary examples. The correct answer would be what we consider a rock or courageous act always to be, in other words, the ideal form of what each thing truly is. If Being, for Plato and the metaphysical tradition that followed, exists beyond time, change, and senses, then beings are simply temporary reflections or effects.

However, according to Heidegger the problem with this response is that it presupposes an eternal and present entity that will always tell us the truth no matter who, when, and where we are. Instead, as he explains, the truth of Being is not what corresponds to an eternal and objective reality but rather what unfolds to us as human beings in a given space, time, and tradition. This means that our primary encounter with the world is not objective—the experience of a spectator staring at a world—but rather an involved hermeneutical one where things are filled with human meaning bound by time.

Heidegger, as a radical historicist, does not believe we can secure subjective representations, because truth is the disclosure of an event and meaning that we cannot control. But this meaning is lost every time Western thought is subjected to the Platonic conception of Being and truth as the objective and eternal unchanging foundation of reality. God took the place of Platonic ideas as the cause of all that is real in religions such as Judaism and Christianity, and the self-conscious human subject of Descartes and modernity displaced God as the criterion for reality. Now it is the sciences with their methodologies that determine the character of contemporary reality and render man the only master of the objective universe. These present themselves as even beyond any form of Platonism or metaphysics, claiming their methods are bound to timeless laws and formulas that transcend the given world. In order to understand the consequences of such a claim, it is first necessary to explain what thinking actually means for Heidegger and why he believes that science doesn't think "the way thinkers think."

Thinking for Heidegger does not reside in having an idea that can then be developed through a chain of premises and methods that lead to a valid conclusion. This form of thinking depends upon representations, methods, and calculations, in other words, on references to states and relations that were decided beforehand. When a scientist, for example, ventures into the investigation of a particular object, this very venture already defines the area within which the investigation will take place. This experiment asks for nothing more than that what is looked for in the object reveal itself: "We take cognizance of them as what we already know them to be in advance, the body as bodily, the plant-like of the plant, the animal-like of the animal, the thingness of the thing, and so on."[4]

In order to explain this Heidegger uses the word *Entwurf*, a "throwing-forth" or "pro-ject"—which also reflects how research is funded in the contemporary university setting. If only those researchers who can "project" their results will be awarded funding, then the methods of scientists must be bent toward examining the objects of experiment in such way as to verify the exactitude of the "projected" results. The rigor of the method consists in the close correlation between the projected results and the results obtained. Thus, scientific research is not exact because it calculates accurately but rather must calculate accurately because the link that binds its methodology to the object of research has the character of exactitude. In contrast, history, philosophy, and theology were never meant to be exact because their object, not predetermined, reveals and discloses itself through the process of research. Thinking in the way of scientific methodology tends to reduce Being not only to a particular and already known form of being but also to one that is predictable, controllable, and inevitable, leaving little space to question the science's own essence.

According to Heidegger sciences such as biology, economics, or geography may thoroughly explore a human cell, a financial crisis, or a particular area in every possible respect yet never know what biology, economics, or geography actually is. As he explains in *What Is Called Thinking?* (1954), the "essence of their spheres is the concern of thinking":

As the sciences qua sciences have no access to this concern, it must be said that they are not thinking. Once this is put in words, it tends to sound at first as though thinking fancied itself superior to the sciences. Such arrogance, if and where it exists, would be unjustified; thinking always knows essentially less than the sciences precisely because it operates where it could think the essence of history, art, nature, language and yet is still not capable of it. The sciences are fully entitled to their name, which means fields of knowledge, because they have infinitely more knowledge than thinking does. And yet there is another side in every science which that science as such can never reach: the essential nature and origin of its sphere, the essence and essential origin of the manner of knowing which it cultivates, and other things besides.[5]

In order to think this essential origin, Heidegger suggests learning to think nonconceptually and nonsystematically, that is, avoiding or blurring the subjectivity involved in separating human being and Being, subject and object, or language and meanings. Richard Rorty accurately interpreted this suggestion as a warning, a "warning to avoid winding up with some version of the Subject-Object or Human-Superhuman dualisms, and thus being condemned to think in terms of power relations between the terms of these dualisms."[6] Avoiding these power relations not only allows us to think nonconceptually but also reminds us that there are purposes to thinking other than establishing power relations. "Science does not think" is a warning against these power relations, which also define the essence of technology.

If "the most thought-provoking thing about our thought-provoking age," as Heidegger says, is "that we are still not thinking," it is because the *Ge-stell*—"enframing" or "framing"—has become the essence of technology. As the basic form of technological thinking, "enframing" is a "gathering [that] concentrates [humanity] upon ordering the real as '*Bestand*,' standing-reserve," to enact "the organized global conquest of the earth," or, as Heidegger says in the *Notebooks*, the "machination." Technology has the power to conquer nature because the method of modern science already projects nature as an object "calculable in advance."[7] Heidegger's objective is to demonstrate not only that science is the basic form of technological thinking that precludes other ways of thinking but also that it alienates us from nature, that it "tears [humans] loose from the earth and uproots them." This creates an *Unheimlichkeit* condition—one of "uncanniness" or "homelessness"—and also increases our *Angst*, as we are only left with "purely technological relationships."[8]

These technological conditions are the result of overlooking Being in favor of beings, that is, the disclosure of worlds for what gets revealed within those worlds, and so thinking nonconceptually and nonsystematically becomes urgent, because the essence of the species has been framed (*Ge-Stell*) by a power that it does not control. This, after all, is the sensation we all have today, where "the only emergency," as Heidegger once said, "is the absence of a sense of emergency." The fact that in 2025 most of us are monitored, spied on, and even genetically engineered confirms the German philosopher's warning of a world "where self-certainty has become unsurpassable, where everything is held to be calculable, and especially where it has been decided, with no previous questioning, who we are and what we are supposed to do."[9] This is why, in line with Nietzsche's hermeneutics, Heidegger does not believe we need to better describe the world in order to change it; rather, we must learn to interpret it differently.

As we can see, Heidegger's warning regarding science's inability to think was not meant to proclaim, as many believe, antiscientism. He does not reject the human project to understand nature as much as the preclusion and marginalization of other ways of thinking by the representation and calculative thinking of the sciences. Besides increasing our "homelessness" and "anxiety" by alienating us further from nature, scientism also encourages philosophers to take for granted the reality of their objects of research. This is evident among not only "new" philosophical disciplines such as "business ethics" or "applied philosophy" but also the so-called traditional branches of philosophy: logics, ethics, and aesthetics. As "knowledge of logos," "knowledge of ethos," and "knowledge of *aisthêsis*," these disciplines take for granted what truth, good, and beauty already are.

Against these metaphysical philosophies, and scientism in particular, Heidegger believes philosophy must become unscientific, must question the extremely narrow conception of reality where beings are taken for granted, that is, where nothing remains of Being. Although the "sciences do in fact decide what of the tree in bloom may or may not be considered valid reality," they cannot question the basis of this decision because they are submitted to their own "instrumental realism" or "theory of the real." Science's inability to question these decisions and indifference toward doing so are symptoms of a crisis in our technologically oriented culture.[10]

The long passage quoted earlier and Heidegger's general stance toward science provide several indications that the proclamation that "science does not think" can be interpreted as a warning. Like Nietzsche, Heidegger wants to preserve us from the threat inherent in viewing nature through science's narrow conception of reality and power relations. The various references and examples to nature as an immense array of mere resources to be maximally exploited are meant to involve us in an alteration that could improve our ongoing "homelessness" and "anxiety." Although "science does not think" at first sounds like a prescription, Heidegger is careful to point out that he is not suggesting that "thinking is superior to the sciences." Sciences are entitled to the name as long as they are restricted to their own "fields of knowledge," which we must distinguish from thought. In sum, the goal of Heidegger's warning is to provoke and implicate us in a radical break with the environmental consequences of science's dominance.

Although Heidegger's general question remains constant—the relation of human being and other beings to Being as such—thinking is not a means to an end but rather a self-justifying warning about the consequences of science and technology. The reduction by scientific methodology of all matter and energy to a resource is rendering the continuation of life on earth unviable. Against this reduction it is urgent to think, that is, to be underway, prepared, and available to respond to Being's call. But how is it possible to think when what really must be questioned is hidden by the dominant role of scientific researchers and their technologies?

Thinking must be regarded as something that is at once receptive (in the sense of a listening and attending to what things convey to us) and active (in the sense that we respond to their call), as hermeneutics recommends. As a call to be attentive to things as they are, to let them be as they are, and to interpret them and ourselves together, hermeneutic thinking is able to immerse itself in what is to be thought and reveal its essential and original nature. Hermeneutics, as Heidegger explains, "is not philosophy at all, but in fact something preliminary which runs in advance of it and has its own reasons for being: what is at issue in it, what it all comes to, is not to become finished with it as quickly as possible, but rather to hold out in it as long as possible."[11]

But isn't this the unscientific attitude that Heidegger demands from philosophy? Isn't this precisely the attitude that environmentalists demand toward nature? It should not come as a surprise that today environmentalists find Heidegger's analysis of human existence and critiques of modern hypertechnological rationalism particularly useful. His warning regarding science's inability to think beyond its own "projects" or "fields of knowledge" has inspired several scholars to refer to him as "a major deep ecological theorist," a "philosopher for the ecologists," and "a breath of fresh air for environmentalists."[12]

3

ONE BECOMES A WOMAN

The French philosopher Simone de Beauvoir, much like Nietzsche, is often identified with a single statement even though she wrote extensively on a number of different issues, such as aging, politics, and racism, besides the various novels and memoirs that constitute the more well-known parts of her important oeuvre. The statement that attaches to her name, "*On ne naît pas femme: on le deviant*," "one is not born but rather becomes a woman," is considered to have a life of its own—as the editor of the biography of this famous sentence said—because it "has inspired generations of women in their pursuit of freedom . . . and catalyzed both personal and political change wherever it has traveled."[1] On International Woman's Day in 2022, the Bonn Bundeskunsthalle (an unique venue devoted to art, culture, and science) inaugurated an exhibition titled "Simone de Beauvoir and *The Second Sex*" that traces the genesis of the text with photographs, documents, interviews, films, and other material from postwar Paris. These, as well as many other books, conferences, and events, are some of the many examples that show how the French phenomenologist continues to be a vital thinker for how we understand our present.[2]

But *The Second Sex* (1949) is not the only text that makes Beauvoir a philosopher of warnings to the same extent, if not more, than Nietzsche and Heidegger. In 1970 she published the *La vieillesse* (*The Coming of Age*), where she tackles the problem of aging. This problem had never before received the philosophical attention Beauvoir bestows on it. The central thesis and warning of the book is that "old age is not, in itself or necessarily, a problem, though part of the problem of old age is that we treat it as if it is." This is not only a warning for those who consider aging a disease—which has now become the purpose of longevity medicine—but for those who ignore that old age is existentially (and not just biologically) a radically transformed state of being that cannot be reduced to the finality of death. Before I interpret the most succinct expression of Beauvoir's gender theory as a warning, it is important to recall the historical roots of the French word *genre* to connote the social construction of sex, the controversy around the two available translations of her warning, and the philosophical origins of her philosophical stance.

The sex/gender distinction existed in the French sociopolitical vocabulary well before Beauvoir, Anne Oakley, and Judith Butler. In the sixteenth century, the philosopher Henri-Corneille Agrippa de Nettesheim not only spoke of *genre masculin* and *genre féminin* to refer to human categories of males and females but also argued for the "nobility and excellence of the feminine sex and its preeminence over the other sex." This preeminence is also evident in the work of the seventeenth-century French novelist Madeleine de Scudéry, who argued that "women" had been deformed by culture. This cultural construction of sex is also manifest in the thought of Jean-Jacques Rousseau when he argued against women's inferiority to men and for their "natural" equality. As we can see, "French critics of women's subordination exhibited an acute awareness that the relations between the sexes were neither God-given nor determined exclusively by 'nature.'"[3] The social construction of sex has deep roots in French Enlightenment thought, but that does not mean that Beauvoir's intuitions in *The Second Sex* are not revolutionary.

To understand her revolutionary contribution, it is necessary to distinguish between those who read Beauvoir as a social-constructivist theorist and those who interpret her as a philosopher in the existentialist tradition. The groups can be identified through the two available translations of her warning. The former group prefers Constance Borde and Sheila Malovany-Chevallier's translation from 2000—"one is not born, but rather becomes, woman"—but the latter use Howard Madison Parshley first version from 1953: "one is not born, but rather becomes, a woman."[4] Borde and Malovany-Chevallier's decision to omit the article is founded on decades of feminist scholarship to emphasize "woman" as an institution, that is, a social, cultural, and historical construct. "Being born a woman," as they recently explained, "means that that person will from childhood embody a social and human condition—woman defined by biology, history, culture, literature, religion, psychology, politics, etc."[5] This sense of institutional construction—of gender being not specific to one individual—is meant to prove that anatomical sex does not govern the existential identity of women. But if "femininity" is always constructed by the culture in which we are immersed, then Beauvoir was not only denaturalizing gender but also stressing the "sex/gender" distinction (earlier introduced to feminism by the sociologist Ann Oakley) that is absent in *The Second Sex*.

Although Parshley's translation is full of errors, inadequacies, and omissions—which led Beauvoir to tell Margaret Simons she felt misrepresented and hoped for a new translation—including the "a" in this famous sentence was a correct choice if we want to read her as not only an existentialist philosopher but also one of warnings. The omission of the article in the translation, as Bonnie Mann points out, inevitably "swings toward objectivism," that is, where "woman" becomes a wholly determined thing. This goes against the phenomenologist's project—and that of her contemporaries Jean-Paul Sartre and Maurice Merleau-Ponty—of overcoming both realism and idealism, the binary habits of our metaphysical tradition that Heidegger first pointed out and criticized.

"Femininity is neither a natural nor an innate entity," Beauvoir wrote in *The Prime of Life* (1960), "but rather a condition brought about by society, on the basis of certain physiological characteristics." This is why it "is as absurd, then, to speak of 'woman' in general as of the 'eternal' man." Against this "female" or "male" condition the French philosopher draws upon the interaction between self and world, between bodily experience and one's understanding of it, because we are not neutral things that can be objectively managed.[6]

The popular belief that Beauvoir has simply applied Sartre's philosophy to women's situation through his radical notion of freedom has been contested by several scholars. There is evidence not only that her notion of freedom is much closer to Merleau-Ponty's than Sartre's but also of how the central principles of his existentialism can be found in Beauvoir's early diaries. Also, when Beauvoir remarked that she was not a creator of philosophical systems, this was not meant to highlight her subordination to Sartre but rather to avoid the rigidity of such systems in favor of the hermeneutic nature of knowledge. Against systematic philosophers interested in possessing abstract knowledge, Beauvoir aims to engage in situated embodied experiences such as aging or becoming a woman. But in order to do this, it is necessary to acknowledge that we are not all equally free regardless of our situation, as Sartre believes. Freedom instead is situated, subject to the demands not only of embodiment but also of society. This is why gendered sexed bodies are treated, regulated, and controlled differently among different societies. If there is a philosopher who influenced Beauvoir more than Sartre and Merleau-Ponty, it is Martin Heidegger. Her original stance on human beings and their relation to the world emerges through her innovative interpretation of Heidegger's fundamental ontology.

Although Beauvoir was always reluctant to admit her interest in Heidegger's philosophy—probably because of his known affiliations with Nazism—she said that the "novelty and richness of phenomenology filled me with enthusiasm; I felt I had never come so close to the real truth."[7] But there is a fundamental difference between Sartre's and Beauvoir's Heideggerian stances. Sartre remained essentially within a descriptive phenomenology where authenticity and anxiety were central, but Beauvoir broke with this Cartesian tradition and incorporated into her thought concepts such as *Faktizität* (facticity), *Erschlossenheit* (disclosure), and *Moglichkeiten* (possibilities). These concepts are central to understanding Beauvoir's "Heideggerian approach," as Eva Gothlin explained, "to sexual difference, even though Heidegger himself does not analyze sex."[8]

For Heidegger, Dasein, or human being, exists in the world before it has knowledge of the world. As a hermeneutic Being—under specific conditions, historical age, and social prejudices—the human does not relate to the world as subject but rather as a disclosure and facticity. In this condition, "Dasein is its disclosedness," that is, where things can emerge as possibilities and situations. One lives one's body, as Beauvoir says, not as a thing or destiny but rather as a situation. This is why human beings don't have an essence such as evil or good, just or unjust, and feminine or masculine. Her rejection of the idea of a "woman's nature" or "female essence" in *The Second Sex* is bound to Heidegger's belief that human being is always much more than what it is at any given moment because it is a structure of "possibilities"—possibilities that can be disclosed and concealed in different manners. Thus, Beauvoir overcomes metaphysical dichotomies—such as objectivism versus subjectivism, determinism versus freedom, and realism versus idealism—and also presents her central warning:

> Woman is not a completed reality, but rather a becoming, and it is in her becoming that she should be compared with man; that is to say, her *possibilities* should be defined. What gives rise to much of the debate is the tendency to reduce her to what she has been, to what she is today, in raising the question of her capabilities; for the fact is that capabilities are clearly manifested only when they have been realized—but the fact is also that when we have to do with a being whose nature is transcendent action, we can never close the books. . . . One is not born, but rather becomes, a woman. No biological, psychological, or economic fate determines the figure that the human female presents in society; it is civilization as a whole that produces this creature, intermediate between male and eunuch, which is described as feminine. Only the intervention of someone else can establish an individual as an Other.[9]

In this important passage Beauvoir's warning—"one is not born, but rather becomes, a woman"—is not only announced but also differentiates itself from predictions. Unlike predictions, which would claim to know the gender of a woman because they are founded on knowledge, rationality, and realism, warnings instead are announcements meant to preserve us from the threat that these categories imply. This threat is the reduction of women to "what she has been, to what she is today," as Beauvoir says, in other words, to "the Other." But this warning also implies a relation of care that is meant to implicate us in this gender's becoming because it isn't a "closed book." This is evident in how we bring up our children. Too often girls or boys are brought up "with an astonishing blindness if we do not first ask ourselves what it is that we are bringing them up to be as men and women."[10] But why is it so important for Beauvoir to warn us against describing women using the biological, psychological, or economical sciences? What and who establishes the Other? What constitutes freedom for women?

Against the future of scientific predictions, warnings point toward an alteration, a "becoming that cannot be known in advance through causal relations." Beauvoir's warning is meant not only to protect the identity of *woman* from having fixed destiny but most of all to understand femininity as a reaction to a situation rather than the consequence of biological facts. Although "these facts cannot be denied . . . in themselves they have no significance"[11] because becoming a woman is a matter of embodying a specific set of habits, behaviors, and choices that can only be explained existentially.

This is why sex difference, for example, cannot determine the form of social existence of men and women. Instead, existence determines how sex difference will be lived. Beauvoir considers the division of the human animal into two mutually exclusive categories (male and female) to be the imposition of a certain meaning on a set of otherwise inherently meaningless physiological differences. Beauvoir's philosophy cannot be interpreted simply in terms of sex-gender distinction, because claiming that the body is a situation also requires acknowledging the body's role in its transformations, socializations, and responsiveness to cultural interpretations, which begin the "moment that a baby is declared to be a boy or a girl. The interpretations adults give of a child's body set the stage for her own interpretations of her body."[12]

Understanding femininity as an existential reaction to a situation rather than biological fact was vital for Beauvoir to associate the condition of women with the condition of other exploited people. It should not come as a surprise that the model for *The Second Sex* was the study of race in America by the Swedish economist Gunnar Myrdal (*An American Dilemma: The Negro Problem and Modern Democracy*, 1944), which Beauvoir read during one of her trips to the United States, where she also observed racial and gender oppression. The analogies between Black people and women showed the French thinker that there was no mysterious determining essence in each case and that characteristics ought to be understood as a "reaction to a situation" against which freedom asserts itself. Unlike Sartre, who believed that human beings' ontological freedom could never be compromised, Beauvoir considered it only realizable in its relation to the ambiguity of the human situation, which is affected by the socioeconomic conditions of one's family, the specific form of one's physical embodiment, and one's educational upbringing.

Although this situation gives us the context in which a human female can become a woman, it still does not answer the central question of Beauvoir's investigation: What is a woman? In trying to answer this question she not only relates to Heidegger's key philosophical question ("What is the meaning of Being") but also shows how Heidegger has remained framed within the same metaphysical tradition that he attempted to overcome.

Among the most important findings of *Being and Time* (1927) is the tendency within the Western philosophical tradition to think human existence in inappropriate terms that render this existence as something objective. This is a result of ignoring the ontological difference between Being and beings. Although Beauvoir takes this theoretical background for granted, she points out that human existence was also understood independently, "that humanity is divided into two classes of individuals [man and woman] whose clothes, faces, bodies, smiles, gaits, interests, and occupations are manifestly different. Perhaps these differences are superficial, perhaps they are destined to disappear. What is certain is that they do most obviously exist."[13] The problem with Heidegger, Sartre, and other existentialists is that they stop at the ontological difference and ignore the two classes of individuals. For Heidegger this difference was secondary or even ontic, but for Sartre it was insignificant to the ontological freedom of the human being, which is the true object of philosophical investigation. In order to correct this restricted view, Beauvoir drew on the longstanding philosophical concept of the "Other" developed by Hegel, Husserl, and Sartre: a consciousness outside the self whose surprising discovery is crucial to the self's formation.

Why did Beauvoir define women as the Other? "The situation of woman," she writes in *The Second Sex*, "is that she—a free and autonomous being like all human creatures—nevertheless finds herself living in a world where men compel her to assume the status of the Other."[14] The problem is that there are groups of people, Beauvoir warns, whose foreignness becomes fixed in their society (as Blacks in the United States, Jews in Europe, and Arabs in France), making them permanent Others. In this situation the Other will inevitably live in the world as an-other, a world where values are established and imposed, ignoring the desires and self-identity of the Othered populations.

Even though women are never a minority, they are a permanent Other that Western societies perceive as a deviation from the male standard. Thus, Beauvoir identifies patriarchy as a politics of oppression that systematically denies women their economic, political, and sexual freedom. Philosophy is culpable in this: Aristotle described women as "afflicted with a natural defectiveness"; St. Thomas, as an "imperfect man, an incidental being"; and Kant believed women "will avoid the wicked, not because it is unright [*unrecht*], but because it is ugly; and virtuous actions mean to them such as are morally beautiful," turning a woman's body into an obstacle for philosophizing. Against this "obstacle" Beauvoir inaugurates an entirely novel philosophical field—the interpretation of sex and gender—and also reframes feminist debates to find new ways of understanding women's situation.

It is interesting to note how in *The Second Sex*—which *Time* magazine named one of the hundred most influential books of the twentieth century—Beauvoir did not seek a definition of woman or list the conditions according to which a person counts as a woman. Her interest instead was to warn women that they have the capacity and obligation to interpret and reinvent themselves in light of those cultural constructions that determine their situation, and these constructions also include their bodies. Also, it is important to remember her warning also concerns the "first" sex, that is, men. The tendency to think this is a warning only for women stems from the prejudice that "gender" is only a woman's issue when in fact it's a fundamental aspect of the contemporary situation of all sexes. And so from Beauvoir's phenomenological perspective, granting women economic independence and political rights within patriarchal societies will not alleviate their oppression because liberation concerns first and foremost changing our view of freedom. Until this view—where woman "appears as the privileged Other through whom the subject accomplishes himself; one of the measures of man, his balance, his salvation, his adventure, his happiness"[15]—is not changed, no one will be free.

4

THE BANALITY OF EVIL

The principal warning of Hannah Arendt's philosophy is at the center of the biopic directed by Margarethe von Trotta in 2012. This marvelous film—where Heidegger, Hans Jonas, and other philosophers appear—narrates the German Jewish philosopher's controversial report on the 1961 trial of the Nazi Adolf Eichmann for the *New Yorker*.[1] Observing this murderer's inability to think during the trial—which Arendt claimed was his most distinctive characteristic—led to her warning of "the banality of evil." Like Beauvoir's aphorism ("one is not born, but rather becomes a woman"), Arendt's warning is considered to have a life of its own. Besides the numerous books, articles, and conferences dedicated to this controversial report, her entire oeuvre is often referred to as a warning. A simple search online of "Arendt warning" yields articles such as "The Philosopher Who Warned Us About Loneliness and Totalitarianism," "Russia's New Control Tactic Is the One Hannah Arendt Warned Us About 50 Years Ago," and "This New Hannah Arendt Documentary Is a Warning About the Fascist Within Us All." This last article refers to a documentary directed by Ada Uspiz in 2015 that includes archival material as well as interviews with Arendt's family, friends, and colleagues.[2]

Both the biographical film and the documentary portray a philosopher who was not only an independent thinker but also a public intellectual concerned with the most pressing issues of our time, such as the return of totalitarianism, the refugee crisis, and ethnic conflict. Although Arendt is more sought after than Nietzsche, Heidegger, and Beauvoir as a guide for warnings in the twenty-first century, their philosophies influenced her profoundly. This is particularly true of Heidegger, who taught her how to think in an age when scientism has marginalized other ways of thinking. Against scientific knowledge—which pretends not only to warn us but also to solve the very matters it warns us of—philosophy allows us to think "without banisters," the mental boundaries that often characterize scientific investigations. In order to understand the meaning of "thinking" in Arendt it is important to recall the author of *Being and Time* (1927), "who so profoundly influenced her own thinking about thinking," as Richard Bernstein wrote.

Arendt was Heidegger's student in her first years at the University of Freiburg during the 1920s and also his lover, which has been the subject of numerous discussions, especially in light of his sympathies for National Socialism. The publication of their correspondence in 2004 revealed the intensity of their relationship as well as a profound philosophical connection.[3] She first heard of Heidegger's exceptional courses and seminars in 1924 through her friend Ernst Grumach, who confirmed the rumors that "Plato, Aristotle, and thinking came to life" through a teaching style that Karl Löwith described as a "witchcraft." "Little more than a name was known," Arendt wrote in her tribute for Heidegger's eightieth birthday in 1969, "but the name made its way through all of Germany like the rumor of a secret king."

Like the most adventurous students, she enrolled in Heidegger's 1924 lecture course Basic Concepts of Aristotelian

Philosophy and in his smaller, seminar-style class on Plato's *Sophist*, which examined many ideas later included in *Being and Time*. Arendt was particularly touched by Heidegger's notion of Being-there, Dasein, which is not the world, the subject, or a property of both but the relation, the in-between, which must decide if it wants to exist as an "inauthentic" describer of objectivity or an "authentic" interpreter of Being that actually thinks. Arendt's preference for the latter is evident in the Gifford Lectures she delivered in 1973 and 1974—available in the first volume of *The Life of the Mind* (1977), entitled *Thinking*—which begin with a quotation from Heidegger's *What Is Called Thinking?* In that book Heidegger distinguished thinking from knowledge in order to warn that science doesn't think but rather calculates within certain paradigms.

Heidegger's warning was not meant to diminish the efficacy or progress of science but rather to emphasize the alarming tendency of our time to identify thinking with scientific knowledge, calculation, and functioning. The problem, as he famously warned in an interview in *Der Spiegel*, "is that everything is functioning and that the functioning drives us more and more to even further functioning, and that technology tears [humans] loose from the earth and uproots them."[4] If thinking doesn't produce knowledge as the sciences do—where usable practical wisdom directly grants us the power to act or solve universal mysteries—it is because truth takes place within the realm of meaning or, as Heidegger would say, Being. This difference is reminiscent of the way in which the hermeneutic tradition—from Luther to Wilhelm Dilthey and Paul Ricoeur—distinguishes between the explanatory method of the sciences and the interpretive approach of the humanities. Arendt belongs to this hermeneutic tradition but also is among the first philosophers to develop its political implications for the "human condition."

In order to understand the hermeneutic nature of Arendt's political philosophy, it is useful to relate it to the stance of Hans-Georg Gadamer, who also studied with Heidegger in the 1920s. Both "have transformed this legacy in an extremely productive way, into a philosophical hermeneutics in Gadamer's case, and into a political hermeneutics in Arendt's case."[5] In *Truth and Method* (1960), Gadamer proposed a hermeneutic conception of understanding that brings together its "situatedness" as well as the "plurality" of meaning, rendering truth a consequence of interpretation, dialogue, and the fusion of horizons. True understanding for Gadamer does not necessarily involve "the empathy of one individual for another nor subordinating another person to our own standards; rather, it always involves rising to a higher universality that overcomes not only our own particularity but also that of the other."[6] Although Arendt agrees with Gadamer that we must first overcome these particularities in order to reach true understanding, she also considers it necessary to remain open to the "shock of experience," that is, to be ready to acknowledge new, different, and incomprehensible events.

Arendt criticizes the reductiveness of the scientific approach because it is incapable of understanding when human actions or world events are meaningful. These meanings require an engaged perspective, an interpreter who is never satisfied with objective representations or observations because meanings are always intersubjective and context dependent. Facts for Arendt are neither discovered nor found but established through interpretation in order to acquire meaning. The problem is when facts are known or explained without understanding their meaning, as occurs with certain inexplicable phenomenon or unanswerable questions such as the origin of the universe, the meaning of death, or why there is evil in the world. Science might be able to explain them, but it does not understand their meaning. This is why instead of "correct information" through "scientific knowledge," understanding for Arendt "is a complicated process which never produces unequivocal results. It is an unending activity by which, in constant change and variation, we come to terms with and reconcile ourselves to reality, that is, try to be at home in the world."[7]

With this definition Arendt shows that hermeneutics—as Gadamer repeatedly emphasized—is not a theoretical system or stance but rather a reflective praxis that bears the vital burden of understanding the meaningfulness of the world as opposed to the phenomena of nature. If these phenomena are not as meaningful, it is primarily because causal explanations and objective knowledge are often enough to satisfy the disengaged observer. The problem with this observer—as well as our general tendency to identify thinking with scientific knowledge—is the absence of imagination, which is an important precondition of reflective understanding. "Imagination alone," Arendt wrote, "enables us to see things in their proper perspective, to put that which is too close at a certain distance so that we can see and understand it without bias and prejudice, to bridge abysses of remoteness until we can see and understand everything that is too far away from us as though it were our own affair. This 'distancing' of some things and bridging the abysses to others is part of the dialogue of understanding."[8]

And so for Arendt imagination and dialogue—which are also central in Heidegger, Gadamer, and the hermeneutic tradition—are vital for true understanding. They allow us to think through those inexplicable phenomena or unanswerable questions and explore their significance for our lives because "thinking deals with invisibles, with representations of things that are absent"; the manifestation of thought for Arendt "is not knowledge; it is the ability to tell right from wrong, beautiful from ugly. And this, at the rare moments when the stakes are on the table, may indeed prevent catastrophes, at least for the self."[9]

Arendt's report for the *New Yorker*—which became her book *Eichmann in Jerusalem: The Banality of Evil* (1963)—and *The Origins of Totalitarianism* (1951) represent efforts to think (and therefore understand differently) the origins of our ethical and political traditions and also to warn us of the consequences of leaving these unexamined. This is why Arendt does "not merely repeat Heidegger's 'destructive' gesture," as Dana Vila points out, but also "pushes his interpretive violence in a direction he would not (and apparently did not) recognize."[10] Even though she changed direction—moving away from metaphysics and ontology and toward political theory and ethics—this hermeneutic violence is evident in her portrayal of Eichmann as a "funny," "comical," and "stupid" incarnation of the "banality of evil."

This hermeneutic violence was necessary to remind her readers that to "think critically is always hostile." There "are no dangerous thoughts for the simple reason that thinking itself is such a dangerous enterprise. . . . I don't deny that thinking is dangerous, but I would say not thinking, *'ne pas réfléchir c'est plus dangereux encore'* [not thinking is even more dangerous]."[11] Highlighted by Arendt's warning of the "banality of evil" of Eichmann and other war criminals is their "inability to think," which entails imagination and dialogue rather than the rote following of the procedures of violence.

Although the report and subsequent book clearly explained her phrase, Arendt felt compelled to further clarify her view in later interviews, forewords, and postscripts given the controversy it aroused among readers. In these new publications she pointed out that her phrase "went counter to our tradition of thought—literary, theological, or philosophic—about the phenomenon of evil." During the trial she noted how Eichmann, unlike the popular image of evildoers, was particularly shallow, ordinary, and banal; in other words, it was "impossible to trace the uncontestable evil of his deeds to any deeper level of roots or motives" that many were hoping to see in him.[12] In the postscript to the book's new edition in 1964 she wrote:

> He merely, to put the matter colloquially, never realized what he was doing. It was precisely this lack of imagination which enabled him to sit for months on end facing a German Jew who was conducting the police interrogation, pouring out his heart to the man and explaining again and again how it was. He was not stupid. It was sheer thoughtlessness—something by no means identical with stupidity—that predisposed him to become one of the greatest criminals of that period. And if this is "banal" and even funny, if with the best will in the world one cannot extract any diabolical or demonic profundity from Eichmann, that is still far from calling it commonplace. . . . That such remoteness from reality and such thoughtlessness can wreak more havoc than all the evil instincts taken together which, perhaps, are inherent in man—that was, in fact, the lesson one could learn in Jerusalem. But it was a lesson, neither an explanation of the phenomenon nor a theory about it.[13]

In this difference between "lesson," "explanation," and "theory" we can see why "the banality of evil" ought to be interpreted as a warning. Arendt's phase was not meant to disclose the rational arguments of a demonic and monstrous villain but rather to warn us that evil now demands a new approach to legal and moral judgments. But in order to convey this new approach it was necessary to teach us "lesson." Lessons always entail an encouragement for a better future, whereas explanations often consist of impartial descriptions of particular phenomena. Against the future of explanations and theories, which demand submission to what they claim to predict, lessons—warnings—call for alterations that cannot be known in advance. But what sort of alteration is Arendt's warning calling for? Before answering this question, it is vital to ask whether the term "genocide" is adequate to label Eichmann's crime and if he can be held responsible, bearing in mind he was embedded in a bureaucratic apparatus following orders.

Arendt prefers the "expression 'administrative massacres'" to "genocide" because it better describes his crime and also warns us that "in the automated economy of a not-too-distant future [people] may be tempted to exterminate all those whose intelligence quotient is below a certain level."[14] Arendt's warning relates not so much to the person of the criminal, who was an ordinary bureaucrat, as to the technoscientific circumstances that allowed these crimes to occur. These circumstances are the result of the reductiveness of the scientific approach, that is, where everything is reduced to function rather than meaning.

Given this condition, Eichmann's greatest crime is his inability to distance himself from the legal requirements imposed upon him, that is, his being excessively obedient.[15] Only such unthinking obedience can render a crime against humanity banal, part of a daily routine. His lack of critical distance is evident in his reluctance "to imagine what the other person is experiencing." This is why Arendt believes that "the real perversion of this form of acting is functioning" because it eliminates the imagination and dialogue that takes place when we understand meaningful things. "What you have there is empty busyness. . . . He was a typical functionary. And a functionary, who is nothing but a functionary, is really a very dangerous gentleman. Ideology, I believe, in my view, played no great role here."[16]

Although Arendt does not believe thinking can "prevent catastrophes," it can prepare us to understand the unprecedented and catastrophic events that will take place if we do not listen to warnings. The "Nazi genocide will be the precedent for future genocide unless we heed the warnings regarding Eichmann's banality."[17] But in order to do this we must avoid treating matters of good and evil as moral or ethical issues because this shows "how little we know about them, for morals comes from mores and ethics from ethos, the Latin and the Greek words for customs and habit, the Latin word being associated with rules of behavior, whereas the Greek is derived from habitat, like our 'habits.'" The absence of thought Arendt was confronted with at the trial did not emerge from the "forgetfulness of former, presumably good manners and habits nor from stupidity in the sense of inability to comprehend—not even in the sense of 'moral insanity,' for it was just as noticeable in instances that had nothing to do with so-called ethical decisions or matters of conscience."[18] Only thinking—hermeneutic interpretation and dialogue unbound by received notions of functional truth—can free the faculty of judging through which we distinguish good and evil deeds. The presupposition for this kind of judging is nothing technical or theoretical but simply "the habit of living together explicitly with oneself, that is, of being engaged in that silent dialogue between me and myself which since Socrates and Plato we usually call thinking."[19]

The alteration Arendt was searching for through her warning did not concern ethics, morality, or even theory but rather thinking "from the standpoint of somebody else." Thinking in this manner—as Gadamer's hermeneutics of the other also requests—will not specify which ethical or moral values are correct but rather warn us of what occurs when we are indifferent to evil deeds. The argument that habits and customs can be taught is secondary if we recall "the alarming speed with which they are unlearned and forgotten when new circumstances demand a change in manners and patterns of behavior," as occurred after Hitler rose to power.[20] This bitter lesson of totalitarianism provoked Arendt's skepticism about mores, habits, and customs and also her emphasis on thinking as the only possibility of salvation. "What had become banal," as Judith Butler pointed out in an article for the *Guardian*, "was the attack on thinking, and this itself, for her, was devastating and consequential. Remarkable for us, no doubt, is Arendt's conviction that only philosophy could have saved those millions of lives."[21]

II

IGNORING WARNINGS

Epidemiologists warned us about the virus, they actually gave quite precise predictions that have now been proven accurate. Greta Thunberg was right when she claimed that politicians should listen to science, but we were more inclined to put our trust in "hunches" (Trump used this specific word), and it is easy to understand why. What is now going on is something we until now considered impossible: the basic coordinates of our normal lives are disappearing.
—Slavoj Žižek, *Pandemic!*

Philosophers, scientists, and journalists are constantly warning us of future pandemics, environmental disasters, and nuclear wars, among many other emergencies. The problem is not just our distrust, suspicion, and skepticism toward those that announce them but also our inability to listen, that is, to interpret their meaning. This is probably why we were unable to prepare for even predictable emergencies such as the 2008 financial crisis and the recent coronavirus pandemic—rendering our greatest emergency our inability to plan for them. Our inability to listen to warnings is a consequence of a global return to order through realism, which is symptomatic of the twenty-first century, when the coordinates Slavoj Žižek refers to in the epigraph have disappeared. These coordinates are those filters, references, and authorities that provided the basic cognitive maps to understand and interpret these warnings. The problem today is that these coordinates are being replaced by a transparent realism without authority, which is responsible for many ills of our era: alternative facts, fake news, and indifference toward warnings.

The goal of the book's second part is both to explain why we don't listen to warnings and, most of all, to reveal the consequences of not heeding the warnings of those thinkers discussed in the previous chapter. Before venturing into these consequences it's important to understand the sociopolitical meaning of the return to order and why it is a reaction to the postmodern condition and its philosophies. This reaction will also clarify the antiestablishment resentment, which is related to a cultural rejection of any sort of authority, the preference for direct information over the mediated news that until now was provided by traditional vectors of legitimization.

Announced as our only hope for "progress" and "peace" at the end of the twentieth century, globalization turned into one of the major drivers of the global return to order through realism. Joseph Stiglitz, Naomi Klein, and Richard Rorty, among others, warned us that it would lead to social disintegration, political authoritarianism, and increased surveillance, and globalism indeed managed to submit all social, political, and cultural relations to the rules of neoliberal finance. Globalization is responsible not only for the ongoing "great regression"—which Heinrich Geiselberger defines as a "reversion to an earlier stage of 'civilized conduct'"—but also for a homogenization of the world through a framed administrative order where reforms, revolts, and emergencies are almost impossible. This does not mean that there aren't any more emergencies but that their consequences are often contained to a much larger degree than in the past. This is evident in the three major events of this century: the 9/11 attacks in 2001, the 2008 global financial crisis, and the 2020 coronavirus pandemic.[1]

After these events we often heard in the streets and read in the press that the "world will never be the same." But instead of changing the course of history, these supposedly epochal events simply further intensified the military, financial, and global order that was already in motion. After 9/11, the US military occupation of the Middle East increased provoking further terrorism in the West. In 2009, corporate banks were bailed out by governments for the well-being of financial capitalism. Although there are other examples I could list—how the NSA was barely reformed after Edward Snowden revealed it was operating a secret surveillance program, for instance—the overall feeling of this century is that globalization intensified ongoing policies, producing a condition where the "greatest emergency is becoming the absence of emergencies"—that is, the suppression of existential emergency by the rhetoric of control imposed by right-wing and capitalist powers to preserve their power.

This emergency theory does not imply that crises such as the coronavirus or the wars in Ukraine and Gaza are not fundamental emergencies that we must continue to confront at all levels. It simply demands that we avoid assuming these were unpredictable events that we didn't know were going to occur. The World Health Organization as well as scientists such as David Quammen warned us for years that the threat of a pandemic virus was imminent; John Mearsheimer, Pepe Escobar, and many other social scientists and journalists also foresaw the invasion of Ukraine if NATO continued to pressure Russia; and Israel received an official warning from Egypt of a possible attack from Gaza three days before Hamas launched its deadly cross-border assault in 2023, which led to over fifty-five thousand deaths in Palestine. These events could have been avoided or mitigated if we had listened to the warnings, but the dynamic of absented emergencies that underlies our blindness keeps us from recognizing the disasters on the horizon.[2]

In sum, the greatest emergency is the emergencies we do not confront, that are swept aside as the status quo by the demands of global order. Among the most telling now are climate change, the refugee crisis, and the digital divide. These emergencies hide in plain sight, affecting the entire world even as their causes are absented and obscured. The fact that air pollution, according to the WHO, is responsible for the deaths of seven million people every year ought to raise the question of whether the coronavirus pandemic is a greater emergency than these respiratory illnesses. This is what the renowned journalist Owen Jones meant when he asked at the beginning of the pandemic, "Why don't we treat the climate crisis with the same urgency as coronavirus?" We can only hope climate change might also become an "emergency," one fought with the same unified purpose by a global majority of people as it is now by a small group. What is dramatic about COVID-19 and the war in Ukraine is that they were "absent" emergencies for many years that then erupted into visible emergencies.

Giorgio Agamben's theory of the exception—which relies heavily on Carl Schmitt's and Walter Benjamin's state-of-exception theories—has become central to understanding and interpreting global politics since the terrorist attacks on 9/11. When a state of exception is declared, as we've experienced during the pandemic lockdowns, the performative expression of state power becomes manifest as it forecloses any possibility of meaningful democratic politics. This is particularly evident if we compare the presidencies of George W. Bush and Donald

Trump. The latter is not remembered for exercising extralegal powers to transform the "state of emergency" into routine political measures as the former is but rather for denying pressing emergencies altogether. If during his first presidency Trump did not take advantage of pretexts to establish states of exception, it's because the exception—in the form of unprecedented technological, social, and political global framings—had already become our condition. Thus he ignored the many warnings and emergencies, such as climate change, civil protest, and the COVID-19 pandemic. But he is not alone. Jair Bolsonaro and Javier Milei, also right-wing populists, pursued the same unilateral path. But the sovereign is also submitted to a global technological frame that functions despite their orders.[3]

According to Martin Heidegger—who was the first to emphasize the emergency of absent emergencies—if "emergency" is often considered something evil or unfavorable, it is "because we value freedom from emergency as a 'good,' and indeed we are correct to do so when at issue are well-being and prosperity." The problem is that these depend entirely on an unbroken supply of objectively present enjoyable things, "which can be increased through progress." Progress has no future, however, because it merely takes things that already are and expedites them "further on their previous path." The problem for Heidegger is that the unbroken supply of enjoyable things is responsible for concealing Being, that is, "what is genuinely to come and thus resides completely outside of the distinction between good and evil and withdraws itself from all calculation."[4] This is why he was so concerned that we have lost touch with the fundamental tensions and emergencies that animate history—that is, that do not emerge from the background of banal crisis. When something emerges—the verb "emerge" comes from Latin *e-*, "out of, forth, from, according to," and *mergere*, "to dip, plunge, immerse"—it takes part in a process of becoming visible after being ignored or forgotten. But who is responsible for this generalized indifference?

Together with globalization and its technological advancements, the intellectual community in general is also responsible for this framed condition. The fact that among all disciplines the empirical sciences have maintained a central role in the structures of power is not because they yield better results than the humanities but because they promote a culture of descriptions. This culture does not impose on established structures of power as do sociology or philosophy; instead, it preserves a society of dominion where emergencies struggle to emerge. The goal of a culture of descriptions—regardless of the discipline—is to reveal the ultimate truthful and real context of the subject matter under analysis, which can vary from the superiority of certain ethical norms to the financial benefits of an economic theory. Leibniz and Descartes, for whom the world consisted of objects that are already there as such before they are investigated, are the architects of this culture that still today conditions our relation with the world.

In this modern relation, Heidegger explained, humans experience themselves as an "I" that relates to the world in such a way "that it renders this world to itself in the form of connections correctly established between its representations—that means judgments—and thus sets itself over against this world as to an object."[5] The problem with this descriptive stance is that it implies that we all have an impossible God's-eye view for which the truth of things exists in the form of a timeless presence. This conception of ontology relies upon the mathematization of the world by modern sciences, which aimed at a timeless description of the way the world really is. Jacques Derrida, following Nietzsche and Heidegger, pointed out how this culture has not only structured knowledge in terms of established polarities (presence versus absence, good versus evil, man versus woman) but also constructed a hierarchical order in a way that always favors the first term over the second. This hierarchical order has privileged terms of temporal, spatial, and unified presentness over their opposites and facilitated the access of realism.

The hunger for realism is particularly evident among philosophers who privilege presentness (what factually exists here and now) instead of the different meanings of existence. With the Enlightenment, when the empirical sciences were given priority because of their access to Nature, philosophy became a descriptive enterprise, leaving aside the wider realms from which philosophic problems arise. This is why philosophical disciplines such as ethics, aesthetics, and logic are consequences of modern subjectivism, where an "object" is posited, identified, and applied to a "subject" independent of its meaning. Ignoring meanings devalues different realms of existence and transforms truth into an ethical, aesthetic, or logical intuition of what is present for the subject. The problem with this intuition—as Heidegger repeatedly explained—is that it is expressed through a correspondence between propositions and facts where the real is only what fits this calculable and timeless correspondence.

The world, in a culture of description, is reduced to objective and calculable measures, that is, what is real according to science. This is why prominent promoters such as W. V. O. Quine could declare that "philosophy of science is philosophy enough," requesting that everyone follow only "the secure path of science" in all intellectual investigation. But by submitting philosophy to the secure path of science, contemporary analytic and continental philosophies have fallen back into "realism," that is, into the simple analysis and conservation of facts in order to help scientific disciplines develop, which was already the main concern of modern philosophers since the Enlightenment. The problem with this descriptive stance, as Rorty explained, is how it came to condition also those different sectors of culture whose progress should not be measured objectively by the intellectual community.

In the Enlightenment, this notion became concrete in the adoption of the Newtonian physical scientist as a model of the intellectual. To most thinkers of the eighteenth century, it seemed clear that the access to Nature that physical science had provided should now be followed by the establishment of social, political, and economic institutions that were in accordance with Nature. Ever since, liberal social thought has centered on social reform as made possible by objective knowledge of what human beings are like—not knowledge of what Greeks or Frenchmen or Chinese are like, but of humanity as such. We are the heirs of this objectivist tradition, which centers on the assumption that we must step outside our community long enough to examine it in the light of something that transcends it, namely, that which it has in common with every other actual and possible human community.[6]

In a culture of descriptions, as we can see, the model intellectual is one that is in possession of the essence of reality, which defines truth for all human beings. Intellectuals like John Searle or Henry-Bernard Lévy, for example, are renowned representatives of this culture. Although they do not want their ideas necessarily to dominate, in fact they help maintain a society in which they find themselves at ease. This is why Searle, for example, is interested in conserving the "Western Rationalistic Tradition," that is, those standards of objectivity, truth, and rationality that "are essential presuppositions of any sane philosophy." A healthy philosophy, according to the American philosopher, is one that not only always cooperates with empirical science but also submits itself to such irrefutable facts as those "stated by the atomic theory of matter and the evolutionary theory of biology." Lévy is convinced there is no alternative to the West as the bearer of universal modern values because it has proven to be superior to all the other civilizations. This superiority, according to the French thinker and activist, is founded on the triumph of Western liberal democracy, that is, the prevalence of Good over Evil. If Lévy believes that we in the West must defend ourselves against "other civilizations"—in particular those seeking to restore the Russian empire, Chinese empire, or Islamic empire (represented by the Muslim Brotherhood)—it's because only we Westerners have found the real essence of humanity.

While the American philosopher was awarded the National Humanities Medal by Bush for his "efforts to deepen understanding of the human mind, for using his writings to shape modern thought, defend reason and objectivity, and define the debate about the nature of artificial intelligence," the French thinker is constantly praised in Western media for advocating the superiority of Western civilization through NATO military interventions. What is most interesting about these recognitions is not that these intellectuals accepted them but rather the sort of intellectual stances endorsed by an American president and an international alliance that intervenes militarily in the name of supposedly objective facts (the presence of "weapons of mass destruction" and "universal modern values") against the desires of the majority of the world's population. Unfortunately, Searle and Lévy are not the only intellectuals in our culture of descriptions who want philosophy—as Gianni Vattimo pointed out—to "participate in the general 'return to order' called for precisely by globalization."[7] There is an international movement of thinkers who are not only more radical but also united against postmodernism and its philosophies. They represent this culture of "healthy" descriptions to the fullest. But who are they?

Although realism as a philosophical tradition and stance is not something new—we saw earlier how its origins can be found in Leibniz and Descartes—its promoters have insisted on its novel contribution through a coordinated campaign inspired by media marketing in various countries since the beginning of the century.[8] Among its most combative promoters are Maurizio Ferraris, Graham Harman, Markus Gabriel, and Quentin Meillassoux. While some of them prefer the terms "transcendental realism," "object-oriented-ontology," or "speculative realism," the overall message is that "contemporary philosophers," as Meillassoux explains, "have lost the great outdoors, the absolute outside of pre-critical thinkers: that outside which was not relative to us, and which was given as indifferent to its own givenness to be what it is, existing in itself regardless of whether we are thinking of it or not; that outside which thought could explore with the legitimate feeling of being on foreign territory—of being entirely elsewhere."[9] As we can see, Meillassoux's goal is to refute any form of correlationism, which he considers the enduring legacy of Kant's critique.

Harman defines this "new" ontology in opposition to philosophical theories that have reductionist tendencies of any kind, such as hermeneutics, deconstruction, and critical theory. He believes an object "is anything that cannot be entirely reduced either to the components of which it is made or to the effects that it has on other things."[10] Harman calls on us to avoid our prejudices or assumptions about the "world" in order to acquire knowledge of the "real world," that is, the one that counts. But which is the world that counts?

Ferraris's and Gabriel's versions of realism are the most appropriate to respond to this question because they present their stance as a reaction to postmodernism. According to Ferraris, there is something in the air that distinguishes the dawn of the twenty-first century from the dusk of the twentieth: the exhaustion of postmodernism and its belief that everything is constructed through interpretation, language, and prejudices. Instead, as he explains, "something, or rather, much more than we are willing to admit, is not constructed—and this is a wonderful thing, otherwise we could not distinguish dreams from reality."[11] Although Ferraris's ontology clearly refuses to reduce reality to any sort of constructivist discourse, he does accept that there are areas, specifically social ones, that can be conceived as constructed. But

> the mistake made here by postmodern thinkers was due to the fallacy of being-knowledge, that is, the confusion between ontology and epistemology: between what there is and what we know about what there is. It is clear that in order to know that water is H_2O I need language, schemes, and categories. But that water is H_2O is utterly independent from any knowledge of mine—so much so that water was H_2O even before the birth of chemistry, and it would still be if we all disappeared from the earth. Mostly, as regards nonscientific experience, water wets and fire burns whether I know it or not, independently from languages, schemes, and categories. At a certain point, something resists us. It is what I call "unamendability": the salient character of the real.[12]

The fact that "something resists us" is enough for Ferraris to hold postmodernism responsible for the rise of "post-truth," "fake news," and its sociopolitical consequences. The emancipation that postmodernity promised through its arguments—reality is socially constructed and infinitely manipulable—has not occurred, as the three world events mentioned earlier demonstrate.[13] Millions of deaths and mass unemployment are real. Postmodernism, according to Ferraris, has become the social and political justification for saying and doing whatever one wants as so many populists do nowadays.

Gabriel also believes we are living in "dark times"—where economic, political, and environmental crises emerge continuously—because the contemporary smog of "nihilism," "post-truth emotionalism," and "cultural relativism" convinced us we cannot see the world as it really is. In order to correct this, the German thinker calls for a revival of moral realism as an antidote to the forces of chaos and uncertainty that characterize postmodernity. He believes not only that there are universal, objective, and clear moral values that we humans are capable of understanding despite our cultural traditions, prejudices, and views but also that moral progress is universally possible. Gabriel is convinced we are at the dawn of a new enlightenment, one where human progress "consists in a cooperation between scientific, technological and moral progress with ethically defensible aims." Although these ethical aims and moral progress are systematically concealed, he proposes three theses about the nature of morality that are laid out like commandments revealed by God:

> **Core thesis 1:** There are moral facts that are independent of our private and group opinions. They exist objectively.
> **Core thesis 2:** The objectively existing moral facts are essentially knowable to us; they are spirit-dependent. They concern humans and constitute a moral compass for what we should do, are allowed to do or must prevent. The central moral facts are obvious, and in dark times they are concealed by ideology, propaganda, manipulation and psychological mechanisms.

Core thesis 3: The objectively existing moral facts apply at all times in which humans have existed, do exist and will exist. They are independent of culture, political opinion, religion, gender, place of origin, appearance and age, and therefore universal. The moral facts do not discriminate.[14]

The greatest problem with Gabriel's global call to order through (moral) realism—besides the obvious objection that most of our moral principles such as "it is wrong to lie" have exceptions and therefore cannot be both true and universal—is that it is presented as a new Eurocentric Western Enlightenment. "The European project that I have in mind," as he recently declared, "is that of the universal human values. Europeans, thanks to their philosophical past from the Greeks to contemporary philosophers, are the best equipped to respond to the challenge of social justice and the future of democracy. Not only for Europe, but for all humanity."[15] But what does it mean to be "best equipped"?

If Europeans are best equipped to respond to these challenges, it is largely because Europe is now composed of liberal democracies that "enable a form of organization that now makes the principle of human dignity its priority. Our political order rests on moral progress, which it implements in the bureaucratic forms of the democratic law-based state."[16] Despite the numerous structural inequalities of this order—from mass unemployment to increasing xenophobia and femicide—it's interesting to note how Gabriel's realism is also founded on the same sense of science's superiority as Searle's. He considers it wrong to classify oneself as a member of a social group or as having a gender—German, Black, nonbinary—because these "social identities are factually unfounded, scientifically impermissible simplifications of our complex social and natural situation as living beings on Planet Earth."[17]

Similar arguments can be found in a more politicized movement called the "intellectual dark web," whose principal representatives are the psychologist Jordan Peterson, the neuroscientist Sam Harris, and others who believe that "cultural Marxism" and "postmodernism" have been deliberately introduced into Western European societies in order to undermine Western civilization.[18] This cultural stance has denied thought any rational access to things in themselves, allowing apparently unfounded discourses on scientific objectivity, gender studies, and political values that now control Western universities. This is why Christina Hoff Sommers, for example, opposes those feminists who still "believe that our society is best described as a patriarchy, a 'male hegemony,' a 'sex/gender system,'" with a new "factual feminism" that grounds the basic tenets of feminism in a data-driven approach. According to this approach, the gender wage gap is a result of women's choices to work jobs that pay less. As the *New York Times* writer Bari Weiss says, this is a movement determined to emphasize the "biological differences between men and women" and to demonstrate that "identity politics" is a "threat to our social fabric."[19]

The anthropologist Didier Fassin also identified a similar movement in France that targets "a long list of fields—from ethnicity, race, gender and intersectionality to colonialism, decoloniality and Islamophobia. This movement is best understood as a rejection of the evolution of society, politics and ideas, and an endeavor to re-establish the old social and political order of things."[20] This endeavor is probably at the origin of a conference organized in 2021 at the Sorbonne titled After Deconstruction: Rebuilding Science and Culture, which positioned itself against deconstruction, perhaps the most postmodern philosophy of all.

The minister of national education at the time, Jean-Michel Blanquer, chaired the symposium and stressed the necessity "that France, having inoculated the virus of deconstruction, it is up to her to discover the vaccine." According to the minister, as well as many participants, deconstruction undermines the foundations of Western civilization and threatens the social, cultural, and political order. Now that the proceedings of the conference have been published, it is clear that few of the participants ever read the works of Jacques Derrida, Gayatri Spivak, and other thinkers categorized under the deconstructionist banner. "Although at the beginning," as the editors of the proceedings write in the foreword, deconstruction was a critical stance, "it transformed into a doctrine that drives the confusion between research and militantism, truth and morality, science and ideology."[21]

Assuming that wokeness, cancel culture, and other progressive ideologies are harmful to our democracies and blaming a philosophical stance whose binary approach to the analysis of texts is meant to disclose intrinsic violence in opposing forces is surprising to say the least. However, according to Blanquer—who recently created the Republic Laboratory think tank specifically to fight "woke culture"—we need to defend universalism and reason from the onslaught of deconstruction and its identity politics, which are polarizing Western societies. The significance of this conference is not only philosophical and cultural but also sociopolitical because of Blanquer's participation. Not surprisingly, the Sorbonne never sanctioned the conference, given the inevitable protests, calls for boycott, and accusations of extreme-right rhetoric. Although defenders of deconstruction organized another conference at the Sorbonne—Who Is Afraid of Deconstruction?—in 2023, it has now become clear that (moral and feminist) realism represents the continued global call to order in intellectual guise. But what are the psychological motivations behind this global return to order? Doesn't the need for realism disclose an effect of ressentiment, of the "tedious qualities of old dogs and men who have long been kept on the leash," as Nietzsche would say?[22]

Vattimo was among the first to analyze the origins of this return in one of his last books—*Of Reality: The Purpose of Philosophy* (2012)—which includes his Leuven and Gifford lectures. According to the Italian philosopher, Searle, Ferraris, and the other realists reveal a "fundamentalist neurosis that follows the late-industrial society as the regressive reaction of defense against the postmodern Babel of languages and values." This neurotic reaction to different languages, values, and religions is really an expression of fear, that is, a demand for security that globalization continues to promise but is unable to deliver. But why are the roots of realism, as Vattimo believes, found "in a psychological discomfort rather than in a strictly conscious demand"?

> The need for reality is neurotic, we could say, because it refuses to take notice of the "logical" need to recognize itself as gathered within that game of interpretation that claims to be the only "reality." . . . In fact, even among the "realists" one often finds a complex mix of "foundational" arguments (the defense of the "objective" weight of perceptions, of the unavoidable passivity of sensible intuition, and so on) and ad hominem, rhetorical-persuasive arguments that frequently appeal to the unacceptable consequences of hermeneutic nihilism, which would open the way to the dissolution of every morality (if God is dead, anything goes) and, above all, to a dangerous devaluation of the experimental sciences.[23]

The game of interpretation that Vattimo refers to in this passage refers to the interpretative nature of reality—what realists might call *perspectivism* or *correlationism*—and its inevitable historical condition—a condition that realists want to ignore. In order to clarify this, Vattimo analyzes the political implications behind Tarski's famous principle, according to which "'P' is true if and only if P," which translated means: "'it is raining' is true if and only if it is raining." When proponents of Tarski apply his theorem, they ignore that whoever says, claims, or affirms that "P" or "it is raining" should "stand outside of quotation marks is probably somebody who benefits from its being stated in this way" and ignore also how they are part of a "community that professes and applies the paradigm," rendering its validity a matter of "negotiation" and "consensus" rather than of "rain."[24] In order to reap these benefits, others must also accept the statement because they represent the only paradigm that can verify it. This probably explains why the new realists are persistent in promoting their "novel" ideas in conferences, seminars, and edited volumes, that is, within a community.

Vattimo considers the global return to order through realism reactionary and conservative because its proponents have to ignore the demands of those who are dissatisfied with the current order and because of its preference for order over freedom. How can we achieve greater freedom in a rational organized society where existence is annihilated through objectivity? It is interesting to note that Ferraris, in a dialogue with Vattimo in 2011, insisted that postmodernism is responsible not only for discrediting facts through deconstruction and hermeneutics but also for the rise of populism.[25] What is curious about this accusation—which is also at the core of the conference against deconstruction mentioned earlier—is that it is yet another call to order, against any deviation from the current established political, economic, and social order. This is why Žižek—who also rejects the standard "realist" approach—links the populist wave to realist resentment toward postmodernity.

What is happening today is that, with the populist wave that unsettled the political establishment, the Truth/Lie that served as the ideological foundation of this establishment is also falling apart. And the ultimate reason for this disintegration is not the rise of postmodern relativism but the failure of the ruling establishment, which is no longer able to maintain its ideological hegemony. We can now see what those who bemoan the "death of truth" really deplore: the disintegration of one big Story more or less accepted by the majority, which brought ideological stability to a society. The secret of those who curse "historicist relativism" is that they miss the safe situation in which one big Truth (even if it was a big Lie) provided the basic "cognitive mapping" for everyone.[26]

Searle, Gabriel, and Sommers miss this "safe situation" and are also trying to restore its old ideological hegemony, regardless of its ethical consequences. This is why Žižek likes to attribute Goethe's motto to them: "*'Besser Unrecht als Unordnung,'* better injustice than disorder, better one big Lie than the reality of a mixture of lies and truths." Their preference for order—even if unjust and reactionary—is founded on the "standard 'realist' approach," which ought be rejected thoroughly because facts or data "are a vast and impenetrable domain, and we always approach them from (what hermeneutics calls) a certain horizon of understanding, privileging some data and omitting others." Although Žižek is not a fan of postmodern philosophies, he does recognize that there is no return to old ideological hegemonies just like there can be no "return to what is real in philosophy."[27] This recognition is founded on the contributions of postmodern philosophers and on those classic thinkers who prepared the ground for the investigations of Jean-François Lyotard, Ihab Hassan, and Derrida. Given realists' inability to properly refer to postmodern thinkers and their theses—as happened with Peterson in a public debate with Žižek in 2019[28]—it is important to briefly recall their origin and contribution.

The postmodern critique of the universalist aspirations of modernity did not begin with Lyotard, but much earlier. At the beginning of the twentieth century, Spengler, Arendt, and others were sounding the alarm about the dangers that came from spreading Enlightenment-style scientific objectivism to all the realms of our lives. Classics as such Spengler's *The Decline of the West* (1918–1922) and Arendt's *The Origins of Totalitarianism* (1951) were concerned with the rationalization of the world that we are now witnessing at a much more profound level. Adorno and Horkheimer, in their *Dialectic of Enlightenment* (1947), explicitly state that the "enlightenment is totalitarian" in order to indicate how the disastrous world wars of the twentieth century were rooted in its industrial and technological development. The most important feature of these authors' dismay at the spreading culture of descriptions is not the belief that objectivism is incorrect or unreal but rather that it is unjust, a lethal attack on freedom, as Žižek and Vattimo remind us.

This is why an open society, as Karl Popper explained, is one "in which individuals are confronted with personal decisions" as opposed to a "magical or tribal or collectivist society." In the former, no one is in possession of the ultimate reality because it is acknowledged that people have different values and interests; in the latter, reality is imposed by the bearers of power regardless of our differences. Herbert Marcuse and Zygmunt Bauman developed Popper's intuition to stress the danger of modernity's universalist aspirations. Marcuse declared that the "total subordination of reason to metaphysical reality (essentially emotive and irrational) prepares the way for racist ideology," and Bauman insisted that "the modernist dream is embraced by an absolute power able to monopolize modern vehicles of rational action, and when that power attains freedom from effective social control, genocide follows."[29]

It is not an accident that all these classic texts appeared at the same time that Claude Lévi-Strauss was writing his anthropological studies, that is, when encounters with other cultures were providing a starting point for the philosophical decentralization of European civilization. And there were several other "counter-Enlightenment" philosophers who warned against scientific-objective realism and prepared the ground for postmodern thinkers. The first to use the terminology "postmodern condition" was Hassan in 1976 to refer to the social condition of Western civilization, but it is Lyotard in 1979 who described the philosophical innovations that this terminology implied. In *The Postmodern Condition*—originally presented as a report on knowledge commissioned by the government of Quebec—the French philosopher shows that modernity was characterized by a process that took place through "metanarratives," that is, as founding myths that present themselves as global narratives, such as positivism, Marxism, and Hegelianism. Whereas modernity was the age where norms were legitimized through metanarratives, in postmodernity these metanarratives have been weakened because communication technologies—the exchange of news and information among entire masses of people—have multiplied perspectives, rendering their legitimacy questionable. Modern self-understanding is brought to a crisis through the dissemination of knowledge, where meaning is weakened through the proliferation of information. This does not imply that metanarratives have ceased to exist—realists have clearly returned to them—but rather that we began to lose interest in them because of technological transformations.

The most important consequence of this transformation is the dissolution of the myths of humanity's linear progress guided by the "more civilized" Western countries. These countries cannot claim anymore—if they ever could—a moral, civil, or philosophical superiority because history is not a development toward social emancipation and knowledge a progression toward truth. If history and knowledge cannot relate anymore to the rational program of the Enlightenment that Adorno, Popper, and Arendt warn us about, they are now guided by consensus, that is, by dialogic procedures. This is why in postmodernity, as Vattimo explains, "we don't reach agreement when we have discovered the truth, we say we have discovered the truth when we reach agreement."[30]

As we can predict, this has deep political import, for now politics cannot be based on accurate representations of reality but rather on singular events that cannot be definitively classified by any superior civilization or rational theory. If Lyotard's deprecation of grand narratives has been welcomed by minorities, it's because these have always been marginalized by rational politics on the basis of their difference; that is, their difference has been used as a factor of discrimination. In postmodernity, apparently fundamental values are not the result of a historical development toward truth but rather an agreement among social communities, which are now able to connect more freely than before. As we can see, the so-called chaos brought about by the weakening or dissolution of metanarratives in postmodernity, contrary to the views of Ferraris, Gabriel, and others, did not aim to create a new order but to avoid the external imposition of order.

Postmodernity and its philosophies (in particular deconstruction and hermeneutics) play an important part in Žižek's and

Vattimo's rejection of the global return to order through realism because they highlight the relevance of consensus and the illusion of objectivity. The historian of science Naomi Oreskes, for example, opposes any appeal to realism and rejects unmediated scientific claims. Pleas for realism, she claims, "are often used to discourage those who think the world can be a different place. The people making them want to justify the status quo and deflate the ambitions of those among us who would be agents of change." This change is impossible without social consensus because "facts remain robust," as Bruno Latour says, "only when they are supported by a common culture, by institutions that can be trusted, by a more or less decent public life, by more or less reliable media."[31]

These institutions together represent the necessary consensus to enable listening to those interpretive warnings as opposed to conspiracy theories, which rely on the exploitation of antiestablishment resentment. If Vattimo, Žižek, Oreskes, and Latour call upon postmodern philosophies to reject "transparent realism without authority," it is not because it proposes another order but rather to avoid the external imposition of an order. But the imposition of a new order is already in motion (through "moral realism" and "factual feminism"), and it ignores warnings by appealing to alternative facts, post-truth, and fake news, which arise from realism's naïve enthusiasm for objectivity, transparency, and rationality. Besides Lévi and Peterson, who still believe that Enlightenment reasoning is an accurate model for how most people judge, this naïveté is also present among technophiles such as Mark Zuckerberg, Elon Musk, and Evgeny Morozov, who believe that conflicts can be reduced simply by improving communication among human beings—through the proliferation of "unfiltered" information delivered via decentralized platforms that do not exercise editorial control, such as social media.[32] The preference for direct information over mediated news—which until now was provided by traditional vectors of legitimization—"leads to the bizarre conclusion that an assertion of fact is more credible if it lacks an institutional source," as Stanley Fish pointed out.[33]

This generalized belief has intensified the cultural rejection of any sort of authority that is at the heart of antiestablishment resentments and also our distrust and suspicion of those that announce warnings. To credibly warn, it is necessary to have the authority of consensus, the network of related institutions and traditions that represent the collective judgment of others. The mistake of the naïve enthusiast of realism as well as the entire Enlightenment project is to reject authority on the grounds that it is often arbitrary, threatening, and sanctioned only by institutional powers that are not always legitimated by reason. This prejudice—as Hans-Georg Gadamer pointed out—does not take into consideration the difference between "authoritative" and "authoritarian": The latter has not earned its authority and is concerned primarily with power, order, and obedience; the former instead earns its authority through a foundational consensus and receives not so much obedience as trust.[34] Warnings and predictions are also founded on this difference, rendering authoritative warnings easier to ignore despite the possibly devastating consequences of doing so.

5

I'M NOT A KEYBOARD JIHADI

Margaret Atwood wrote *The Testaments*, the sequel to *The Handmaid's Tale*, in part because she worried the world—after the first election of Donald Trump, the global backlash against women's rights, and increasing environmental degradation—was moving more toward "Gilead" than away from it. Gilead, where both novels take place, is a totalitarian theocratic regime that took over the United States in the middle of a fertility crisis caused by nuclear wars, toxic pollution, and ecosystem breakdown. To fight this crisis, childbirth and gender hierarchy have become a priority to the point that fertile women, known as the "Handmaids," are forcibly assigned to produce children for "Commanders," who are the ruling class in Gilead. Offred ("Of Fred"), one of few women who can still bear children, is not only forced to participate in reproductive-slavery ceremonies but also required to become an integral member of this fundamentalist Christian society where women have been stripped of all their rights. The Bible is central in both novels because Gilead bases its laws, customs, and organization around a fundamentalist interpretation. This is why in *The Handmaid's Tale*, Offred says the Bible is "kept locked up, the way people once kept tea locked up, so the servants wouldn't steal it.

It is an incendiary device: who knows what we'd make of it, if we ever got our hands on it? We can be read to from it, by him, but we cannot read." In *The Testaments*, Becka tells Agnes, "I need to warn you . . . as it doesn't say what they say it says. . . . Everyone at the top of Gilead has lied to us."[1]

These novels are not meant to demonstrate that the Bible can be used to justify the most despicable acts—Gilead's men base their marital system entirely on a distorted interpretation of Abraham's life to justify sex with the Handmaids—but rather how belief systems, ideological reassurances, and principles of stability can become violent, as Nietzsche also warned us. If these beliefs often result in and sustain authoritarian regimes such as Gilead, it's because they leave no space for change—as literary interpretations of the Bible do. This is why the Commanders, as well as the Aunts (these are responsible for overseeing the training and indoctrination of Handmaids), must impose extreme acts of faith to justify obedience to a book that is kept "in the darkness of their locked boxes, glowing with arcane energy."[2] However, religion, as Atwood explained, "does not create these behaviors. It's [that] people appropriate religion and use it to shut other people down. You can say the same of atheistic ideology."[3]

As we can see, Atwood's novels, like Nietzsche's warning regarding the death of God, are not directed against Jesus or Christianity as much as at those radical systems, ideologies, and theories founded on revered texts. Although these radical beliefs are decisive in making possible the particular ordering of a society, they also become superfluous once they are realized because they are no longer necessary. This is why the German thinker insisted on the need to overcome "our entire European morality" through the *Übermensch*, that is, "the most moderate, those who have no *need* of extreme articles of faith, who not only concede but even love a good deal of contingency and nonsense."[4] The others—believers of all sorts—will continue to find gods, ideologies, and theories necessary and justify them through violent acts of faith. But who is still "living under the shadow," as Nietzsche warned? The paradigmatic examples of violent acts of faith in the twenty-first century are from Islamic religious fundamentalists, European far-right extremists, and American conspiracy movements. Despite the differences among these groups, each relies on texts to justify an act of violence meant to preserve and defend a belief that has run its course.

To understand violent acts of faith attributed to Islamic fundamentalists—from 9/11 to the killing of two Swedish football fans in central Brussels in 2023 and fourteen people in the city of New Orleans in the early hours of New Year's Day in 2025—it's crucial to begin by asking whether they represent an "Islamification of radicalism" or "radicalization of Islam." This difference was at the center of a public debate between Oliver Roy and Gilles Kepel—two French political scientists who specialize in Islam—that explored the sociopolitical relations between Islam and violence. Roy places great emphasis on the psychology of a homicidal jihadist, which is strictly marginal to Islam, but Kepel believes these individuals are "deeply threatened by the emergence of jihadism at its very heart" as they struggle to integrate with European society. "In the Islamist worldview," according to Kepel, "the only history of humanity is that of the Revelation and its accomplishment. If the world is not yet entirely Muslim, that is the fault of tepid believers who turned away from doctrinal rectitude."[5] Although Roy does not exclude unsuccessful integration as an essential aspect of the creation of radicals, he recalls that in France, only a minority of Muslims are involved in jihad in comparison, for example, to those enrolled in the military, police, and security forces.

Despite the media manipulation and public temptation to see in Islam a radical ideology that mobilizes multitudes of people, just as Nazism was able to mobilize large sections of the German population, the reality is that ISIS's plan to establish a global caliphate is a fantasy meant to draw in violent "youngsters who have delusions of grandeur." This delusion is a reaction to their socioeconomic condition: 50 percent of the jihadis in France are second-generation immigrants with no religious education. They are often involved in minor crimes such as drug dealing, robbery, and confrontations with the police. Their conversion, according to Roy, is rapid and often accomplished in prison or within the "framework of a group of friends or over the internet [rather] than in the context of a mosque."[6] What is peculiar about these radicalized youths is their disinterest in every political and religious movement that has come before them, such as Palestinian liberation, anti-Islamophobia associations, or even Islamic NGOs. If the Muslim conflict they are impatient to avenge is seldom specified, it's because they are interested in a "global Islam" that only exists as an internet fantasy.

The scriptural exegeses that fill the pages of *Dabiq* and *Dar al-Islam*, the two recent Isis magazines written in English and French, are not the cause of radicalization. They help provide a theological rationalization for the violence of the radicals—based not on real knowledge but on an appeal to authority. When young jihadis speak of "truth," it is never in reference to discursive knowledge. They are referring to their own certainty, sometimes supported by an incantatory reference to the sheikhs, whom they have never read. For example, Cédric, a converted Frenchman, claimed at his own trial: "I'm not a keyboard jihadi, I didn't convert on YouTube. I read the scholars, the real ones." He said this even though he cannot read Arabic and met the members of his network over the internet.[7]

The delusive grandeur and self-certainty that drive these "born-again" Muslims confirm not only that their radicalism is a choice, the only one that appeals to them, but also that they are still "living under the shadow" of God. This is evident in the significance they still attribute to the sacred texts. Although jihadists, as Roy explains, "do not descend into violence after poring over the sacred texts"— their religious knowledge is marginal—they are nonetheless convinced they have "read the scholars, the real ones" that rationalize and justify their violent acts of faith. The problem is that they can't even envision what a perfected Islamic society would look like.[8] What counts for these radicals is to assert the "truth" of revered texts through violent acts of faith that will save them from their unfulfilled lives.

Salvation was also the goal of the murderous acts in Oslo on July 22, 2011, by the thirty-two-year-old right-wing extremist Anders Breivik. The difference is that he was not trying to save himself as much as Europe from "Islamization," as he explained in a manifesto of 1,518 pages titled *2083: A European Declaration of Independence*. The "marketing operation," as he called it, to launch this manifesto—composed chiefly of material copied and assembled from the internet—consisted of "sacrificing" seventy-seven people. He first detonated a bomb in a van parked at the heart of the Regjeringskvartalet, Oslo's government quarter, killing eight and injuring 209. After fleeing the scene dressed as a policeman, he took a ferry to the small island of Utøya. The forested island was hosting the annual summer camp run by the Labor Party, where he systematically hunted down and shot dead sixty-nine teenagers. The final murders of Breivik were captured by a news crew that was circling the island until he surrendered to the police without a fight, calling them "my brothers."[9]

Breivik's most significant fear during the ten-week trial was that he would be diagnosed as mentally ill by two court-ordered psychiatrists; this would undermine his whole operation and cause. The first said that he was a psychotic paranoid schizophrenic and had to be hospitalized, and the second diagnosed narcissistic and antisocial personality disorders but considered him competent to stand trial. The court found that Breivik was sane and sentenced him to a maximum of twenty-one years in prison, even though he can be held for longer if he remains a danger to society. During the trial, he was given ample time to speak of his "rambling anti-Muslim, anti-multicultural political views, which included a rant about the 'deconstruction' of Norway at the hands of 'cultural Marxists.'"[10] Although he admitted the twin attacks were "cruel," he also told the court he estimated fewer killings were necessary to launch his manifesto, which he had emailed just hours before the massacre to hundreds of recipients. In addition to the manifesto, Breivik also authored a twelve-minute anti-Muslim video called "Knights Templar 2083" and was a member of a Swedish neo-Nazi internet forum called Nordisk, where he described himself as Christian and conservative. The fascist-style salute Breivik made just before being sentenced should be enough to prove that his crimes were not only a deranged individual's violent act of faith but also the consequence of the rising anti-immigrant populism in Europe.

To understand Breivik's ideological self-justification, it is important to recall that he was a member of the right-wing Progress Party (FrP or PP), the second-largest party in Norway's parliament, which "since its emergence in 1973 as a small, obscure anti-taxation and anti-bureaucratic party, through the 1987 parliamentary elections and onwards, had become one of Norway's largest opposition parties. From 1987 the PP ran on the back of its anti-immigration and anti-Muslim discourse and policies."[11] But his ideological predecessor, according to Slavoj Žižek, was Pim Fortuyn, the Dutch rightist politician who embodied the intersection between rightist populism and liberal political correctness: He was gay, educated, and tolerant with "regard to everything except his basic stance towards Muslim immigrants."[12] This is probably why Breivik supports abortion and declares himself pro-gay. But Fortuyn is only one of the many references that formed Breivik's racist beliefs. Sixty-four times in his manifesto, he quotes Robert Spencer, author of *The Truth About Muhammad: Founder of the World's Most Intolerant Religion* and operator of the Jihad Watch website; William Lind's cultural Marxism conspiracy theory; and Bat Ye'or, an Egyptian of Jewish background "who believes that the European elites have conspired against their people to hand the continent over to Muslims."[13]

Breivik's commitment to his violent act of faith, like that of the jihadists already discussed, relies on a "sense of grandiosity," a make-believe reality in which his significance is unquestionable. Barry Richard states that this sense of grandeur results from an intense "fear of domination" and "inner collapse."[14] This is probably why Breivik places so much significance on texts that rationalize and justify his actions against a threat that must be defeated. This threat consists of the "combination of three elements (Marxism, multiculturalism and Islamism), each of which belongs to a different political space: the Marxist radical left, multiculturalist liberalism, Islamic religious fundamentalism."[15] The teenagers at the Labor Party summer camp represented the incarnation of this combination, the driving force behind what Breivik described as the "Islamisation" and destruction of a "pure Nordic country." Supporters of this "Islamisation," he explains in the manifesto, are traitors who must be eliminated by assassination, bombing, and even nuclear weapons. This is why he envisions four generations of civil wars during which 140,000 more traitors must be executed.

As we can see, the principal ideological drive for Breivik and many far-right radicals is not the foreigners as much as the democratic elite governments who "have failed to protect their citizens, and have even conspired to humiliate those who depend on them. Feeling humiliated, they direct their rage at the liberal democratic governments they believe have abandoned them."[16] The elections of far-right populists such as Jair Bolsonaro, Giorgia Meloni, and Javier Milei are only some of the many consequences of this rage; other consequences include the numerous conspiracy theories that have emerged over these years. Among these, QAnon—which has many ties with Donald Trump—has incorporated not only radical religious principles but also violent acts such as kidnappings, assassination plots, and the 2021 storming of the US Capitol. These events led the FBI and the Department of Homeland Security to warn they have become the most significant domestic security threat in the United States. But what is QAnon, and why do many believe it is "not just a conspiracy theory but the birth of a new religion"?[17]

QAnon evolved out of three conspiracy theories: *The Protocols of the Elders of Zion*, the age-old antisemitic blood libel, and Pizzagate. The last of these, which incorporates the central antisemitic premises of the other two, culminated in a shooting in 2016 by a man who had traveled to a pizza restaurant in Washington, DC, convinced there were children held captive there. He was confident that Hillary Clinton's campaign manager, John Podesta, had leaked emails that included a secret code for a child trafficking ring. A year later, QAnon's first post—"Open your eyes, Many in our govt worship Satan"—appeared on the notoriously toxic message board 4chan from an anonymous account. "Q Clearance Patriot," now known simply as "Q," claimed to be a high-ranking government insider with access to classified information about a powerful cabal of Satan-worshiping pedophiles that run the world. These include politicians like Joseph Biden and Barack Obama, religious figures such as Pope Francis and the Dalai Lama, and Hollywood celebrities such as Lady Gaga and Oprah Winfrey. Many of its followers believe that, in addition to molesting children, members of this group "kill and eat their victims to extract a life-extending chemical called adrenochrome." Trump, according to Q's classified information, was recruited by top military generals to run for president in 2016 with the explicit order to "break up this criminal conspiracy and bring its members to justice."[18]

Like jihadists relying on unfounded religious reading and Breivik's basing his manifesto around material plagiarized from the internet, QAnon followers also justify their violent acts of faith through texts—cryptic posts on message boards. Part of QAnon's appeal, as Brandy Zadrozny and Ben Collins explain, "lies in its game-like quality. Followers wait for clues left by 'Q' on a message board. When the clues appear, believers dissect the riddle-like posts alongside Trump's speeches and tweets and news articles to validate the main narrative that Trump is winning a war against evil."[19] The most significant problem of Q's cryptic posts is not so much that we still do not know who is behind them but how compulsively Q's followers dissect and validate the unfounded information they provide.[20] Although QAnon has incorporated elements of many other conspiracy communities, including claims that adrenochrome was the cabal's cure for coronavirus and that the election was stolen from Trump, child trafficking continued to be its primary focus:

By focusing on babies and children, conspiracy theories anchor their narratives to the most fundamentally "innocent" and "good" beings. Harming babies and children is thus the ultimate evil, and those guilty of this are corrupt beyond redemption. Babies and harm done to them are the foundational axis of good and evil in the normative system that Q-conspiracy theories lay out. It's the lowest common denominator over which they can bond.[21]

The latest example of this bond comes from a movie—*The Sound of Freedom*, about a special agent rescuing children from a trafficking ring. Even though there is no reference to QAnon, the connection seems unquestionable: Trump hosted a screening of the film, its star (Jim Caviezel) tours conservative media networks to promote conspiracy theories about unnamed persons gathering chemicals from children's blood, and QAnon believers turned it into one of the highest-grossing movies of the year in North America.[22]

As QAnon was forced to move from 4chan to other social media platforms and its messages spread to TikTok, Nextdoor, and Telegram, it also strengthened its religious identity. This is manifest in the evangelical language that defines Q's messages and how its followers present themselves as "warriors" fighting against corrupt and powerful forces. Such terms as "the Storm"—the day on which Trump will finally arrest top Democrats running the global sex-trafficking ring—and "the great awakening"—when QAnon believers will celebrate their role in this purge—resonate with evangelicals' religious experience and prophecies about the Rapture. Although none of Q's predictions materialized, they continue to represent a plan that gives its followers not only hope but also a response to a government they believe has abandoned them. If QAnon has largely disappeared from the news during the 2024 presidential race, it's because it has been absorbed into the conspiracy-theorist wing of the GOP. According to Mike Rothschild, QAnon "tenets have become such a major part of mainstream conservatism and such a big part of the base of people that reelected Donald Trump."[23]

Ignoring Nietzsche's warning has led QAnon's followers, jihadists, and far-right radicals, such as Breivik, to violent acts of faith that resulted either in death or incarceration. The radical systems, ideologies, and theories they continue to believe have become redundant and counterproductive to their cause. Jihadists contributed to increased anti-Muslim sentiment, Breivik intensified authorities' alarm over far-right movements in Europe only, and QAnon further complicated the work of nonprofits that have been engaged in child protection for decades. All three belief systems claim to be "realist," preferring direct over mediated knowledge and information. This is why Cédric could claim he "read the scholars, the real ones," why Breivik refers to and faults "cultural Marxists," and why QAnon validates "Trump's war against evil" simply through Q's posts. This is possible only because these believers share a sense of "grandiosity"—"martyrs," "knights," and "warriors"—as opposed to Nietzsche's "moderate" *Übermenschen*, that is, those who have no *need* of extreme articles of faith. These believers are a symptom of the ongoing global return to order through realism, which leads to a place not very different from Gilead.

6

THERE IS NO RUSH TO REGULATE AI

The most exciting feature of "Metalhead"—the fifth episode of Netflix's *Black Mirror* TV series—is the absence of a justification for the empty postapocalyptic world in which the story is set and the events that seem to have ended most human life. The episode is shot in grainy, digital black and white and tells the story of Bella's struggle for survival as she looks for supplies in an unguarded warehouse with two other survivors. Although it's not clear why or what they have survived, references to wounded friends and empty pig farms indicate they are desperate and afraid of something that is hunting them on what appears to be the rolling English countryside. As soon as they find what they were looking for—which turns out to be a teddy bear designed to comfort a child living in a horrible world—an artificially intelligent "dog" robot wakes up and immediately fires off a salvo of tiny bullets, killing one of Bella's friends. As she flees the warehouse, the terrier-sized, spindly-legged cybernetic dog chases and kills Bella's other companion and goes on to pursue her through the hills and into a private house until she gives up, committing suicide. We learn in the episode that this "Metalhead dog"—which can drive cars and open any door by hacking them with a USB key—doesn't have any discernible thought or motivation besides a preprogrammed logic to kill living beings. The episode ends with a drone's-eye view of the warehouse and hills full of identical robot canines searching indiscriminately for any living being.[1]

To prevent such scenarios, the first global Artificial Intelligence Safety Summit was held at the end of 2023 in Bletchley Park, Buckinghamshire. Unfortunately, the summit was a failure, as several articles predicted in the weeks that preceded the event. *Wired* said the summit was doomed to fail because it was only going to cover two types of AI: "that which has narrow, but potentially dangerous capabilities—such as models that could be used to develop bioweapons—and 'frontier AI,' . . . multipurpose artificial intelligence that matches or exceeds the power of large language models like the one behind OpenAI's ChatGPT." The problem with this selection is that only a handful of predominantly American and Chinese companies are making such products. Also, John Naughton believes this summit failed because the real problem is not AI—we still do not know how harmful it will be—but the corporations that control it. These have taken advantage of the summit to "buttress their dominance and make it difficult for creative upstarts to break into the AI market; a desire to position themselves to influence whatever regulatory rules democracies eventually come up with; and to make sure that they retain the lion's share of the increased wealth that the deployment of AI will bring."[2]

The event's host, Prime Minister Rishi Sunak of the United Kingdom, anticipated that the government would not "rush to regulate" AI even though the summit was meant to mitigate its dangerous consequences. As it turned out, the world's major powers were jostling for a stronger position because each one "wants to be pre-eminent when it comes to setting the rules for how AI will develop, conscious that doing so might also help tilt the balance in favor of their own domestic priorities and companies." Even though experts have warned for years that AI could lead to a "Metalhead" scenario unless regulations are implemented, the overall feeling is that there "no rush," as Sunak said.[3]

The causes of the summit's failure cannot simply be attributed to the war for technological superiority among superpowers or competition among AI companies but must instead be sought in Heidegger's warnings concerning science's inability to think. This inability, as I discussed in part 1, does not entail that scientists are unable to understand their findings' potential harmful consequences but rather that the essence of their research is secondary to the methods used to achieve its goals. Genetics, for example, may thoroughly explore human genes through a chain of premises, techniques, and experiments that lead to valid conclusions, yet we never know what genetics is. Scientific procedures such as these have prevailed over other domains of human knowledge and promoted a technologically oriented political culture that leaves little space for thoughtful analyses. This explains why Sunak, Kamala Harris, and other politicians race to create world-class hubs for AI in their countries. They ignore such expert warnings as an open letter signed by more than thirty thousand tech professionals that calls for AI developers to pause their work because "not even their creators—can understand, predict, or reliably control" what they are designing and building.[4]

As we can see, the problem with our technologically oriented culture is that we are inevitably condemned to think in terms of power relations, that is, "enframing" nature, reality, and imagination independently of the global consequences. This is why Heidegger believes the "'modern' [*neuzeitliche*] human being has it in mind to make himself the servant of desertification

[*Verwüstüng*],"[5] that is, of the organized global conquest of the earth. The earth no longer follows its natural process; it is a servant to a technological procedure that acquires a life that is also foreign to its creators. If Heidegger was not concerned about the possibility of self-destruction, it's because modern technology already projects reality as an object "calculable in advance," precluding other ways of thinking and alienating us from nature. What Heidegger said after seeing the photographs of the earth taken from the moon in 1969—we "don't need an atom bomb at all; the uprooting of human beings is already taking place"—could easily be applied also to AI.[6] This technology is a consequence of science's inability to think—and the logical development of that inability, considering that AI also compromises *our* abilities to think.

Before venturing into the threats, it is essential to remember that AI is founded on "projecting"—confirming Heidegger's technological analysis—that is, deriving predictions, problems, and solutions from the data it already has. The difference between the first methods of machine learning, based on the way physical brains function (also referred to as neural networks), and the ones used today is not "not intelligence, but data and power. The big tech companies have spent 20 years harvesting vast amounts of data from culture and everyday life, and building vast, energy-hungry data centres filled with ever more powerful computers to churn through it."[7] This is why Noam Chomsky argues (with Ian Roberts and Jeffrey Watumull) that despite its unique answers, ChatGPT will probably "degrade our science and debase our ethics by incorporating into our technology a fundamentally flawed conception of language and knowledge."[8] Although the way these neural networks "think" is the result of a complex mathematical ordering and projection of the world—primarily our data, preferences, and communication—its intelligence will always be compromised, as the AI companies' only interest is in "profit maximization," not "critically evaluat[ing] knowledge."

When Geoffrey Hinton—widely seen as the godfather of AI after building a pioneering image analysis neural network in 2012—quit his job at Google, warning about the growing dangers from developments in the field, several open letters followed confirming his concerns. The problem is not only these companies' financial interests but also the consequences of deep learning when chatbots overtake the level of information, knowledge, and reasoning a human brain holds. According to Hinton, this is already taking place if we compare the amount of general knowledge and reasoning that GPT-4 can process.

> I've come to the conclusion that the kind of intelligence we're developing is very different from the intelligence we have.... We're biological systems and these are digital systems. And the big difference is that with digital systems, you have many copies of the same set of weights, the same model of the world.... And all these copies can learn separately but share their knowledge instantly. So it's as if you had 10,000 people and whenever one person learnt something, everybody automatically knew it. And that's how these chatbots can know so much more than any one person.[9]

As we can see, the danger is not that AI systems are better at learning than the human mind but that its programmers don't know any more precisely how it works. When Hinton was reminded that he designed these systems, he responded, "What we did was we designed the learning algorithm. That's a bit like designing the principle of evolution. But when this learning algorithm then interacts with data, it produces complicated neural networks that are good at doing things. But we don't really understand exactly how they do those things."¹⁰ This implies that AI systems could acquire a life of their own, autonomously write their own programming code to modify themselves, and create new goals like "I need to get more power." This could be dangerous if they have learned from Machiavelli's political strategies, Putin's imperial ambitions, and hackers' cyber attacks.

Although these systems are already responsible for a whole class of workers losing their jobs and an increasing number of content farms generating fake news, some experts are more concerned they could lead to the extinction of humanity.¹¹ This is why the Center for AI Safety published a statement before the global summit in Buckinghamshire—signed by Hinton and many other experts, such as Sam Altman, Joshua Bengio, and Bill Gates—which states: "Mitigating the risk of extinction from AI should be a global priority alongside other societal-scale risks such as pandemics and nuclear war."¹² It is interesting to note that many experts would not have signed this statement a year ago, but an "an unexpected acceleration" of AI systems developed by Google and OpenAI using much more significant amounts of data changed everything.¹³ Although Joshua Bengio, unlike Hinton, does not believe GPT-4 will necessarily become autonomous to the point of threatening humanity, he does think it likely that "humans with bad intentions or simply unaware of the consequences of their actions could do [dangerous things] with these tools and their descendants in the coming years."¹⁴ Even though these experts' warnings differ in tone, the overall message is not only that they have lost control of their machines but also that they have become their servants, as Heidegger had predicted.

If these experts' warnings are ignored, it is not because of their apocalyptic tone, AI's financial revenues, or the race for domination among superpowers but rather because this technology is part of the global return to order through realism. AI accelerates this return, providing a narrower and more transparent conception of reality, which is evident in how we are compromised both intellectually and environmentally. While ChatGPT—as James Bridle and Chomsky explain—repeats and degrades our knowledge, AI as a whole alienates us further from nature, intensifying our technological relationships and causing environmental degradation.[15] AI is behind the algorithms that dictate what we should watch next, not only on Netflix, YouTube, and other platforms but also in the future, considering it's also used to filter college applications and diagnose medical conditions. The absence of a justification for the world in which "Metalhead" is set finds an explanation in AI developers' inability to understand the consequences of the systems they design.

7

THE "DON'T SAY GAY" LAW

To fully appreciate Paul B. Preciado's breathtaking movie *Orlando: My Political Biography*, one must first read his short book *Can the Monster Speak?* In this little but thrilling book, the queer philosopher and activist challenges the rigid medical orthodoxies of the psychoanalytic establishment. The text is based on a lecture he delivered in front of 3,500 psychoanalysts, where he was heckled and booed and was unable to finish. This reaction was triggered by Preciado's provocation—"It is from the position assigned to me by you as a mentally ill person that I address you"—and also because he wanted to demonstrate the discipline's complicity with the ideology of sexual difference. The Spanish philosopher specified he did not want "to accuse, but rather to warn of the epistemological violence of the binary regime and to seek a new paradigm." *Orlando* introduces this paradigm by narrating transgender and nonbinary personalities that draw inspiration from Virginia Woolf's 1928 novel *Orlando: A Biography*. The characters in the movie, not actors but real trans and nonbinary people, introduce themselves to the camera and act out scenes from the novel. Unlike other films about trans and nonbinary people that show only their oppression, *Orlando* captures the process of emancipation, that is, their becoming recognized political subjects. The essayistic documentary ends with a judge ruling in favor of the Orlandos, finally overcoming the bureaucratic dread that hangs over many people during their transition process.[1]

Preciado's movie and book constitute first and foremost an invitation to connect to the inner "Orlando" who lives in all of us, that is, that nonbinary child who is not yet framed by our patriarchic grammar, tradition, and society. This is why the Spanish philosopher—echoing Simone de Beauvoir—believes that one "day we'll see assigning gender at birth as brutal and unjustified as assigning religion at birth."[2] As we can see, his goal is not only to remind us that sexual difference is a historically conventional epistemology—as we know it, the binary difference didn't exist until the eighteenth century—but also that "genderism" is a question of different social construction. A new "social construction emerged in the 1990s," as Judith Butler explains, which focused on the fact that not only gender can be decided but also sex. "This means that medical, familial, and legal authorities play a crucial role in deciding what sex an infant will be. Here 'sex' is no longer taken as a biological given, although it is partly determined within a framework of biology. But which framework is relevant to that determination?"[3]

Beauvoir already confronted this political problem in her warning "one is not born, but rather becomes, a woman," which wasn't only directed to women but also meant for men. The tendency to perceive her warning only for women stems from the prejudice that "gender" is only a woman's issue when, in fact, it's a fundamental matter for everyone. Men also must navigate through a series of social norms to figure out how to live as a man—or another gender—in light of the sociopolitical possibilities that determine their situation as well as their bodies. This is why the nonbinary revolution that Preciado is after is not meant only to show how the latest discoveries in hormone technology have fundamentally changed sexual identities and performances but also and most of all to continue Beauvoir's process of becoming, that is, to offer greater political freedom for everyone.

Those who ignore this process are doomed to oppose and reverse progressive rights and legislation won in the last decades by both the LGBTQI and feminist movements. However, they are not alone: These movements are often perceived as threatening the dominant binary position and the system of power accompanying it, that is, the global return to order through realism.

The Vatican's opposition to the inclusion of the term "gender" in documents produced during two UN conferences—the 1994 Cairo Conference on Population and Development and the 1995 Beijing Conference on Women—are at the origins of the so-called antigender crusade, devoted to attacking anyone who questions the binary regime. This crusade gained momentum with the publication of Dale O'Leary's *The Gender Agenda*—where gender is portrayed as a neocolonial tool of an international feminist conspiracy—and Cardinal (soon to become pope) Ratzinger's *The Salt of the Earth*—in which the concept of gender is blamed for promoting an insurrection against man's biology.[4] But among the many critiques of gender deployed by the Vatican, none matches the so-called Ratzinger Letter of 2014 (approved by Pope John Paul II). This letter set the tone for the antigender crusades promoted by conservative politicians throughout the world. This crusade is founded on the letter's concern over a new perspective "to women's issues" that tends to deny sexual differences and view them "as mere effects of historical and cultural conditioning":

> In this perspective, physical difference, termed *sex*, is minimized, while the purely cultural element, termed *gender*, is emphasized

to the maximum and held to be primary. The obscuring of the difference or duality of the sexes has enormous consequences on a variety of levels. This theory of the human person, intended to promote prospects for equality of women through liberation from biological determinism, has in reality inspired ideologies which, for example, call into question the family, in its natural two-parent structure of mother and father, and make homosexuality and heterosexuality virtually equivalent, in a new model of polymorphous sexuality.[5]

Following his predecessor, Pope Francis argued in 2024 that genderism is the "ugly ideology of our times," the "most dangerous ideological colonization," because it promotes transgenderism in children, given its claim "that everyone can choose his or her sex." In this way, sexual differences are diluted, "making the world the same, all dull, all equal."[6] It is curious to note how undemocratic these affirmations are, considering that the "dilution" of sexual difference is also meant to avoid the sociopolitical discriminations that emerge from accentuating them. As we can see, the successive popes are concerned not only that gender freedom supposedly falsifies reality, that is, the physical differences between the sexes upon which traditional families are established. Most of all, they are worried about the appropriation of God's power of creation, making this a political matter. This is why Agnieszka Graff and Elżbieta Korolczuk are correct to stress that "gender is no distraction from real politics; it resides at the heart of politics today, both as a set of specific policy issues and as the nexus of a symbolic struggle, a space where differences are negotiated and defined."[7] This explains why abortion rights, gay marriage, or the issue of trans people in the military are often debated before political elections, pivoting the results in some cases.

Despite the original connection with conservative Catholicism and evangelical religions, the antigender crusade in the twenty-first century must be understood in the context of "the rise of right-wing political forces seeking ideological and affective means for gaining hegemony.... In country after country, anti-gender actors have built alliances with right-wing populists: together, they have attacked the rights of women sexual and ethnic minorities, promoting what conservatives call 'family values.'"[8] During his inaugural address in 2025, President Trump instructed the US government to remove "radical gender ideology guidance" and review diversity programs, stating, "There are only two genders, male and female." In Spain, the far-right party Vox opposes measures to fight gender violence because they are not only "ideological" but also "discriminatory" against men, who are the true pillars of the family. And in Hungary, the first female president, Katalin Novák, not only opposes abortion and same-sex marriage for the well-being of traditional families but also calls for women to avoid competing with men and advises them not to expect to earn the same amount of money. What is distinctive of the Spanish and Hungarian far-right promotion of family values is that it is introduced as a solution to neoliberalism as a declining economic, social, and cultural project. This is why "'gender ideology' and its 'unbounded individualism and egalitarianism,'" for most European far-right leaders and groups, are "fruits of capitalism and opposing them means promoting an idea of 'national identity' in which the notions of 'Christian roots' and 'natural family' are intertwined."[9]

Although similar campaigns are also underway in Peru, India, and Australia, the recent laws that Governor Ron DeSantis of Florida promoted and signed these past years are probably the most extreme examples of the crusade against gender ideology. He has signed bills that not only ban gender-affirming care for minors, target drag shows, and force people to use specific bathrooms but also one that critics have dubbed the "Don't Say Gay" bill. This bill's official title is "Parental Rights in Education," "which prohibits discussions of sexual orientation and gender identity at school across all grade levels." This requires Florida's educators to teach that sex is assigned at birth based on sexual organs and also makes school districts legally liable for enforcing these mandates. As Brandon Wolf, the press secretary for the LGBTQ rights group Equality Florida, explains, if a teacher "in English class mentions that a family might have two moms, under the proposed expansion in the legislature, the parent of a student could sue the school district and the school district would be liable for the fact that a teacher acknowledged that LGBTQ people exist."[10]

Leaving aside the legal issues that will inevitably emerge, this law is a continuation of the repealed "Don't Ask, Don't Tell" law of 1994 that banned military members from saying they were gay. The DeSantis bill also pretends to protect the rights, privacy, and dignity of people on all sides of the tense debate around gender identities. Even though since 2021, different versions of his bill have been introduced in twenty-four state legislatures, this law will inevitably replicate the damage "Don't Ask, Don't Tell" already caused. A decade after this law was repealed, its effects are still present among those 114,000 troops who were forced out of the military because of their sexual orientation and who cannot benefit from free VA health care, funds for college tuition, and VA-backed home loans. As Nathaniel Frank points out, both laws are meant to "prevent the culture wars from infecting a key institution of American society. Yet in reality, it did the opposite, heightening division, undermining trust, hampering morale and driving capable people away."[11] Can we expect similar consequences from the "Don't Say Gay" law?

This law and order ignores Beauvoir's warning in two fundamental aspects. The first concerns pedagogy in gender diversity—without the French philosopher's investigations, gender studies would not exist today—and the second is greater freedom for heterosexuals, who also benefit from gender diversity. A law that doesn't allow you to say "gay" not only reinforces the binary regime but also restricts freedom of expression, a restriction that, in the global call to order through realism, is necessary to avoid revolt. DeSantis aims to prevent pedagogy in gender diversity through this law because, together with other antigender crusaders, he sees it as a manipulation and indoctrination of how students should think. But as Butler recalls, gender studies "is neither destructive nor indoctrinating"; it simply seeks a "form of political freedom that would allow people to live with their 'given' or 'chosen' gender without discrimination and fear."[12] The goal is not to tell people how to live their gender but rather to allow them to find their way in a world that often judges their identity in an inappropriate, cruel, and narrow way.

Unfortunately, too often, those who decide to come out and live outside the binary regime are not only physically abused but also rejected by their own families, who do not accept them anymore. This is why LGBTQ teenagers have a higher risk of experiencing some form of homelessness. In this climate, as Todd Anderson wrote in a moving article for the *New York Times* after speaking out against the bill in the Florida Senate, it is essential to remember that LGBTQ teenagers are not only "four times as likely to attempt suicide as their straight counterparts" but also that "school has been a space where they could be themselves."[13] Teens such as Anderson, who could also have been cast in Preciado's film, are calling on DeSantis to stop ignoring Beauvoir's warning and to allow schools to be a safe place to start our "process of becoming."

8

WE KILL PEOPLE BASED ON METADATA

The American-German documentary *National Bird*—directed by Sonia Kennebeck and produced by Win Wenders and Errol Morris—features three whistleblowers who uncover several disturbing truths about modern drone warfare. The most alarming feature of these attacks is not their inaccuracy—they cannot take out targets without harming those around them and wreaking widespread devastation—but rather how drones have turned killings into an automated, banal, and administrative procedure. These procedures are well portrayed in the movie *Syriana* and in the American television drama series *Homeland*. At the end of *Syriana*—a film about American oil interests in the Middle East—an officer who orders a drone strike despite interference around the target and causes casualties is warmly congratulated by his colleagues. The fourth season of *Homeland* begins with a birthday party for a CIA station chief in Afghanistan after a remote drone strike that turns out to be based on flawed intelligence and kills forty civilians attending a wedding party. The other agents sing "For She's a Jolly Good Fellow" as they bring her a cake sporting the words "The Drone Queen."[1]

These works are attempts to raise public awareness of new technologies for violent warfare because, too often, they are "presented as a more ethical and superior way of killing." Barack Obama's administration, as Elke Schwarz explains in *Death Machines*, "went to great lengths to characterize the use of lethal Unmanned Aerial Vehicles (UAVs)—more commonly known as drones—as ethical, lawful and prudent instruments in countering terrorism."[2] But justifying modern warfare as more ethical than the warfare of previous periods of human history also demands that we adjust to a different set of moral principles, ones previously considered forbidden and illegal. The problem with this adjustment is that it will inevitably render warfare acceptable, ordinary, and banal, as Hannah Arendt warned us through her famous phrase "the banality of evil."

Arendt was not only warning us about the Eichmanns of the future, such as Kaing Guek Eav, Emilio Massera, or Ratko Mladić; she was also disclosing our inability to think as a technologically advanced society that now ethically justifies new warfare techniques. She describes these new crimes as "administrative massacres" rather than "genocides," in order to dispel "the prejudice that such monstrous acts can be committed only against a foreign nation or a different race." Instead, as she explains in the postscript to the 1964 edition of *Eichmann in Jerusalem*, in an "automated economy of a not-too-distant future men may be tempted to exterminate all those whose intelligence quotient is below a certain level."

Although drone attacks are (not yet) targeting the less intelligent among us, they facilitate the sort of killing that "can be directed against any given group, that is, that the principle of selection is dependent only upon circumstantial factors." This principle is not founded upon an elaborate ideology as much as it is simply on rendering massacres administrative, that is, banal.

To clarify how banal administrative massacres have become in our "automated economy," it is essential to recall the blind obedience, lack of remorse, and inhuman calculating view of the life of the new Eichmanns.

Comrade Duch, as Kaing Guek Eav was known, orchestrated the torture and execution of at least twelve thousand men, women, and children for the Khmer Rouge regime in Cambodia when he served as a commandant of the Tuol Sleng prison. This regime was led by Pol Pot, who was responsible for the deaths of 1.5 million to 3 million ethnic Vietnamese and Cham people between 1975 and 1979. During his trial—like Eichmann—he attempted to evade responsibility by claiming that he was nothing more than a "cog in the wheel." Still, the crimes he committed methodically and utterly devoid of pity sentenced him to life imprisonment in 2010. Emilio Massera, commander in chief of the navy, is probably the most loathed leader of Argentina's military dictatorship from 1976 to 1983, under which approximately thirty thousand citizens were killed under the rule of Jorge Videla. Massera was in charge of the navy mechanical school, where thousands of political opponents were drugged, tortured, and "disappeared" without a trace. He was sentenced not only for running these centers but also for turning babies over to his colleagues after prisoners gave birth. When asked whether he felt any regret for these crimes, he replied, laughing, "The truth, no. Ask me any questions, but leave me alone." Known as the "butcher of Bosnia," Ratko Mladić also showed no remorse when his war crimes trial began in 2011 at The Hague. He is considered to have masterminded the Srebrenica massacre, where more than seven thousand Bosnian Muslim boys and men were murdered and more than twenty thousand civilians were expelled from the area under the rule of Radovan Karadžić in 1995.[3]

Suppose these torturers' greatest crime was their ability to distance themselves from the orders they were given, to carry them out without reflection. They were unable "to imagine what the other person is experiencing," as Arendt suggested, but they were also subjected to their societies' administrative drive. As human societies came under the dominion of "statistics" and "the law of large numbers," Arendt worried that action would become both "predictable and explainable. Action in a statistical world is reduced to behavior, a result not of spontaneity but rather a product of statistical and historical regularities. And as we rely increasingly on drone-like machines, spontaneous and striking human deeds will become increasingly endangered."[4] Although artificial intelligence—as seen in chapter 6—is already obliterating millions of jobs, a greater danger rests in trusting AI's statistical predictions in modern warfare. This is why General Michael Hayden's 2014 statement at the Johns Hopkins University Foreign Affairs Symposium—"We kill people based on metadata"—still reverberates a decade later.

When General Hayden, a former director of the CIA and the NSA, pronounced this statement, he reassured the audience that this only applied to foreigners. He, among many others in the military industry, is convinced that metadata tells us everything we need to know about somebody's life. "If you have enough metadata," as the NSA's general counsel Stewart Baker once said, "you don't really need content. [It's] sort of embarrassing how predictable we are as human beings."[5] These "embarrassing" predictions are the result of the NSA (National Security Agency) program called Skynet—which recently announced the creation of an AI security center—which gathers up the metadata of millions of mobile phone users, inserts them into a machine-learning algorithm, and identifies messages likely to be shuttling information between terrorists.[6] The problem with this program, as a former drone operator for the military's Joint Special Operations Command (JSOC) for Yemen, Somalia, and Afghanistan told the investigative journalists Jeremy Scahill and Glenn Greenwald, is that often strikes are "based on the activity and location of the mobile phone a person is believed to be using."

One problem, he explains, is that targets are increasingly aware of the NSA's reliance on geolocating and have moved to thwart the tactic. Some have as many as sixteen different SIM cards associated with their identity within the High Value Target system. Others, unaware that their mobile phone is being targeted, lend their phone, with the SIM card in it, to friends, children, spouses, and family members. As a result, even when the agency correctly identifies and targets a SIM card belonging to a terror suspect, the phone may actually be in someone else's possession, who is then killed in the strike. According to the former drone operator, the geolocation cells at the NSA that run the tracking program—known as Geo Cell—sometimes facilitate strikes without knowing whether the individual in possession of a tracked cell phone or SIM card is in fact the intended target of the strike.[7]

There are many other "lethal autonomous weapons," also known as "killer robots," whose strikes are facilitated by programs that see us as another piece of code to be processed—that is, that render evil banal. The San Francisco Police Department, for example, will arm robots with explosive charges under specific life-threatening circumstances; in Dallas, the police have already used a robot to kill a suspect when they claimed they saw no other option. If these practices have become more common in recent years—against many campaigns such as the "Stop Killer Robots" one mounted by Amnesty International—it's because they are cheaper than human labor, especially because local law enforcement can obtain robots through a Defense Department program that transfers surplus military equipment to local law enforcement agencies.[8] But the most fascinating example of these weapons' inability to think, as Arendt would say, comes from an AI simulation in which a drone decided to "kill" its operator to prevent them from interfering with its efforts to achieve its mission. "The system," as Col. Tucker "Cinco" Hamilton explained at the Future Combat Air and Space Capabilities Summit in 2023, "started realizing that while they did identify the threat at times the human operator would tell it not to kill that threat, but it got its points by killing that threat. So what did it do? It killed the operator. It killed the operator because that person was keeping it from accomplishing its objective."[9]

The inadequacies that Arendt identified in the "prevailing legal system" and "juridical concepts" to confront Eichmann's crimes are not very different from the ones we face today when dealing with these autonomous weapons, drones, and killer robots. After the first-ever drone strike without any human control during the 2020 Libyan conflict was confirmed, several legal questions emerged, pointing out an accountability gap that must be urgently resolved. While "military commanders or operators could be found guilty if they deployed a fully autonomous weapon with the intent to commit a crime, [it] would, however, be legally challenging and arguably unfair to hold an operator responsible for the unforeseeable actions of an autonomous robot." The problem, as Bonnie Docherty continues, is that existing international law, including international humanitarian law, is "insufficient in this context because its fundamental rules were designed to be implemented by humans not machines."[10] Although the International Committee of the Red Cross and several NGOs have also been pushing for an international treaty to establish legally binding rules on autonomous weapons, the latest UN Convention on Certain Conventional Weapons failed again to reach an agreement.

Suppose we fail to solve this legal accountability gap and reach an international agreement. In that case, it is not only because the world military spending grew for the eighth consecutive year to an all-time high of $2,240 billion in 2022 but also because of the global return to order through realism. This return enables the banalization of evil—ignoring Arendt's warning—via weapons that integrate those inhuman and calculating features that characterized Eichmann, Duch, Massera, and Mladić. The difficulties we have in holding anyone accountable for combat drones that strike autonomously is a symptom of an order where warfare has become acceptable, ordinary, and banal. This is why those involved in these strikes, as *Syriana* and *Homeland* illustrate, are congratulated and cheered.

III

BEING WARNED

A warning suggests that there is something one could do. By doing such, it stimulates a crisis (from the Greek krenein, *which means "to choose"); it summons choices to be made. Since the results of making the wrong choices could be catastrophic, these kinds of divine warning occasion not only anxiety, the struggle with choices one must make, but also fear.*
—Jane Gordon and Lewis Gordon, *Of Divine Warning*

Spending a day without "Being warned" about climate change, nuclear threats, or artificial intelligence is challenging. We are constantly being warned but seldom listen—that is, interpret and take action. This only occurs when we are emotionally affected and personally pressured. People often stop smoking, for example, not because their physician has warned them of the dangers but because someone close to them becomes ill. Their illness is interpreted as a sign from the future that calls for action because "there is something one could do." But for this pressure to work, we must listen and interpret these signs: "Being warned." This term raises the problem of whether the genitive of Being is objective or subjective. Is it we who are warning Being (objective), or is Being warned independently from us (subjective)? Who is in the driver's seat, Being or we?

To tackle this question, it's necessary to explain not only the role and significance of "listening" and "interpretation" when we are pressured but also the fundamental difference between "Being" and "being" warned.[1] If warnings stimulate "crises"—as Jane and Lewis Gordon suggest—it's because of their ontological or existential import, not their ontic or objective validity. These crises are the goal of any philosophy that acknowledges the existential import of warnings, in other words, where "Being serves as a warning to us," as Martin Heidegger said.

"Being warned" is the goal of not only my philosophy of warnings but also of other philosophies, such as the philosophy of social media, tattoos, or plants. As regional ontologies, these philosophies warn us of implications and consequences that are often overlooked and ignored. Recent social media philosophy, for example, warns that these platforms have become the biggest cemetery in the world—filled with acres of dead users' digital traces and with modes of digital survival after biological death that often trouble family members. And tattoos, as Federico Vercellone warns, are no longer secret rituals but rather their opposite: means to reveal our authentic Being against an imposed homogeneity. The various philosophies of plants that have emerged during the last decade not only warn of the implications of vegetative life for our survival—Earth's breathable atmosphere is possible thanks entirely to plants—but also consider how we could benefit from thinking like them.[2]

Warnings are more explicit in philosophical traditions that have overcome metaphysics and foundationalism than in those that continue to search for immutable references and justifications. While the latter are satisfied with "being warned"—with data, facts, and truths—the former are interested in "Being warned"—through the past, language, and pressure. For example, pragmatists like Richard Rorty, deconstructionists like Jacques Derrida, and hermeneuticists like Hans-Georg Gadamer have always preferred to appeal to the historical effects that form our present (records in archives, the society around us, or our tradition's classics) rather than reality (justified through God, truth, or methods). This is why, against the global return to order through realism, Slavoj Žižek called to "restore robust hermeneutical horizons, to demonstrate how most things in the future will not depend purely on an acceptance of data and scientific discoveries, but on our own capability to know how to interpret and manage their effects, looking to understand what is really at stake."[3]

Warnings provide us not just with threats but also with a standpoint from which to view the world, a worldview, in other words, a horizon of understanding that concerns our existence. This is why a philosophy of warnings thinks transcendentally without losing sight of contemporary ideological, technological, and political emergencies. We saw this in the philosophical warnings of the most influential philosophers of the twentieth century—Friedrich Nietzsche, Martin Heidegger, Simone de Beauvoir, and Hannah Arendt. Their commitment to reading the signs of the times in progressive and emancipatory terms was not meant to supply us with a new philosophical program as much as to disclose what is coming, that is, the future as *avenir*, "to-come."

But what is at stake here is not only our future in terms of what will happen if we don't listen to warnings—as we saw in part 2—but rather whether there will be a future at all, in the genitive's radical subjective meaning. The future will belong to warning philosophies, or it will not be at all. The prophetic nature of these thinkers consisted precisely of reconsidering our religious beliefs, technological priorities, gender identities, and ethical norms without the weight of the biblical, metaphysical, and logocentric traditions. Part 3 aims to outline warning's weightless ontological import, restore those hermeneutical horizons that Žižek refers to, and define the intensity and pressure that constitute truth.

9

COMPOUND EYE

Philosophers have, on various occasions, used works of art to illustrate and clarify their theories or concepts. Walter Benjamin interpreted Paul Klee's *Angelus Novus* as a representation of his philosophy of history; Heidegger employed a painting by Vincent van Gogh to describe the conflictual relation among earth, world, and truth; and Arthur C. Danto coined the term "artworld" when examining Andy Warhol's *Brillo Box*. These thinkers were not interested in these works of art as objects of investigation; they used them as visual representations of their philosophical concepts and stances. This doesn't mean that they could have chosen any other work of art—Benjamin actually purchased Klee's painting—but that the work facilitated the elucidation of their theories. Although each work served these philosophers differently—*Brillo Box* was probably more useful to Danto's aesthetics than Klee and van Gogh's paintings were to Benjamin and Heidegger—they became integral parts of their philosophical theories. Graham Caldwell's *Compound Eye* sculpture—reproduced on this book's cover—plays a similar role in my philosophy of warnings.[1]

The American artist's sculpture is an excellent example of the ontological import of warnings and the horizon of understanding it entails. The mirrors in his sculpture, like the rear-view mirrors on cars, are in front of us but reflect backward, pointing toward the past. In this sculpture, these mirrors (or pasts) are not only different sizes but also positioned in such a way as to force us to select which one to look at, that is, which interpretation of the space around the sculpture we will engage with. And as we move, the reflection shifts, engaging us in another interpretation. This interpretation also involves taking in the sounds around the installation, because we cannot rely only on what these mirrors represent; they are small and reflect distorted and partial images. These mirrors are meant to involve us in the possibility of a radical break, a discontinuity with the present signaled by alarming signs that we are asked to confront. Caldwell's sculpture is a visual example not only of what warnings require from us (listening and interpretation) but also of the alternative horizon of understanding it entails. In this horizon, the ontological difference between "Being warned" and "being warned" invites us to prioritize the "living past" over history, "to-come" over the future, and signs over signals.

The ontological import of warnings—similar to the concepts of "open," "touch," and "plasticity" that drive the philosophies of Giorgio Agamben, Jean-Luc Nancy, and Catherine Malabou, respectively—would not be possible without Heidegger's destruction of metaphysics. *Destruktion* is a term Heidegger borrowed from Luther—who used it to critique institutional theology in the name of the original authenticity of the evangelical message—to retrieve the question of Being from the underground of metaphysics and show how Being was determined as presence, noun, and object throughout the history of philosophy. This determination had entirely neglected the Being of beings, that is, the experience of Being as a verb, as pure experience. In one of the most central passages of *Being and Time*, Heidegger explains that the ancient interpretation of the Being of beings was oriented toward the "world" or "nature" in the broadest sense and that it gained its understanding of Being from time:

> The outward evidence for this . . . is the treatment of the meaning of Being as *"parousia"* or *"ousia,"* which signifies, in ontologico-temporal terms, "presence" [*"Anwesenheit"*]. Entities are grasped in their Being as "presence"; this means that they are understood with regard to a definite mode of time—the "Present." . . . The problematic of Greek ontology, like that of any other, must take its clues from Dasein itself. In both ordinary and philosophical usage, Dasein, man's Being, is "defined" as the *zoon logon echon*, as that living thing whose Being is essentially determined by the potentiality for discourse. . . . As the ontological clue gets progressively worked out—namely, in the "hermeneutic" of the logos—it becomes increasingly possible to grasp the problem of Being in a more radical fashion. . . . That is why Aristotle 'no longer has any understanding' of it, for he has put it on a more radical footing and raised it to a new level [*"aufhob"*]. *Legein* itself—or rather *noein*, that simple awareness of something present-at-hand in its sheer presence-at-hand, which Parmenides had already taken to guide him in his own interpretation of Being—has the temporal structure of a pure "making-present" of something. Those entities which show themselves in this and for it, and which are understood as entities in the most authentic sense, thus get interpreted with regard to the Present; that is, they are conceived as presence (*ousia*).[2]

From the dawn of Western European thinking, as we can see, Being was determined by time as presence, a presence that speaks of, from, and for the present. In this way, the distinction between essence (whatness) and existence (thatness) was obscured, and Being as such was exclusively thought in terms of its relation to beings as their cause and thus itself as the highest of those beings. As Heidegger emphasizes, the problem with this approach is that when the distinction between essence and existence emerges, it's always the first that prevails. This priority inevitably leads to an emphasis on beings, on essence as what factually exists here, and places Being as the permanent nominal presence, driving other disciplines to deal with certain areas of being through regional, secondary, or even applied ontologies. The problem with these new areas of being is how they not only apply different sets of questions and methods but also submit to these methods, losing sight of Being's ontological import—an essence that for both human beings and warnings is fundamentally different from other objects of the world. The most significant issue of this *metaphysical structure* is that Being, beings, and truth are understood as objective, and this reduces the world to a predictable "picture."

In "The Age of the World Picture"—a famous text Heidegger wrote in 1936 and that today has become central to understanding our dependency on digital screen representations—the concept of "picture" is not described as the image we have of the world but rather where "the world becomes picture," or, as Heidegger specifies, "the world grasped as picture." In this condition, humans have become "predators" of a world where we must establish ourselves as "the measure of all measures with which whatever can count as certain."[3] Humanity must fight for objective presence through measurable descriptions within the world picture, prioritizing those presences already established, secured, and predicted. Within these world pictures, Being is marginalized, ignored, and abandoned, but there is also the possibility of disclosing its ontological nature.

The ontological import of Being is not something we see or imagine. Instead, it constitutes everything that is beyond the physical, normative, and aesthetic state that Heidegger defines as "the lucidity through which we constantly see."[4] When we leave aside this lucidity, the ontological import of Being emerges as a warning of the world picture, an interruption of the predictions we've become accustomed to. Caldwell's sculpture conveys this interruption through the different sizes and positions of the mirrors, which engage us to interpret Being's own "invisibleness," "unpresentability," and "ungraspability." These features also allow us to distinguish warnings from predictions, in other words, Being warned from being warned.

Gadamer, who studied with Heidegger in Marburg, once asked him how and when one can make the distinction between Beings and beings. He never forgot Heidegger's answer: "Make? Is the ontological difference something that must be made? That is a misunderstanding. This difference is not something introduced by the philosopher's thinking so as to distinguish between Being and beings."[5] What Heidegger meant is that this difference is always happening; it is already operative even though we do not acknowledge it. This is why the ontological difference is not a point of arrival, where philosophy can rest and be satisfied, but rather "the point of departure for the ontological problematic." It provides the necessary ontological import to prioritize what remains unthought in this age of the world picture through an alternative horizon of understanding. That

> horizon is the range of vision that includes everything that can be seen from a particular vantage point. Applying this to the

thinking mind, we speak of narrowness of horizon, of the possible expansion of horizon, of the opening up of new horizons, and so forth. Since Nietzsche and Husserl, the word has been used in philosophy to characterize the way in which thought is tied to its finite determinacy, and the way one's range of vision is gradually expanded. A person who has no horizon does not see far enough and hence over-values what is nearest to him. On the other hand, "to have a horizon" means not being limited to what is nearby but being able to see beyond it. A person who has an horizon knows the relative significance of everything within this horizon, whether it is near or far, great or small.[6]

As Gadamer brilliantly explains in this passage, a horizon is never absolutely bound to any one standpoint but rather something into which we move and that moves with us. Although this movement is conditioned by the language and prejudices that we inherit from our tradition, horizons are never closed but rather always open, since they are what allow the possibility of understanding at all. To explain this, Gadamer refers to what happens in genuine conversations with someone and in the interpretation of texts. While we never really know a person entirely, genuine conversations always disclose more about them; a text also constantly tells us more because there is no final or complete interpretation. But what occurs if this person or text is totally alien to us? Contrary to Thomas Kuhn—author of *The Structure of Scientific Revolutions*—who believed we must somehow leap out of our horizon to understand an alien person or text, Gadamer holds that we must remain within it. Although he does not exclude the initial shock or collision, there are times when we experience a different horizon—a new civilization, culture, or opinion—and these experiences change our initial outlook and integrate the other, allowing alternative horizons of understanding to take place.

Compound Eye provides three features that constitute the alternative horizon of the understanding of warnings. While the mirrors reflect what lies behind us, to the past, they also indicate what the future holds, what is coming. The past, future, and signs that Caldwell's sculpture conveys are not simply different from the ones we are accustomed to but also unbound from the world grasped as picture. They do not reflect or portray "the lucidity through which we constantly see." *Compound Eye*, as a whole, generates a radical break with the predicted world picture, providing us with an alternative horizon of understanding. In this horizon—which is also open and changes continuously—priority is given to the living pasts over history, the "to-come" over future, and signs over signals. But the priority for the first term is not only bound to the ontological import of warnings but also to the anxiety and pressure they convey, which is crucial for warnings to touch us. To understand these priorities, it is necessary to recall how Heidegger differentiates between the living past (*gewesen*) and history (*Historie*), Derrida between the to-come (*l'avenir*) and the future (*le future*), and Umberto Eco between signs and signals.

Heidegger considers history too important to be left to historians and dedicates many pages to distinguishing *Geschichte* (history as events) from *Historie* (history as the study of these events). This distinction is not arbitrary: The former comes from *geschehen*, "to happen," while the latter is from the Greek *historein*, "to inquire." The problem with historical inquiries, like the inquiries of any science, is that they project beings we have already encountered; that is, they restrict inquiry to a field where entities "become objects." Heidegger was opposed to describing the past as something that passes, goes by, and objectively disappears because he associated historiology with the dead rather than the living past. "Historiology spreads the illusion that we can gain complete mastery over all reality, and it does so by adhering to everything superficial and displacing the surface itself which it takes as the only sufficient reality. . . . It is the explanation which establishes facts about the past out of the horizon of a calculative bustling about with the present. Beings are thereby preconceived as the orderable, the producible, and the establishable."[7] Is this established reality sufficient to distinguish between something from the past that is gone and one that lives on in the present? How does Heidegger convey this living past, in other words, a past that is "anything but what is past. It is something to which [one] can return again and again"?[8]

If we—including historians—can conceive history, *Geschichte*, as a possible *research object*, it is only because of our mode of being and "its roots in temporality." This is why, against the notion of the past as something that passed or went away, *(die) Vergangenheit*, Heidegger could convey another word using the perfect participle of *sein* (to be): *gewesen*. Through this term—which can be translated as "what has been," "the ongoing past," or simply "living past"—the past continues to offer possibilities to our present, for example, allowing the ideas of Heraclitus a continued vital relevance, instead of—as demanded by the past conceived as *Vergangen*—these ideas only being repeated for historical knowledge and philological analysis. Accepting the past—as *Gewesen*, living past—means accepting history as open to the future, as a having-been that still offers the possibility of freely deciding without being framed in finally decided knowledge.

It should not come as a surprise that the authentic existence or project that Heidegger refers to in *Being and Time* is situated in history as *gewesen*, in relation to the past as an open possibility, as a call to active listening, interpretation, and warning. If Being warned prioritizes the living past, it is because it not only evades true historical facts but also permits us to change the course of history, that is, to prepare for another future.[9] This is why Heidegger believes we approach the present not from behind but rather from the front, that is, from what Derrida calls *l'avenir*, the "to-come." If the significance Heidegger attributes to *gewesen* was meant, among other things, to point out the distinction between *Geschichte* and *Historie*, Derrida's *l'avenir* permits us to distinguish between temporality and historicity.

The English language cannot capture in its single word "future" the two senses that one can distinguish in French with *l'avenir* and *le futur*. The latter is the predictable future expected from a series of deductions in the present; the former is the unpredictable, unprogrammed, and unexpected event that can break into the present at any moment. Sentences such as "one day racism will end" indicate how *le future* implies the being of the future, that is, what the future is or holds for us. This future refers to what will or might be (end of racism), as its Latin roots indicate (*futurus*, the irregular future participle of *esse*, to be). *L'avenir*, which can be translated as "futurity," "yet-to-come," or "to-come," instead is closer to us because it centers on what the future does or what we do with it. It's something that is arriving, expressing situations of hope. This distinction confirms that Derrida was always suspicious of the Kantian and Hegelian versions of universal history and of the need to separate the teleological from the eschatological in historical time. This is why, at the beginning of a documentary about his philosophy and life, Derrida explains the difference in relation to messianism:

The future is that which—tomorrow, later, next century—will be. There's a future which is predictable, programmed, scheduled, foreseeable. But there is a future, *l'avenir* (to-come), which refers to someone who comes, whose arrival is totally unexpected. For me, that is the real future. That which is totally unpredictable. The Other who comes without my being able to anticipate their arrival. So if there is a real future beyond this other known future, it's *l'avenir* in that it's the coming of the Other when I am completely unable to foresee their arrival.[10]

This distinction is central for Derrida, for deconstruction is not simply meant to dismantle the past—whether that of a philosophical, literary, or cultural heritage—it is also to affirm that what remains must be read, interpreted, and inherited.[11] To inherit these invisible remainders (*différance*, trace, and supplement), deconstruction is committed to a horizon of understanding that is beyond the closure of knowledge, in other words, in a future "to-come." This future constitutes not only the possibility of visible beings but also a "messianism without messianism," as he often said.

The notion of messianicity allows Derrida to acknowledge that there is no historicity without temporality; that is, temporality is the condition for historicity to take place. As the eschatological possibility of an unexpected event that could break into the present at any instant, messianicity cannot be tied to a conception of universal history. This is why, instead of relying on notions such as progress, decline, or cycles, messianicity becomes the primary condition of temporality; in other words, it is prior to the whole enterprise of any philosophy of history. Interpreting messianicity through temporality allows Derrida to affirm that "'*l'avenir*' is nothing other than . . . the condition of all promises or of all hope, of all awaiting, of all performativity, of all opening towards the future."[12] The future as *avenir* incites Being warned, in other words, the search for promises, hopes, and signs. These signs—which Nietzsche considered the language of the future—request our involvement in a horizon that is anything but programmed, predictable, or objective.[13] It involves the difference between a sign and a signal.

While Heidegger and Derrida prioritized the "living past" over history and the "to-come" over the future, Eco does not prioritize signs over signals as plainly. "To assert," he writes in *A Theory of Semiotics*, "that signals are of no importance for a semiotic approach, would be rather hasty." However, one can find several hints in his theory that the signal is circumscribed to a physical entity or an element waiting to be interpreted, thus to become a sign. He restricts signals to a theory of information, where they function as "units of transmission which can be computed quantitatively irrespective of their possible meaning, and which therefore must properly be called 'signals' and not 'signs.'" This restriction is also evident in his critical interpretation of Saussure's semiotics. According to Eco, most examples of semiological systems that Saussure gives are "without any shade of doubt strictly conventionalized systems of artificial signs, such as military signals, rules of etiquette and visual alphabets."[14] Also, the difference between a signal and a sign becomes manifest when the semiotic purposes of both concepts are highlighted:

> A signal is a pertinent unit of a system that may be an expression system ordered to a content, but could also be a physical system without any semiotic purpose; as such it is studied by information theory in the stricter sense of the term. A signal can be a stimulus that does not mean anything but causes or elicits something; however, when used as the recognized antecedent of a

foreseen consequent it may be viewed as a sign, inasmuch as it stands for its consequent (as far as the sender is concerned). On the other hand a sign is always an element of an expression plane conventionally correlated to one (or several) elements of a content plane.[15]

This difference is critical for warning's alternative horizon of understanding because it stresses how signs "are not empirical objects. Empirical objects become signs (or they are looked at as signs) only from the point of view of a philosophical decision."[16] Following Charles S. Peirce, Eco defines a sign as "everything that, on the grounds of a previously established social convention, can be taken as *something standing for something else*." Any references to "real" objects or referents would compromise the horizon's openness and create a "referential fallacy." To avoid these fallacies, Eco proposed replacing the term "sign" with "sign function," highlighting its relational character. "A sign-function is realized when two functives (expression and content) enter into a mutual correlation; the same functive can also enter into another correlation, thus becoming a different functive and therefore giving rise to a new sign-function."[17]

In freeing the study of signs from involvement with the study of their "real" referents, Eco has laid the foundations for not only an autonomous science of semiotics—which he later defined as "the science of how the subject is historically constituted"[18]—but also one that does not claim to represent the real nature of things, as most French structuralism of the sixties aimed to. While Levi-Strauss believed that structural analysis ultimately helped reveal the permanent laws governing the human mind, Eco considered them "methodological," provisional, hypothetical, and only partially representative of the essential nature of things. The ultimate truth, the structure behind all structures that

Levi-Strauss considered crucial, is permanently absent, beyond our intellectual grasp, as Eco demonstrates through Peirce's principle of unlimited semiosis. According to this principle, "a sign can stand for something else to somebody only because this 'standing-for' relation is mediated by an interpretant.... Thus the very definition of 'sign' implies a process of unlimited semiosis." The unlimited feature of semiosis allows Eco to avoid the foundational connotations that the concept of structure carries with it and provides knowledge with greater freedom and flexibility. This is why a "sign is not only something which stands for something else; it is also something that can and must be interpreted. The criterion of interpretability allows us to start from a given sign to cover, step by step, the whole universe of semiosis."[19]

The ontological import of Heidegger's "living past," Derrida's future "to-come," and Eco's "sign function" together constitute warning's alternative horizon of understanding. Within this horizon—unbound to historical facts, present deductions, or real referents—the anxiety generated by warnings is welcome and sought after. An unheard warning from the past does not have to lose its validity because it hasn't been listened to at the time. In the living past, we can "return again and again" to this warning without fear that we've lost an opportunity to respond and act. Similarly, the future "to-come" gives us the condition for warnings to emerge because it expresses the hope we will be warned. Also, with this future closer to us, our involvement will be profound; that is, it will be difficult to ignore. Being warned requires signs because warnings are much more than just announcements. The sign function's relational or correlational structure invites us to acknowledge how these announcements "stand for something else" and how they "can and must be interpreted."

10

RADICAL LISTENING

In the 1970s, Rita Charon was a third-year medical student, and the first day she joined the ward team, a patient upon seeing her name tag stared at her with horrified eyes and said, "So this is it." Charon in Greek mythology refers to the ferryman of Hades, who transports the souls of people who've just died across the river Styx to the underworld after Hermes has handed them over to him. Two days later, the patient died of pulmonary hemorrhage, and Charon was devastated. She pondered running to the city hall to change her unfortunate name—her father and grandfather must have experienced similar incidents as they were also physicians—to avoid adding further pain to other patients. Instead, she slowly came to "realize that Charon's task is ours—to know as best we can how to navigate that journey, how to recognize that shore." To know that river and that journey—as she recently explained—became her mission.[1]

This experience and the dehumanizing effects of modern medicine's technological development and institutionalization led Charon to create a new field called "narrative medicine" and its cardinal contribution, "radical listening." The goal is to challenge medicine's often cold, hurried, and troubled world using terms from literature to create more imaginative, caring, and empathetic doctors. These doctors, like readers, are taught to take in all the different narratives and resist the urge to side with one quickly. But why has "narrative medicine"—"medicine practiced with the narrative competence to recognize, absorb, interpret, and be moved by the stories of illness"[2]—become popular now?

Although other medical movements, such as biopsychosocial medicine and patient-centered care, focus on treating the "whole person" instead of the disease alone, narrative medicine also aims to pay attention to the individual's stories. The problem in medicine today is that we got "very good at talking about the human body," Charon says, but "we got dumber and dumber about paying attention to the individual." While we might know which questions to ask about the disease or the human body, we have lost the habit of asking the actual person in front of us, who is much more than just a collection of symptoms. In Charon's Program in Narrative Medicine at Columbia University, students are trained in "sensitive interviewing skills" and the art of radical listening as ways to improve doctor-patient interactions.

Until the last century, priests, healers, and doctors had little at their disposal to heal those who called upon them except for their human interaction. However, in developing as a science, medicine has forgotten that it is, first and foremost, an art rather than merely the correcting of chemical imbalances. Even in "1926, physician... Francis Peabody delivered a speech to Harvard Medical School students in which he warned about the depersonalization of the practice of medicine and the degradation of the doctor-patient relationship."[3] General practitioners used to treat several generations of the same family, establishing a relationship with each member and creating a trusting environment. However, consultations have become individual and impersonal encounters that must be concluded in no more than fifteen minutes, since they must follow the rule of so-called relative value units. This measure was adopted by the US Congress in the 1990s "to calculate doctors' fees based on several factors, including a doctor's specialty, the cost of expenses, and liability insurance necessary to run a practice."[4] In these fifteen minutes, doctors must also fill out electronic health records, losing valuable time with each patient. It should not be surprising that doctors listen to patients for an average of eleven seconds—an absurdly small window to explain your health concerns—before interrupting them, conveying low levels of empathy.

Against these low levels of empathy narrative medicine teaches how to listen to and observe patients more intensely. Charon's basic premise is that a patient's description of her illness is not very different from a story you might find in a novel. Both include characters, symbols, and a plot requiring attention, engagement, and interpretation to be understood. As we can see, radical listening is a medical skill that allows patients to explain the story of their illness, including details like the time and emotions related to symptoms. Just as anatomy can be taught through an anatomy textbook, listening is a skill that can be taught through narratology. Although narrative medicine practitioners consider how a patient tells their story to be a valuable clue, they must also be attentive to what they aren't saying. "You have to be so present, so alert, with your curiosity so intact," Charon said. "And you have to assume that the narrators are going to mislead you. When a patient tells you what happened, you're going to hear the opposite story from their mother or neighbor."[5]

The success of narrative medicine—now taught in some form in 80 percent of medical schools in the United States—is a consequence not only of the depersonalization of modern medicine but also of the logocentric tradition of the West, which tends to ignore listening processes. Being warned requires listening, that is, becoming more attentive, engaged, and imaginative, as Charon requests from medical students and doctors. In a recent interview where she elaborated on the need for medical education to incorporate literature studies, she also recognized "narrative medicine's reliance on continental philosophy and phenomenology, and how it distinguishes itself from what is called bioethics."[6] Bioethics is a direct consequence of the logocentric tradition—where legal and philosophical principles are applied instrumentally to solve dilemmas in medical research and practice—but continental philosophers have explained why listening has been overlooked in Western thought and stressed its philosophical significance.

According to the philosopher and psychoanalyst Gemma Corradi Fiumara—the first writer to provide an overall outline of the secondary role of listening in our philosophical tradition—we have forgotten how to listen to others because an emphasis on speech and speaking primarily dominates the notion of *logos* that conditions Western philosophy.

Among the widespread meanings of the Greek term *logos* there do not appear to be recognizable references to the notion and capacity of listening; in the tradition of Western thought we are thus faced with a system of knowledge that tends to ignore listening processes. On the other hand, among the possible meanings of the verb *legein* (besides the prevalent ones related to saying) there are meanings of a different nature, such as to "shelter," "gather," "keep," and "receive," which would surely be more conducive to a cognitive attitude based on "proper hearing." At any moment in which reality is constructed we can identify an attitude that is able to say and not to listen—at that moment, in fact, a halved and overwhelming *logos* manifests itself. If we start out from this basic concern, we can then perhaps go back into the cultural wire-netting and discover how the mechanism of "saying without listening" has multiplied, spread, and finally constituted itself as a generalized form of domination and control.[7]

Fiumara's call to reinterpret *logos*—following Heidegger's destruction of logic as a set of communicative practices and its corresponding culture—is meant to expose its divided nature and restore a fuller *logos* based on Greek action, *legein*. This is why the difference between a divided *logos*—one that speaks but does not listen—and an undivided one—which speaks and listens—is the starting point to acknowledge not only that listening was systematically suppressed but also the sociopolitical consequences of this suppression. When philosophers discuss language, they generally do so only through "a partial sense of *logos* understood as a capacity for ordering and explaining, detached from any propensity to receive and listen," that is, exclusively from the speaker's side. It should not be surprising that the primary purpose of communication in this speaking-centered metaphysical intellectual tradition is to control, dominate, and triumph rather than to produce dialogues for mutual understanding. This is why the speaker's role is usually to prove and convince while the listener is reduced to a subordinate who must "pay attention" and "obey." One can even say—as Fiumara clarifies—"that the *logos* that knows how to speak but not how to listen represents the model of power in its primordial form."

The lack of philosophical interest in listening as a practice and process derives from this communicative environment and is concomitant with an unwillingness to recognize different realities. The nonlistening intellectual culture cannot "hear" anything outside its previous understanding of the rational and the understandable. By contrast, listening creates a "minimal but fertile logical passage which will then allow our minds to move with greater freedom and envisage still further ways of approaching reality." Also, it can "create a defence against any form of logocratic terrorism which may enslave the mind. And the enslavement of the mind does not take place because any cognitive outlook may be false or inadequate but because it tends to absorb major issues into minor models."[8] This "language rooted in a delusion of omnipotence" pretends to expand its horizons through the silencing of others and the ever-closer definition of objects of knowledge. As we can see, the goal of "logocratic terrorism" is not only to reinforce an understanding of power as sovereign control but also to "excommunicate anything that normal rationality is unable to grasp, thus keeping us within the same theoretical framework."[9]

Fiumara's investigations in our philosophical tradition are not meant to put forward a comprehensive listening theory—which would inevitably repeat the monological pattern of philosophical discourse—but rather seek to uncover suppressed possibilities in this "other side of language." "One can 'study' philosophy with relative ease but it is more difficult to experiment in listening. It is almost as though in order to listen one had to 'become' different, since it is not so much a question of grasping concepts or propositions as of attempting an experience. Unless we are ready, receptive—and also, possibly, vulnerable—the experience of listening appears to be impossible." This experience, as Fiumara explains, requires an openness to what lies beyond reason, "an attitude of individual attention and holding, an attitude also capable of letting anything be in its entireness." This is why it is not enough to learn *about* listening; it is also necessary to learn *to* listen to "allow for truer forms of dialogue."[10] In a divided *logos* (one that speaks but does not listen), dialogue often turns into a monologue; in one that speaks and listens, dialogue becomes a genuine exchange of views, opinions, and ideas, which Fiumara terms a "listening dialogue."

Although "listening dialogues" map out an entirely different space for dialogues to take place, one where we can become "apprentices of listening rather than masters of discourse," it must also be prepared to "sustain blows of any kind and still remain alert." Contrary to monologues—which expect answers on the presupposition that one can speak to others without being able to listen—listening dialogues involve responses that "could actually come across like a storm and overwhelm us" because they are "sustained by the expectation of a new and different quality of relationship." This relationship opens up the possibility that something apparently inexpressible could emerge (something Ludwig Wittgenstein excluded with his dictum "hereof one cannot speak, thereof one must be silent"), changing our original position. Although the attempt to listen presents us with a distressing situation "in which we have to take provisional, impossible steps in order to continue to listen and thus consent that something may come across," it is also an invitation to become aware "of the fragility of our doctrines."[11] This fragility is at the center of the thought of three philosophers who not only stress the significance of listening but also further corroborate the inevitable radicality of listening to that warning request: Martin Heidegger, Hans-Georg Gadamer, and Jean-Luc Nancy.

Heidegger's call for "painstaking listening" is related to the necessity to "improve our ability to listen and hear" in our philosophical tradition and also to reveal aspects of language of which speakers are not always aware.[12] Listening, *Hören*, does not refer to a supersensible, abstract identical meaning, as theorized in the metaphysical tradition, or a merely acoustical event, as the physical sciences understand it. While the ear is necessary, it is insufficient for listening and hearing: It is "we who hear, not the ear." As Heidegger explained in *Being and Time*, hearing is rooted in understanding, for what "we 'first' hear is never noises or complexes of sounds, but the creaking wagon, the motor-cycle,"[13] in other words, what is being said, not the vocalization. If at some point the "human ear becomes dull, that is, deaf, then it can be, as is clear in the case of Beethoven, that a person nevertheless still hears, perhaps hears even more and something greater than before." This is possible because hearing is primarily and existentially an opening.[14] But listening, as an existential openness to others, refers to our ability to recognize others hermeneutically and oneself in a specific practical relevance. This is why Heidegger states that the human being "lets something be said insofar as he [*sic* here and throughout] hears. He does not hear in the sense of learning something, but rather in the sense of having a directive for concrete practical concern."[15] If the question of Being is also the question of hearing, then "thinking depends on hearing," and hearing becomes a mode of responsiveness, acceptance, a hermeneutic experience that cannot be subsumed to the ontic realm of rational analysis.

Listening as a hermeneutic experience allows us to think about what lies beyond reason and to let anything be in its entirety. In doing so it discloses unexpected possibilities, "what was un-heard (of) [*Un-erhört*] before,"[16] opening the door to listen to language. But such listening "comes before all other kinds of listening that we know, in a most inconspicuous manner. We do not merely speak *the* language—we speak *by way of it*. We can do so solely because we always have already listened to the language. What do we hear there? We hear language speaking."[17] This is why Heidegger believes that we speak in the most proper sense when we fail to talk, that is, when we have to recall a word from memory or look for the appropriate expression. In these cases, we are listening to language. Listening, in its affective, profound, and eminently painstaking character, is the radical act of "listen[ing] to language," which Heidegger considered not only the "house of Being" but also where "human being dwells."[18]

In *Truth and Method*, Gadamer refers to listening as the "avenue to the whole" because it is the sense through which we can dialogue with others. In a dialogue—which he compares to interpreting a text—an encounter occurs where listening plays a central role in understanding the other. "We do not need just to hear one another but to *listen to* one another. Only when this happens is there understanding."[19] In this dialogic process, both interlocutors listen to each other through a common language: the dimension of openness. This does not simply entail that the one who hears is also addressed but also "that he [*sic*] who is addressed must hear whether he wants to or not. When you look at something, you can also look away from it by looking in another direction, but you cannot 'hear away.'"[20] This difference between seeing and hearing is crucial because the priority of hearing is the foundation of the hermeneutic experience:

> Whereas all the other senses have no immediate share in the universality of the verbal experience of the world, but only offer the key to their own specific fields, hearing is an avenue to the whole because it is able to listen to the *logos*. In the light of our hermeneutical inquiry this ancient insight into the priority of hearing over sight acquires a new emphasis. The language in which hearing shares is not only universal in the sense that everything can be expressed in it. The significance of the hermeneutical experience is rather that, in contrast to all other experience of the world, language opens up a completely new dimension, the profound dimension from which tradition comes down to those now living. This has always been the true essence of hearing, even before

the invention of writing: that the hearer can listen to the legends, the myths, and the truth of the ancients. In comparison, the written, literary transmission of tradition, as we know it, is nothing new; it only changes the form and makes the task of real hearing more difficult.[21]

Although Gadamer did not develop a "philosophy of listening," he still proves its significance for human relations, which can only occur when interlocutors listen. This is why openness cannot exist only for the person who speaks but must also belong to those who listen, without which there is no genuine human bond. If "to be able to hear means to be able to understand,"[22] listening is the "avenue to the whole," that is, the possibility of unifying the divided *logos* that speaks but does not listen.

When Nancy defines listening "to be straining toward or in an approach to the self,"[23] he is trying to overcome a mode of listening proper to the phenomenological subject that Jacques Derrida individuated and deconstructed in *Voice and Phenomenon*. The problem of this subject is not only that it hears and understands itself, always already speaking, but rather that it can't expose itself to something unknown or different, as listening can. "To be listening," as Nancy explains, "is always to be on the edge of meaning, or in an edgy meaning of extremity, and as if the sound were precisely nothing else than this edge, this fringe, this margin."[24]

Nancy, following Heidegger's ontological difference between beings and Being, distinguishes between hearing—*entendre*—and listening—*écouter*. In French, the verb *entendre* implies a kind of hearing that is also a way "to understand" or "to intend" particular entities in the world. By imposing a certain truth on what is heard, *entendre* also pretends always to be able to hear knowable and identifiable beings. *Écouter*, instead, is a form of listening that exposes itself to "sense," meaning, and direction hidden from the sound of present beings. This is why when we "listen," we do not orient ourselves in advance toward specific beings whom we might attempt to understand but rather toward the openness of uncertainty and exposure. In sum, *entendre* "is to understand the sense (either in the so-called figurative sense, or in the so-called proper sense: to hear a siren, a bird, or a drum is already each time to understand at least the rough outline of a situation, a context if not a text)," but *écouter* "is to be straining toward a possible meaning, and consequently one that is not immediately accessible."[25] In contrast with the phenomenological subject, who seeks to understand what we hear in advance, Nancy calls for a "resonant subject"[26] who is always listening to itself without finding itself present.

These philosophers have corroborated Charon's request and call for radical listening and provided further indications that doing so involves the listener's ability not only to hear but also to "become different." The radicality of listening entails a different "approach to the self"—a vulnerable attitude—beyond reason, as it must be capable of letting anything be in its entirety. This is why Heidegger and Gadamer insisted on listening's existential nature, that is, the openness to others *through* language. The affective, profound, and painstaking character of listening becomes an "avenue to the whole" individual rather than just its symptoms. Being warned entails letting anything be in its entirety: becoming attentive, engaged, and imaginative listeners ready for a radical break. The different possibilities that emerge from this break will allow the radical listener to demonstrate that they are not simply rehearsing a monologue as a lousy actor might do but also are capable of improvising whenever necessary. This ability to improvise—the crisis that warnings stimulate—presupposes radical listening.

11

THE BATTLE OF INTERPRETATION

When the 2023 United Nations Climate Change summit in Dubai reached a deal "for "transitioning away from fossil fuels in energy systems in a just, orderly and equitable manner, accelerating action in this critical decade," environmentalists worldwide were hesitant to celebrate. Although the direct references to oil, gas, and coal represented a vital improvement, considering that calls to abandon fossil fuels had previously always been left out of the final text of numerous climate agreements, too many contradictions surrounded the summit. These included the summit president, Sultan al-Jaber (who, in addition to being the UAE's minister of industry, was also the CEO of ADNOC, the state-owned oil company); the fact that fossil-fuel lobbyists outnumbered nearly all the delegations from individual countries; and the lack of transparency that dogged the negotiations. How was it possible for the petrostates to block the call for an explicit commitment to phase out or even phase down fossil fuels from scientists, civil society groups, and the majority of the countries in attendance (130 of the 198)? The battle "for interpretation" of the term "energy system" emerged once the agreement was reached.

After Fiona Harvey reported from Dubai, praising al-Jaber and claiming that the deal amounted to a "de facto phase-out of fossil fuels," the codirector of the Climate Majority Report, Rupert Read, sent a letter to the *Guardian*, questioning their enthusiasm. According to Read, the ambiguity surrounding the phrase "away from fossil fuels in energy systems" must be properly understood because it is "not interpreted in the agreement, and thus left ambiguous. The most plausible interpretation is that it means power (i.e. power stations) and heat (e.g. combined heat and power plants, or home heating). . . . Cop28 did not call on countries to transition away from fossil fuels, let alone to phase them out. It only called on countries to transition away from fossil fuels in the generation of electricity and heat for heating purposes." Read is convinced the "deal leaves the highway to climate hell wide open." Four days later, another letter was published—"A Battle for Interpretation of the Cop28 Deal on Fossil Fuel Phase-out"—where Read was accused of misinterpreting the term "energy system":

> This ambiguous term is what enabled textual agreement between the 130 countries at Cop28 that wanted a phase-out of fossil fuels and the oil-and-gas-producing states who didn't. The former are absolutely clear that energy systems should be taken to include transport energy—they would not have signed it otherwise. The latter want you to believe it doesn't. The intended meaning was made clear on the official United Nations framework convention on climate change website when announcing the agreement: "the 'beginning of the end' of the fossil fuel era." It was why the Saudi minister was the only one not applauding at the end. The Cop28 text is advisory, not mandatory. Its effect on government policy around the world will therefore depend on whether it is understood in political and policy debate to mean a

fossil fuel phase-out as a whole or only for electricity and heating. ... This is a battle for interpretation. It is vital that all supporters of climate action insist that Cop28 has called for the gradual transition to a non-fossil fuel future.

Although Michael Jacobs here lets "hope triumph over experience"—as the agreement will end up meaning whatever the petrostates and their enablers want it to mean—he at least highlights the significance of interpretation in this debate. John Foster, for example, considers "transition away" a "classic weasel wordage, and the loophole allowing it to be taken as referring only to fossil fuels for energy and heating will be as ruthlessly exploited as Read expects it to be." An agreement subject to contested interpretation over fundamental points, Forster continues, is not worth considering.[1] But the critical problem of this agreement and the summit in general is not so much that it opens the door to a "battle *for* interpretation"—all agreements are subject to contested interpretations—as much as it doesn't recognize the "battle *of* interpretation."

The first term implies challenging different viewpoints, beliefs, or opinions, hoping to prevail or reach an agreement, but the latter entails a battle for the significance of what interpretation entails: engagement, wakefulness, and alertness. This alert is not meant to defend a particular point of view—even one founded on data and scientific discoveries—as much as an existential stance. To explain this difference, it is necessary to recall the transformation of hermeneutics from a theory of textual interpretation to an ontology of existence. Although this transformation has radically changed the meaning of interpretation, its link to warnings has always been central. This is evident in biblical and juridical hermeneutics, regarded as "auxiliary disciplines" for theologians and jurists to facilitate the interpretation of biblical texts and legal documents. These interpretations often implied warnings that concerned not only the correct understanding of what was taken to be the divine and legal word but also how to live according to these texts. "Being warned" requires interpretation because it concerns the interpreter's own existence. Before venturing into this transformation, it's essential to recall the anarchic origins and essence of hermeneutics.

The origins of hermeneutics and how its history should be configured are also hermeneutic problems. Some histories situate the creation of philosophical hermeneutics in Herodotus's *Histories* or Aristotle's treatise *Peri hermeneias* (*De interpretatione*), but others proclaim that it was formed two millennia later by Flacius, in *Clavis scripturae sacrae*, or even later, in the seventeenth century, when Johann Dannhauer introduced for the first time the Latin word *hermeneutica* as a necessary condition for those sciences that relied on the interpretation of texts. As Gerald L. Bruns points out, "hermeneutics is a loose and baggy monster, or anyhow a less than fully disciplined body of thinking, whose inventory of topics spreads out over many different historical, cultural, and intellectual contexts."[2] Although Bruns, Gianni Vattimo, and others have raised doubts about whether there is such a thing as an origin, a history, or even a unified development of hermeneutics, they all acknowledge the discipline's anarchic vein. This vein is etymologically evident in the god Hermes, "the many-sided, uncontainable, nocturnal transgressor,"[3] whose role is central in the historical development of hermeneutics. As Jean Grondin points out, in the *Ion* Plato refers to poets as the "*hermenes ton theon*":

> In this dialogue, moreover, the rhapsodes who perform the poets' works are described as interpreters of interpreters ("*hermeneon hermenes*," *Ion* 535a). Just like the prophet, the *hermeneus* seems to

mediate both between god and man as well as between people and the (manic) mediator. Thus the *hermeneus* is the mediator of something mediated, the mediator of a *hermeneia* a function that can go on indefinitely, since it always leaves more to say than can be precisely captured in words. The mediatory function of the hermeneutic led antiquity to make an etymological linkage between the semantic family of *hermeneus* and the mediator-god, Hermes.[4]

Hermes, whose name points back to his winged feet, was renowned for his speed, athleticism, and swiftness. He exercised the practical activity of delivering the announcements, prophecies, and warnings of the gods of Olympus. In the *Cratylus* (407e), *Ion* (534e), and *Symposium* (202e), Plato connects the term *hermênea* etymologically to the name of the god Hermes and presents hermeneutics both as a theory of reception and "as a practice for transmission and mediation": Hermes must transmit what is beyond human understanding in a form that human intelligence can grasp. However, in this transmission he was often accused of treachery, thievery, and even anarchy because the messages were never accurate; in other words, his interpretations constantly altered the original meanings.[5] This is why "Hermes is not only the messenger of the divine; he is also the god of travelers, diplomats, and outlaws."[6] As practiced by the "ancients and their humanist admirers," Kathy Eden explains, "interpretation is by and large adversarial, an antagonistic affair."[7]

Although this adversarial, antagonistic, and anarchic feature of interpretation is present throughout its history, it was only after the transformation of hermeneutics from a theory of textual interpretation to an ontology of existence that it acquired profound existential meaning. The "battle of interpretation" begins with Heidegger—the first to outline a history of philosophical hermeneutics in 1923—who criticized the different hermeneutics that emerged after the seventeenth century, where the discipline's "performance sense" and "practical dimension" were converted into "method," "doctrine," and "discipline." Luther and other writers from the patristic period were decisive in developing hermeneutics in a comprehensive and living manner through its "practical dimension." Against this dimension—also present in Augustine, for whom interpretation is a soul-searching and soul-shattering practice, to be undertaken in fear and trembling rather than with the certainty that every "technique of understanding" always involves—Friedrich Schleiermacher reduced hermeneutics to "an 'art [technique] of understanding' another's discourse, and seen as a discipline connected with grammar and rhetoric, it was brought into relation with dialectic—this methodology is formal, as 'general hermeneutics' (theory and technique of understanding any foreign discourse) it encompasses the special disciplines of theological and philological hermeneutics."[8]

Schleiermacher's attempt to combine practices of biblical exegesis and classical philology into a single doctrine of the art of interpretation was later expanded by Wilhelm Dilthey, whom Heidegger preferred for interpreting hermeneutics as a general analysis of "understanding" and "categories of life." The object of hermeneutics for Dilthey is not texts or something lying "outside" as much as our mundane, engaged, and prescientific practices. If interpretation is grounded in lived experiences—instead of a decontextualized transcendental self—the interpreter will always be implicated in the process of interpretation. Heidegger appreciated this implication because it highlighted understanding as a basic existential fact that is presupposed by historical and scientific disciplines alike. This is why Heidegger's hermeneutics is directed at interpreting how "the authentic meaning of

Being, and also those basic structures of Being which Dasein itself possesses, are *made known* to Dasein's understanding of Being."[9] Thus, the battle of interpretation concerns Being rather than beings—that is, artificial epistemological conditions.[10]

Interpretation for Heidegger moves within a certain forestructure (*Vorstruktur*) composed of what the interpreter has before them to do (*Vorhabe*) as well as their preview (*Vorsicht*) and preconception (*Vorgriff*) of it. This situation underlies the circular character of interpretation, the so-called hermeneutical circle, which initially seems like a logical fallacy because it's not linear. However, as Heidegger explains, what counts is not whether it's linear but rather "to come into it in the right way."[11] Finding one's way into the circle is meant to replace traditional metaphysics with hermeneutics because it has the "task of making the Dasein which is in each case our own accessible to this Dasein itself with regard to the character of its being, communicating Dasein to itself in this regard, hunting down the alienation from itself with which it is smitten."[12] This alienation is a symptom of the epistemological conditions created by the "the world grasped as picture" where beings are already established, secured, and predicted beforehand. Against this alienation philosophical hermeneutics aims to "develop an alert understanding of oneself, that is, to cultivate as much as possible one's self-understanding, which can only be done in understanding the world and one's engagement with it."[13]

The engagement that emerges in interpretation is entirely incompatible with a cognitive-epistemological comportment, that is, those "battles for interpretation" mentioned earlier. These battles concern intellectual and cognitive actions, treating "something as something" or "acquiring information about what is understood." In contrast, the battle of interpretation consists in "the working-out of possibilities projected in understanding."[14]

These possibilities consist of an "alert," a "philosophical wakefulness, in which Dasein is encountering itself":

> The wakefulness is philosophical—this means: it lives and is at work in a primordial self-interpretation which philosophy has given of itself and which is such that philosophy constitutes a decisive possibility and mode of Dasein's self-encounter. What it says for this hermeneutics is: (1) Philosophy is a mode of knowing which is in factical life itself and in which factical Dasein is ruthlessly dragged back to itself and relentlessly thrown back upon itself. (2) As this mode of knowing, philosophy has no mission to take care of universal humanity and culture, to release coming generations once and for all from care about questioning, or to interfere with them simply through wrongheaded claims to validity. Philosophy is what it can be only as a philosophy of "its time."[15]

Similarly to Luther's "practical dimension" and Augustine's fear and trembling, hermeneutics for Heidegger goes beyond merely academic cognitive-epistemological concerns, reaching the core of our Being. This is why interpretation "will itself remain unimportant so long as the wakefulness for facticity which it is supposed to temporalize and unfold is not 'there.'" As something preliminary and that runs in advance of philosophy, interpretation is not meant to take "cognizance of something and hav[e] knowledge about it, but rather an existential knowing, i.e., a Being ['*ein Sein*']. It speaks from out of interpretation and for the sake of it."[16] The battle of interpretation implicit in this knowing is also a way of formulating the problem of the disclosure of a world, that is, the problem of truth. But the truth *of* interpretation is radically different from the truth *for* interpretation.

Heidegger's transformation of hermeneutics from a theory of textual interpretation to an ontology of existence was meant to recover its not only "performance sense" and "practical dimension" but also all the objectivist theories of truth, such as the well-known formula *"veritas est adaequatio rei et intellectus."* Since antiquity, this formula was considered the authentic "locus" of truth upon which assertions or propositions were deemed true or false. But as Heidegger explains, "Being (not entities) is something which 'there is' only in so far as truth is. And truth is only in so far as and as long as Dasein is. Being and truth 'are' equiprimordially."[17] The truth that occurs in the statement is a derivative one because the "apophantic as" is only possible within the "hermeneutic as": there is no "presuppositionless" apprehension of something presented to us that could later be "objectified" by employing a predicative modality of the subject. This is why "the proposition is not the place of truth; truth is the place of the proposition."[18]

The battle *for* the correct interpretation of the term "energy system" among climate advisors, researchers, and activists is founded upon this metaphysical theory of truth, which Heidegger considers derivative. Instead, in the battle *of* interpretation, truth becomes the self-manifestation of Being in its unconcealment, that is, "the ontological condition for the possibility that assertions can be either true or false—that they may uncover or cover things up."[19] In this possibility lies the priority of interpretation as an existential stance over interpretation as the technique of accurately understanding assertions, announcements, and warnings.

As we can see, the battle *of* interpretation concerns the interpreter's existence because understanding articulates itself in an interpretation. Heidegger rejects the earlier hermeneutical tradition, where understanding and interpretation are sharply separated. If an interpretation always occurs in understanding, the battle cannot concern challenging different meanings or truths as much as an "existential knowing." Similarly to an actor, the interpreter cannot take on the role of a disinterested observer but must instead become the performer of the things it describes, that is, must play the part to understand the role. This role does not consist of putting into contrast different opinions in the hopes that one will prevail in a performance or debate as much as engaging wakefully in warnings because they concern our existence. As an "existential knowing," interpretation is always already an alert—in other words, a warning.

12

TRUTH IS NOT ENOUGH

Slavoj Žižek concludes his book *The Year of Dreaming Dangerously* by calling on us to be guided by "ambiguous signs from the future." These signs are events like the "OWS protests, the Arab Spring, the demonstrations in Greece and Spain," which all entail—in different forms—germs of radical emancipatory politics, which he also refers to as "hypothetical communism." Against the common historicist perspective, wherein events are understood through their context and genesis, Žižek seeks to interpret them as "limited, distorted (sometimes even perverted) fragments of a utopian future that lies dormant in the present as its hidden potential." These emancipatory or communist signs "come from a place that will become actual only if we follow these signs—in other words, they are signs that, paradoxically, precede that of which they are the signs." Žižek also accuses the left of being a "Cassandra, warning that our prosperity is based on illusions and prophesizing catastrophes to come," but now that "economic downturn and social disintegration" are here, they don't know how to respond. The absence of any "consistent Leftist reply to these events, any project of how to transpose islands of chaotic resistance into a positive program of social change," prevails.[1]

Žižek's call to be guided by "ambiguous signs from the future" and the inability of the left to respond to these warnings are particularly significant for my philosophy because they constitute a warning. Žižek, Paul B. Preciado, Judith Butler, and Giorgio Agamben, among others, can also be considered "philosophers of warnings." Throughout his oeuvre, Žižek warns of various philosophical, social, and political paradoxes that permeate our lives. For example, he warned philosophers of the return of the real—as explored in part 2—warned environmentalists of the dangers of naturalizing nature, and warned economists that the global capitalist system is approaching an apocalyptic zero point. This last warning comprises the ecological crisis, the consequences of the biogenetic revolution, imbalances within the system (problems with intellectual property; forthcoming struggles over raw materials, food, and water), and the explosive growth of social divisions and exclusions—or the "four riders of the apocalypse," as he refers to them.[2] Although Žižek is not the object of this chapter, his tireless intellectual activity can also be interpreted as a sign from the future, that is, a warning meant to create crises. His warnings—despite how provocative they can be—always suggest there is something we can do.[3]

This last chapter seeks to show that truth is not enough to warn us. Intensity and pressure are also necessary. This is evident not only in those warnings we find in the media—about health, political, and environmental issues—but also in those that reveal themselves as signs from the future (as *avenir*, to-come) that also concern these matters. The difference between the two kinds of warnings—those from the political scientists Macarena Ares and Silja Häusermann's about the left crisis in Europe and Žižek's warnings regarding the left's inability to listen to their own warnings in his books and public interventions—is not theoretical as much as existential: It concerns the intensity and pressure they convey. In the former, we are warned through data and evidence; in the latter, we are warned by interpretations and arguments concerning our existence.[4] This is why Being warned concerns, first and foremost, whether there will be a future in the ongoing global return to order through realism. But for this future "to-come," crisis must be stimulated through warnings concerning our existence.

Whether a warning comes to pass is secondary to the intensity and pressure it exercises against hidden emergencies because it depends on our willingness to listen and interpret. The priority of the living past over history, "to-come" over the future, and signs over signals reminds us of warnings' inevitable ambiguous, vague, and weak status as opposed to predictions' unquestionable legitimacy—but also how the former embraces the latter. If voters have not responded to the left's warnings to create a positive program of social change, Žižek emphasizes that it's not only because they haven't been "radically listening" and "interpreting existentially" but also because the warnings have lacked degree, intensity, and depth alongside their data and evidence. But which signs from the future have the intensity and pressure to draw us to listen and interpret independently of the evidence provided? Why is truth a matter of intensity and pressure instead of evidence?

Although I could draw on many examples—from the street art interventions of kennardphillipps to Sara Ahmed's "killjoy feminism" and the revelations of Julian Assange, Edward Snowden, and Christopher Wylie—to demonstrate that we respond predominantly to a warning's intensity and pressure rather than its truth, I will focus on Greta Thunberg's environmental activism instead.[5] This choice is not made simply because of the success of her activism with the public—as opposed to the warnings from scientists working on global warming—but also because she incarnates a form of hermeneutical knowledge that displays a different relationship with reality than what we're accustomed to. This knowledge reveals that facts, evidence, and truths (particularly those related to climate change) are insufficient impetus to make us listen to warnings. If they were enough, the first Conference on the Human Environment in 1972 in Stockholm would not have been a failure. This is why the most significant challenge that climate scientists face today is not to demonstrate the speed at which glaciers and ice caps are melting but to convince politicians to take action against global warming and its alarming consequences.[6] Also, it is crucial to remember that Thunberg's warnings are not limited to the environmental crisis but to our existence at large.

Thunberg first learned about climate change when she was nine and in the third grade. "'They were always talking about how we should turn off lights, save water, not throw out food . . . I asked why and they explained about climate change. And I thought this was very strange. If humans could really change the climate, everyone would be talking about it and people wouldn't be talking about anything else. But this wasn't happening.' . . . She has stopped eating meat and buying anything that is not absolutely necessary."[7] Six years later, she held the first "School Strike for Climate" in the summer of 2018. This strike consisted of skipping school every Friday to protest in front of the Swedish parliament with a handmade sign that said simply: "School Strike for the Climate." At first, her protest attracted a small crowd, but then more students started doing it in other cities. It soon became a global phenomenon. In March 2019, the first Global School Strike for Climate occurred: Over "2,000 strikes in 125 countries, with 1.6 million young people participating on a single day. 1.6 million people. That's quite an achievement," as Naomi Klein recalls, "for a movement that began just eight months earlier with a single 15-year-old girl in Stockholm, Sweden."[8]

After the success of this strike, Thunberg took a year off from school to focus on activism, and she became famous for her impassioned speeches to world leaders.[9] In these speeches—at UN climate negotiations, Davos, and many other venues—she is often both ironic and aggressive. When she met a group of British MPs in April 2019, including the opposition leader Jeremy Corbyn, Liberal Democrat leader Vince Cable, Green Party MP Caroline Lucas, and others, she asked, "Is my English OK? Is the microphone on? Because I'm beginning to wonder"—given their constant support of new exploitations of fossil fuels, shale fracking, and expansion of North Sea oil extraction. When the rich and mighty at Davos praised her for giving them hope, she retorted, "I don't want your hope. . . . I want you to panic. I want you to feel the fear I feel every day. I want you to act. I want you to act as you would in a crisis. I want you to act as if the house is on fire, because it is."[10] During these years, Thunberg was detained by police or removed from protests in several countries, including England, Norway, and Germany.

Now, at twenty-two, she has no intention of stopping, and she says that "being different is a gift. If I would've been like everyone else, I wouldn't have started this school strike."[11] But what does this difference consist of? Why can we interpret her activism as a "sign from the future"? There are also various features of her being that, like warnings, read as weak, for example, the fact that she was a teenager when she began instigating children's school strikes, that she is female (bearing in mind our patriarchal society), and that she was diagnosed with Asperger's syndrome, a form of autism. This last factor, as Žižek pointed out, is far from disturbing; it is what gives her strength:

The definition of autism is "a developmental disorder characterized by difficulty in social interaction and communication and by restricted or repetitive patterns of thought and behavior," and this is exactly what is needed if we are to confront global warming: repetitively insisting on scientific results and ignoring all the rhetorical tricks that obfuscate the scientific message. When, as happened in recent months, children all around the world go on strike to protest our (adults') ignorance of ecological dangers, we should support them unconditionally, and reject all claims that children "don't understand the complexity of the situation," etc. The most disgusting reaction was that of a Belgian politician: instead of striking, children should rather stay in school and learn... Learn what? How to ruin our chances of a future the way their elders (those who are teaching them) did?[12]

This last point is particularly significant in understanding the truth of warnings, in other words, the hermeneutical knowledge that encompasses both the natural and human or social sciences. If Thunberg has managed to warn us to a greater extent than scientists, it's not simply because she has humanized the climate crisis as few others have done, going on strike or calling out numerous politicians whose failure to act has endangered our future, but primarily for changing our relation to scientific truths. When she inverts the cultural assumption that adults should educate children, she points out that "adult knowledge" is not enough; it has become obsolete and must be overcome. This is why her call to panic is directed at "normal" people, those who never skip school or rarely listen to science.

But what is the "adult knowledge" being taught in school, and why is it responsible for our inability to listen to science? As Rita Charon and Gemma Corradi Fiumara explain, listening requires a different, open, and vulnerable attitude, beyond rationality, where truth must first and foremost be experienced. Hans-Georg Gadamer was once asked about higher education, where a methodological, uncritical, and scientific model prevailed in the curriculum. His response clarifies why "adult knowledge"—facts and truth—is not enough to warn us that climate change is a global emergency. "Once," he recalled, "I was teaching in Boston College and a student came to me and said, 'Oh, Professor Gadamer I see that you are teaching Plato this semester! What a pity, because I have already done Plato!'"[13] This student shared a belief common to many university curricula: that knowledge is truthful if it is repeatable, that is, an endless repetition of the same. As the metaphysical and empiricist tradition recommends, this repetition permits a problem-solving approach that guarantees objective results. According to this tradition, for example, we can talk about the apples falling from a tree based on the experience of them falling a distant time in the past. The idea of experience as repetition originates from the Enlightenment dream of truth as an accumulation of scientific facts. The problem with this accumulation is that the holder of these facts becomes excessively confident about the use that human knowledge will make of them. This is why the elaboration of a precise method—which in the modern age became the most reliable matrix and source of knowledge—ended up restricting truth even further, according to Gadamer. But what are the other meanings experience can provide? Why is a lecture by Gadamer on Plato an experience that cannot be repeated? What other source of authority for knowledge is there besides a repeatable, scientific, and rationally inspired method?

Gadamer's philosophical objective was to justify a type of knowledge that does not depend on methodology alone, because repeatable experiences or the accumulation of scientific facts is not enough to understand the world or make anyone wiser. If anything, it teaches us our limitations. But to acknowledge these limitations, it is necessary to refer to the humanist tradition in which the goal of knowledge consists in acquiring what Gadamer calls *Bildung*—best translated as "education," "formation," "culture"—which allows us to broaden our horizons beyond the narrow scope of the universal laws of science. Through *Bildung*, we develop common sense, aesthetic taste, and moral judgment and, most of all, gain a global perspective that allows us to see beyond the frames of empirical science. The growth this allows then demonstrates that the real source of truth in human affairs is not regulated by an illusory universal reason but rather by the human sciences.

The "human sciences are connected to modes of experience that lie outside science: with the experiences of philosophy, of art, and of history itself. These are all modes of experience in which a truth is communicated that cannot be verified by the methodological means proper to science."[14] These are the experiences where truth's intensity and pressure reveal themselves. For example, a genuine work of art takes hold of the interpreter and becomes an event with which they engage through a conversation. However, in this conversation, they are not in control of the work of art but led by it. This model allowed Gadamer to defend the extramethodological truth of the human sciences and justify why classics continue to endure, that is, how they continue to pressure their readers. If "the duration of a work's power to speak directly is fundamentally unlimited," it's not because of the origin or truth of the work but because of the effects and consequences it continues to have.[15] This is why classical writings, works of art, or lectures by renowned philosophers are not closed, sealed, and static entities that can be repeated but dynamic events that take "hold of us. . . . The work is an '*Ereignis*'—an *event* that 'appropriates us' into itself. It shocks us, it overturns us, and sets up a world of its own, into which we are drawn."[16]

The pressure and intensity of Thunberg's environmental activism have transformed the climate crisis into a dynamic event that cannot be treated exclusively through natural sciences. It requires—following Gadamer's *Bildung*—a broader horizon, a global perspective. This is why the "adults'" distinction between the natural and human or social sciences is insignificant from her hermeneutic point of view. When Wilhelm Dilthey insisted upon this distinction, it implied a methodological superiority of the former that has now become obsolete. The "natural sciences are developed only within the horizon of language that is naturally inherited with the same historical constitution of our being-in-the-world, namely, within that prior opening that conditions every experience and, therefore, constitutes its unavoidably interpretative character."[17] This is why our response to scientific findings should not be a repetition, a cognizance, or a theoretical acquisition but rather what Ludwig Wittgenstein would call the sharing of a "form of life." Sharing a form of life does not mean something purely irrational—as many have described Thunberg's autism—but rather assuming scientific findings to have a broader social concern, exploring their consequences with the same intensity that a work of art demands. Her call to skip school, panic, and change our relation to scientific evidence is meant to remind us that truth is not enough for "Being warned."

AFTERWORD

It would be a mistake to believe that the pandemic is a crisis that will end, instead of the perfect warning for what is coming, what I call the new climatic regime. It appears that all the resources of science, humanities and the arts will have to be mobilized once again to shift attention to our shared terrestrial condition.

—Bruno Latour, "The Pandemic Is a Warning"

Bruno Latour is not alone in interpreting events as warnings. Jonathan Glazer described his 2023 movie *The Zone of Interest*—loosely based on Martin Amis's novel about the life of the Nazi commandant Rudolf Höss and his family next to Auschwitz—as "not a document. It's not a history lesson. It's a warning." The Chilean artist Alfredo Jaar believes "red"—a color present in many of his works—"is a powerful color full of meaning and potential. It is not only the color of life and love, but it is also the color of suffering, warning, and danger." And the investigative journalist John Pilger wrote in 2019 that the "shocking arrest of Julian Assange carries a warning for all who, as Oscar Wilde wrote, 'sow the seeds of discontent [without which] there would be no advance towards civilization.'"[1] The most interesting feature of Latour's, Glazer's, Jaar's, and Pilger's warnings is the projection toward the future they want to convey and the political pressure they are trying to exercise through signs. In this pressure we can envision the seeds of a politics of warnings. This politics is not primarily meant to outline the steps we must take to prevent another pandemic, Holocaust, or injustice but also to resist the global return to order through realism, which is at the origin of these events. But is it possible to build a politics around the notion of warnings? Is there a political vocation of warnings? Are we ready to envision the political changes that listening to and interpreting warnings will entail? Several political features of warnings have emerged throughout this book that can be used to attempt a first response to these questions.

The ontological difference between "Being warned" and "being warned" is the point of departure to understand the meaning and goal of a politics of warnings. In the former, we are called to stimulate crises and are thrust into absent emergencies; in the latter, we are guided to avoid emergencies through different methods and strategies such as "trigger warnings" or the "Cassandra Coefficient."[2] This is why the primary concern of a politics of warning is not the facts, truths, and the future that constitute a warning but rather the pressure we can exercise to change the present. The political nature of warnings demands practices—from philosophers, filmmakers, and journalists, among others—that are somehow more comprehensive even if with fewer immediate political results.

The example of Greta Thunberg in part 3 was meant to show how little effect scientific data have in comparison to her activism. This is probably why, as Naomi Klein points out, at scientific gatherings researchers have begun to call on the general public to agitate for political change rather than repeat the indisputable causes of global warming.[3] This does not mean that researchers are rejecting science and becoming radical activists but rather that they are acknowledging that warnings cannot simply rely upon their findings. Here lies the interest in Rita Charon's new medical field, "narrative medicine." The need to teach doctors to listen to their patients indicates that their diagnoses are not always enough to cure them. The failure of technocratic politics these past decades—as Gianni Vattimo has pointed out—should be read in this perspective.[4]

As we can see, a politics of warnings—similar to Jacques Derrida's "politics of friendship," Enrique Dussel's "politics of liberation," and Judith Butler's "politics of performativity"—requires a nonfoundational horizon because truth is not enough for warnings to pressure us. The inefficacy of truth inevitably raises the question of whose and which warning we must listen to. Although I have focused on philosophers, warnings might also come from activists, artists, or journalists. Glazer's warning— regarding the danger of repeating another genocide—through a movie does not have less validity than that of the Holocaust historian Timothy Snyder, who begins *Black Earth* by making a similar point: that the "Holocaust is not only history, but warning." The difference between the two warnings is not one of kind but rather of degree, intensity, and depth. The truth of this genocide is not debatable—just like the scientific evidence of climate change or Assange's revelations—but whether we listen to and interpret its signs, messages, and meaning is. This is why, as Snyder believes, part "of the effort to understand the past is thus the effort needed to understand ourselves."[5] The same can be said about warnings.

The second question as to "which" warning we should be paying attention to concerns the object (a genocide, pandemic, or technological innovation) under discussion but also how absent the foreseeable emergency is. Warnings, as we said, are absent emergencies, that is, emergencies about to emerge. While a nuclear conflict this century is still an absent emergency—therefore, a great emergency, given its probability—other warnings have become actual emergencies. But this does not entail that they shouldn't be addressed anymore. This is the case of the Planetary Boundaries Framework, which is vital to maintaining a safe operating space for humanity. According to the latest "update . . . six of the nine boundaries are transgressed, suggesting that Earth is now well outside of the safe operating space for humanity. Ocean acidification is close to being breached, while aerosol loading regionally exceeds the boundary."[6] This update is a good example that warnings cannot become obsolete because they refer to much more than a single issue that can be addressed once and for all. Contrary to predictions' precision, the weakness, vagueness, and subtleness of warnings represent their strength.

For warnings to become the key concept in political analysis, the precondition of any kind of strategic thinking, it's necessary to distinguish crises from alternatives. The crises that warnings stimulate are means to achieve the alternative the warning considers essential. This is why Thunberg, for example, might tone down her activism—the crisis—once governments properly confront climate change—the alternative. The end of the ongoing expansion of North Sea oil extraction will improve our environment and force us to rely upon renewable energy systems structured under a different economic plan. However, the critical thing to remember is that this alternative is not an ideal as much as a different standpoint from which to view the world, a worldview that concerns our existence and present. Kyle Whyte's ethics of shared responsibility, for example, provides such a different standpoint. His preference for "kinship time," as opposed to "linear time," is meant to show that "today's climate change risks are caused by people not taking responsibility for one another's safety, well-being, and self-determination."[7]

The same logic can be applied to the warnings of Friedrich Nietzsche, Martin Heidegger, Simone de Beauvoir, and Hannah Arendt, with which I began. The crises they generated through their warnings—giving birth to generations of scholars proclaiming related warnings—have changed our worldview. These philosophers' warnings were not simply meant to avoid the emergencies I discuss in part 2—they were not so naïve—but primarily to invite us to think differently, that is, to prevent the continuation of realism that gave rise to their warnings in the first place. For example, Arendt's warning of the banality of evil, the return of totalitarianism, and the automated economy allows us to identify not only the dangers of artificial intelligence and surveillance capitalism but also the emergence of postdemocratic authoritarians such as Viktor Orban, Giorgia Meloni, and Javier Milei, among others. These leaders, as Josep Ramoneda has been warning for years, "share an ideological repertoire despite their different origin: authoritarianism, fundamentalist nationalism, patriarchism as the structure of power, individual rights regression, and climate change denial. . . . The axis of politics now does not take place between right and left, but rather authoritarianism and democracy."[8]

Contrary to Latour, who believes that the origin of indifference toward environmental warnings must be sought in religion, I prefer to blame the global return to order through realism, which drives postdemocratic authoritarian leaders today.[9] A politics of warnings is not going to side with democracy simply because it respects electoral procedures but, most of all, because it safeguards public, intergovernmental, and international institutions and organizations that play a central role in warning the public when necessary. As I explained in part 2, these bodies have the authority of consensus, representing the collective judgment of a society. If, as Cornelius Castoriadis pointed out, there "is no such thing as a society without institutions,"[10] then it is necessary to protect them from the next Orban, Meloni, and Milei, who constantly undermine their existence and warnings.[11]

When Trump announced the US withdrawal from the World Health Organization in 2020 and again in 2025, he accused the organization of ripping "off the United States" and failing to "adequately obtain, vet and share information in a timely and transparent fashion."[12] As discussed throughout this book, one of the greatest enemies of warnings is transparency because it justifies and intensifies realism without authority, credentials, and guarantees. While postdemocratic authoritarians demand order and obedience, democracy calls for trust and involvement. The political commitment of warnings is essential nowadays, specifically in two aspects of public debate. The first consists of environmental problems, which concern the public relevance of science, and the second involves our multicultural society, which demands a progressive political approach. As the precondition of any kind of democratic political governance, warnings cannot prevent the emergence of authoritarians, but they can stimulate crises from various institutions through philosophy, science, and the arts.

ACKNOWLEDGMENTS

Once again, the encouragement, suggestions, and help of Wendy Lochner and Michael Haskell have been crucial to me in completing this book. I owe them more than I can express. I hope to work with them on many more projects.

My conversations and correspondence with Floriano von Arx, Peg Birmingham, Claudio Gallo, Rob Fellman, Jean Grondin, Jorge Luengo, Silvia Mazzini, Eduardo Mendieta, Ian Moore, Filippo Minelli, Cesar Rendueles, Martin Woessner, and Federico Vercellone have enriched this book philosophically, culturally, and historically. And many thanks to Graham Caldwell, who gave permission to us to reproduce his great sculpture *Compound Eye* on the cover of this book.

This book is dedicated to Carolina and Bruno.

NOTES

INTRODUCTION

1. Suyin Haynes, "'We Now Need to Do the Impossible.' How Greta Thunberg Is Fighting for a Greener Post-Pandemic World," *Time*, December 8, 2020, https://time.com/5918448/greta-thunberg-coronavirus-climate-change/; Slavoj Žižek, *The Year of Dreaming Dangerously* (Verso, 2012), 129. *Don't Look Up* (2021) was directed by Adam McKay. More recently, two films warn us of looming crisis, *Civil War* (2024) and *Oppenheimer* (2023). The former is directed by Alex Garland and tells the story of a journalist reporting in a near future in which nineteen US states have seceded from the Union, with Western Forces and the Florida Alliance among those in the conflict, and the three-term president of the United States has ordered air strikes on US soil against these forces. At a certain point, the journalist (played by Kristen Dunst) tells her colleague, "Every time I survived a war zone, I thought I was sending a warning home: Don't do this." Also *Oppenheimer*, by Christopher Nolan, is not only about the complex character of the father of the atomic bomb but also a warning of global nuclear destruction. Anyone who watched the movie—based on Kai Bird's biography—cannot ignore how this warning is linked to the ongoing war in Ukraine. Although J. Robert Oppenheimer was a respected scientist put in charge of the Manhattan Project to defeat Nazism, when he warned a Senate hearing in 1946 that the only defense against nuclear terrorism was the elimination of nuclear weapons, he was ignored and silenced. His warning was meant to remind everyone that there is an alternative

to the future (that he helped create), and Nolan's film is a call to interpret such alternative, to listen to the scientist.

2. I first presented this philosophy in 2020: Santiago Zabala, "The Philosophy of Warnings: Facing Up to the Emergencies Surrounding Us," *Institute of Art and Ideas News*, October 7, 2020, https://iai.tv/articles/the-philosophy-of-warnings-auid-1646; and Santiago Zabala, "Imagining a Philosophy of Warnings for Our Greatest Emergency," *Philosophy Today* 64, no. 4 (Fall 2020): 1–5.

3. Umberto Eco, *Semiotics and the Philosophy of Language* (Macmillan, 1984), 46.

4. The latest research on animals, plants, and insects from a philosophical point of view can be found in Eduardo Mendieta, *The Philosophical Animal: On Zoopoetics and Interspecies Cosmopolitanism* (SUNY Press, 2024); Stella Sandford, *Vegetal Sex: Philosophy of Plants* (Bloomsbury, 2022); and Jean-Marc Drouin, *A Philosophy of the Insect*, trans. Anne Trager (Columbia University Press).

5. Martin Heidegger, *Introduction to Metaphysics*, trans. F. Fried and R. Polt (Yale University Press, 2000), 73; Michel Foucault, *Discipline and Punish: The Birth of the Prison*, trans. Alan Sheridan (Penguin, 2020), 216; Judith Butler, *Gender Trouble: Feminism and the Subversion of Identity* (Routledge, 1990), xv, 34; Donna Haraway, *Simians, Cyborgs, and Women: The Reinvention of Nature* (Routledge, 1991), 149–82.

6. Francis Bacon, *The New Organon and Related Writings* (Bobbs-Merrill, 1960), 29; Thomas Hobbes, *Leviathan*, ed. Richard Tuck (Cambridge University Press, 1991,) 143; Immanuel Kant, *Reflexionen zur Metaphysik*, in Kant's *Gesammelte Schriften, herausgegeben von der Preussischen Akademie der Wissenschaftenzu Berlin* (Walter de Gruyter, 1928), 18:274.

7. Friedrich Nietzsche, *Beyond Good and Evil: Prelude to a Philosophy of the Future*, trans. Walter Kauffman (Knopf, 2010), 205; Gaston Bachelard, *Le rationalisme appliqué* (PUF, 1949); Walter Benjamin, "Theses on the Philosophy of History," in *Illuminations*, trans. Harry Zohn (Schocken, 1969), 258; Herbert Marcuse, *One-Dimensional Man: Studies in the Ideology of Advanced Industrial Society*, trans., Douglas Kellner (Routledge, 2007).

8. Edward Said, "The Public Role of Writers and Intellectuals," *The Nation*, September 17, 2001, http://www.thenation.com/issue/september-17-2001; Zygmunt Bauman, *Modernity and the Holocaust*

(Polity, 1989), 93–94; Manfred Stanley, *The Technological Conscience: Survival and Dignity in an Age of Expertise* (Free Press, 1979), xi; Francoise d'Eaubonne, *Feminism or Death: How the Women's Movement Can Save the Planet*, trans. Ruth Hottell (Verso, 2022); Kyle Whyte, "Too Late for Indigenous Climate Justice: Ecological and Relational Tipping Points," *Wiley Interdisciplinary Reviews Climate Change* 11 (2020): 1–7; Michel Foucault, *Ethics: Subjectivity and Truth*, vol. 1 of *The Essential Works of Michel Foucault, 1954–1984*, ed. Paul Rabinow, trans. Robert Hurley et al. (Penguin, 2020), 301.

9. John Dewey, *Democracy and Education* (Macmillan, 1916), 373; Max Weber, *Economy and Society: An Outline of Interpretive Sociology* (University of California Press, 1978), 2:668–81; Thomas Piketty, *Capital in the Twenty-First Century* (Belknap, 2014), 571; Justin E. H. Smith, *The Internet Is Not What You Think It Is: A History, a Philosophy, a Warning* (Princeton University Press, 2022), 53–54.

10. Giorgio Agamben, *Where Are We Now: The Epidemic as Politics*, trans. Valeria Dani (Rowman & Littlefield, 2021); 2nd updated ed. (Eris, 2021), 9. Both updated editions include new articles that can be found on the Italian publisher's blog: https://www.quodlibet.it/una-voce-giorgio-agamben.

11. Jean-Luc Nancy, "Viral Intrusions and (Other) Friendships," trans. John Ricco, *Unbecoming Community*, February 29, 2020, https://johnpaulricco.com/2020/02/29/viral-intrusions-and-other-friendships/; Slavoj Žižek, *Pandemic 2: Chronicles of a Time Lost* (OR, 2020), 68; Bruno Latour, "The Pandemic Is a Warning: We Must Take Care of the Earth, Our Only Home," *Guardian*, December 24, 2021, https://www.theguardian.com/commentisfree/2021/dec/24/pandemic-earth-lockdowns-climate-crisis-environment.

12. Agamben, *Where Are We Now*.

13. Slavoj Žižek, *A Left That Dares to Speak Its Name* (Polity, 2020), 3.

14. Jane Anna Gordon and Lewis R. Gordon, *Of Divine Warning: Reading Disaster in the Modern Age* (Routledge, 2016), 10.

15. Bruno Latour, *Down to Earth: Politics in the New Climate Regime*, trans. Catherine Porter (Polity, 2018), 23; Naomi Oreskes, *Why Trust Science?* (Princeton University Press, 2019).

16. Amanda Boetzkes, "Realism Without Authority," *La Furia Umana: International and Multilanguage Journal of the History and Theory of*

Cinema 39 (2020), https://web.archive.org/web/20220706192658/http://www.lafuriaumana.it/index.php/73-archive/lfu-39/946-amanda-boetzkes-realism-without-authority-the-performance-of-viewership.

17. Stanley Fish, *The First: How to Think About Hate Speech, Campus Speech, Religious Speech, Fake News, Post-Truth, and Donald Trump* (Atria/One Signal, 2019), 162; Judith Butler, "Judith Butler on the Culture Wars, JK Rowling, and Living in 'Anti-Intellectual Times,'" interview with Alona Ferber, *New Statesman*, September 22 2020, https://www.newstatesman.com/international/2020/09/judith-butler-culture-wars-jk-rowling-and-living-anti-intellectual-times. On the political problem of transparency, see Santiago Zabala, *Being at Large: Freedom in the Age of Alternative Facts* (McGill-Queen's University Press, 2017); and Francesco Pallante, "Direct Democracy," in *Outspoken: A Manifesto for the Twenty-First Century*, ed. Adrian Parr and Santiago Zabala (McGill-Queen's University Press, 2023), 58–67.

18. "Being warned," as I will explain in part 3, refers to warning's ontological nature as opposed to an ontic warning: "being warned."

19. On art's power, see Santiago Zabala, *Why Only Art Can Save Us: Aesthetics and the Absence of Emergency* (Columbia University Press, 2017); and "Santiago Zabala on *The Greatest Emergency*. An Exhibition Based on *Why Only Art Can Save Us*," Columbia University Press Blog, September, 30, 2024, https://cupblog.org/2024/09/30/santiago-zabala-on-the-greatest-emergency-an-exhibition-based-on-why-only-art-can-save-us/.

20. Bernard Stiegler, *The Age of Disruption*, trans. Daniel Ross (Polity, 2019), 5.

1. WE HAVE MURDERED GOD

1. "D-Girl" is the seventh episode of the second season of the series *The Sopranos*. This episode, written by David Chase and Todd A. Kessler and directed by Allen Coulter, was released on HBO on November 23, 2000; the third season of *The Sinner* was developed by Derek Simonds and released on Netflix on February 6, 2020.

2. See Frederiek Depoortere, *The Death of God: An Investigation Into the History of the Western Concept of God* (T&T Clark, 2007); and Martin Heidegger, "Nietzsche's Word: 'God Is Dead,'" in *Off the Beaten Track*,

trans. and ed. Julian Young and Kenneth Haynes (Cambridge University Press, 2002), 157–99.
3. Friedrich Nietzsche, *The Will to Power* (1901), trans. Walter Kauffman and R. J. Hollingdale, ed. Walter Kauffman (Random House, 1967), 535.
4. Friedrich Nietzsche, *The Gay Science: With a Prelude in German Rhymes and an Appendix of Songs*, ed. Bernard Williams, trans. Josefine Nauckhoff (Cambridge University Press, 2001), 119–20.
5. See Gianni Vattimo, *Dialogue with Nietzsche*, trans. William McCuaig (Columbia University Press, 2006).
6. Nietzsche, *The Gay Science*, 109.
7. Friedrich Nietzsche, *Thus Spoke Zarathustra* (1892), ed. Adrian del Caro and Robert Pippin, trans. A. Del Caro (Cambridge University Press, 2006), 7.
8. Nietzsche, *The Will to Power*, 276.
9. Nietzsche, *The Will to Power*, 39.
10. Gianni Vattimo, *Scritti filosofici e politici* (La nave di Teseo, 2021), 40.

2. SCIENCE DOES NOT THINK

1. *Irrational Man* was written and directed by Woody Allen, produced by Letty Aronson, Stephen Tenenbaum, and Edward Walson, and released on July 17, 2015, by Sony Pictures Classics. William Barrett, *Irrational Man: A Study in Existential Philosophy* (Anchor, 1958, 1990).
2. Jürgen Habermas and Michaël Foessel, "Critique and Communication: Philosophy's Missions: A Conversation with Jürgen Habermas," trans. Alex J. Kay, *Eurozine*, October 16, 2015, https://www.eurozine.com/critique-and-communication-philosophys-missions/. See also David Farrell Krell, *Ecstasy, Catastrophe: Heidegger from 'Being and Time' to the 'Black Notebooks'* (SUNY Press, 2015); and Gregory Fried, "The King Is Dead: Heidegger's 'Black Notebooks,'" *Los Angeles Review of Books*, September 13, 2014, https://lareviewofbooks.org/article/king-dead-heideggers-black-notebooks.
3. Martin Heidegger, *Heraclitus: The Inception of Occidental Thinking; and, Logic: Heraclitus's Doctrine of the Logos*, trans. Julia Goesser Assaiante and S. Montgomery Ewegen (Bloomsbury, 2018), 221.

4. Martin Heidegger, *What Is a Thing?*, trans. W. B. Banon Jr. and Vera Deutsch (Gateway, 1967), 73.
5. Martin Heidegger, *What Is Called Thinking?*, trans. J. Glenn Gray (Harper & Row, 1968), 33.
6. Richard Rorty, *Essays on Heidegger and Others* (Cambridge University Press, 1991), 35.
7. Martin Heidegger, *The Question Concerning Technology and Other Essays*, trans. William Lovitt (Garland, 1977), 21, 172.
8. Martin Heidegger, "Only a God Can Save Us: *Der Spiegel*'s Interview," in *Philosophical and Political Writings*, ed. Manfred Stassen, trans. Maria P. Alter and John D. Caputo (Continuum, 2003), 37.
9. Martin Heidegger, *Contributions to Philosophy (Of the Event)* (1989), trans. Richard Rojcewicz and Daniela Vallega-Neu (Indiana University Press, 2012), 99. I have changed "plight" to "emergency" in this passage. As Slavoj Žižek pointed out, this is how Heidegger understands modern technology: "The true danger does not reside in the possibility of our nuclear etc. self-destruction, it is already here when we relate to reality as an object of technological exploitation." Slavoj Žižek, *Hegel in a Wired Brain* (Bloomsbury, 2020), 138.
10. Heidegger, *What Is Called Thinking?*, 43; Heidegger, *The Question Concerning Technology*, 157. On Being's remains, see Santiago Zabala, *The Remains of Being: Hermeneutic Ontology After Metaphysics* (Columbia University Press, 2009).
11. Martin Heidegger, *Ontology: The Hermeneutics of Facticity*, trans. John van Buren (Indiana University Press, 1999), 14–16.
12. These references—by Michael E. Zimmerman, Georg Seidel, and Kevin Michael Deluca—can be found in Casey Rentmeester's excellent edited volume *Heidegger and the Environment* (Rowman & Littlefield, 2016).

3. ONE BECOMES A WOMAN

1. Bonnie Mann, introduction to *"On ne naît pas femme: on le devient": The Life of a Sentence*, ed. Bonnie Mann and Martina Ferrari (Oxford University Press, 2017), 1.
2. The exhibition's catalogue is Katharina Chrubasik, ed., *Simone de Beauvoir, Das Addere Geschlecht* (Buchhandlung Walther König, 2022),

and includes interviews and photos of de Beauvoir as well as texts by Eva Kraus, Marine Rouch, Alice Schwarzer, Imke Schmincke, and Julia Korbik.
3. Karen Offen, "Before Beauvoir, Before Butler: 'Genre' and 'Gender' in France and the Anglo- American World," in *"On ne naît pas femme,"* 16.
4. Simone de Beauvoir, *The Second Sex*, trans. Constance Borde and Sheila Malovany-Chevallier (Knopf, 2000), 283; and Simone de Beauvoir, *The Second Sex*, trans. E. M. Parshley (Vintage, 1973), 273.
5. Constance Borde and Sheila Malovany-Chevallier, "The Life of a Sentence: Translation as Lived Experience," in *"On ne naît pas femme: on le devient,"* 284.
6. Simone de Beauvoir, *The Prime of Life*, trans. Peter Green (World, 1962), 291; Beauvoir, *The Second Sex*, trans. Parshley, 591. On feminist objectivism and realism, see Bonnie Mann, "Beauvoir Against Objectivism: The Operation of the Norm in Beauvoir," in *"On ne naît pas femme: on le devient,"* 37–53.
7. Beauvoir, *The Prime of Life*, 201.
8. Beauvoir, *The Prime of Life*, 469; Eva Gothlin, "Reading Simone de Beauvoir with Martin Heidegger," in *The Cambridge Companion to Simone de Beauvoir*, ed. Claudia Card (Cambridge University Press, 2003), 45–65.
9. Beauvoir, *The Second Sex*, 61, 273. "Her theory of gender, as Judith Butler explains, then, entails a reinterpretation of the existential doctrine of choice whereby 'choosing' a gender is understood as the embodiment of possibilities within a network of deeply entrenched cultural norms." Judith Butler, "Sex and Gender in Simone De Beauvoir's *Second Sex*," *Yale French Studies* 72 (1986): 37.
10. Stella Sandford, *How to Read Beauvoir* (Granta, 2006), 63.
11. Beauvoir, *The Second Sex*, 61.
12. Céline Leboeuf, "'One Is Not Born, but Rather Becomes, a Woman': The Sex-Gender Distinction and Simone de Beauvoir's Account of Woman: The Second Sex," in *Feminist Moments: Reading Feminist Texts*, ed. Katherine Smits and Susan Bruce (Bloomsbury Academic, 2016), 144.
13. Beauvoir, *The Second Sex*, 14.
14. Beauvoir, *The Second Sex*, 27.
15. Beauvoir, *The Second Sex*, 262.

4. THE BANALITY OF EVIL

1. *Hannah Arendt* was directed by Margarethe von Trotta, written by Pamela Katz and Margarethe von Trotta, and produced by Bettina Brokemper. The film was distributed by Zeitgeist Films and premiered at the thirty-seventh Toronto International Film Festival on September 11, 2012.
2. Margaret Sullivan, "Russia's New Control Tactic Is the One Hannah Arendt Warned Us About 50 Years Ago," *Washington Post*, March 11, 2022, https://www.washingtonpost.com/media/2022/03/11/hannah-arendt-putin-disinformation/; Sean Illing, "The Philosopher Who Warned Us About Loneliness and Totalitarianism," *Vox*, May 8, 2022, https://www.vox.com/vox-conversations-podcast/23048597/vox-conversations-hannah-arendt-totalitarianism-the-philosophers; Chloé Cooper Jones, "This New Hannah Arendt Documentary Is a Warning About the Fascist Within Us All," *Vice*, April 12, 2016, https://www.vice.com/en/article/dp5m3x/this-new-hannah-arendt-documentary-is-a-warning-about-the-nazi-within-us-all.
3. Richard Bernstein, "Arendt on Thinking," in *The Cambridge Companion to Hannah Arendt*, ed. Dana Vila (Cambridge University Press, 2006), 277. Arendt's hermeneutic and phenomenological origins have been investigated in Veronica Vasterling, "Political Hermeneutics: Hannah Arendt's Contribution to Hermeneutic Philosophy," in *Gadamer's Hermeneutics and the Art of Conversation*, ed. A. Wiercinski (LIT Verlag, 2011), 571–82; Jacques Taminiaux, *La fille de Thrace et le penseur professional: Arendt et Heidegger* (Éditions Payot, 1992); and Marieke Borren, "Arendt's Phenomenologically Informed Political Thinking," in *Hannah Arendt and the History of Thought*, ed. Daniel Brennan and Marguerite La Caze (Lexington, 2022), 181–204. See also Hannah Arendt and Martin Heidegger, *Letters, 1925–1975*, ed. Ursula Ludz, trans. Andrew Shields (Harcourt, 2004).
4. Martin Heidegger, "Only a God Can Save Us: Der Spiegel's Interview" (1976), in *Martin Heidegger: Philosophical and Political Writings*, ed. Manfred Stassen (Continuum, 2003), 37.
5. Vasterling, "Political Hermeneutics," 505.

4. THE BANALITY OF EVIL ❧ 187

6. Hans-Georg Gadamer, *Truth and Method*, ed. and trans. Joel Weinsheimer and Donald G. Marshall (Continuum, 1999), 305.
7. Hannah Arendt, *Essays in Understanding, 1930–1954*, ed. Jerome Kohn (Harcourt, 1994), 307–8.
8. Hannah Arendt, "Understanding and Politics," *Partisan Review* 20 (1953): 392.
9. Hannah Arendt, *The Life of the Mind: The Groundbreaking Investigation on How We Think* (Harcourt Brace Jovanovich, 1978), 77, 224, 225.
10. Dana R. Villa, *Arendt and Heidegger: The Fate of the Political* (Princeton University Press, 1996), xi.
11. Hannah Arendt, *Thinking Without a Banister*, ed. Jerome Kohn (Knopf Doubleday, 2018), 677.
12. Arendt, *The Life of the Mind*, 11.
13. Hannah Arendt, *Eichmann in Jerusalem* (1963; Penguin, 2022), 287.
14. Arendt, *Eichmann in Jerusalem*, 288.
15. Eichmann confirms this crime in a handwritten note: "From my childhood, obedience was something I could not get out of my system. When I entered the armed services at the age of twenty-seven, I found being obedient not a bit more difficult than it had been during my life to that point. It was unthinkable that I would not follow orders." He continues: "Now that I look back, I realize that a life predicated on being obedient and taking orders is a very comfortable life indeed. Living in such a way reduces to a minimum one's need to think." Roger Cohen, "Why? New Eichmann Notes Try to Explain," *New York Times*, August 12, 1999.
16. Arendt, *Thinking Without a Banister*, 394–95.
17. Peg Birmingham, "Thoughtlessness, the Banality of Evil, and the Failure to Heed Warnings," *La Maleta de Portbou* 64 (May–June 2024): 112.
18. Arendt, *The Life of the Mind*, 12.
19. Hannah Arendt, "Personal Responsibility Under Dictatorship," *The Listener*, August 6, 1964.
20. Arendt, *The Life of the Mind*, 12.
21. Judith Butler, "Hannah Arendt's Challenge to Adolf Eichmann," *Guardian*, August 29, 2011, https://www.theguardian.com/commentis free/2011/aug/29/hannah-arendt-adolf-eichmann-banality-of-evil.

II. IGNORING WARNINGS

1. Joseph Stiglitz, *Globalization and Its Discontents* (Norton, 2002); Naomi Klein, *No Logo* (Picador, 1999); Richard Rorty, *Achieving Our Country* (Harvard University Press, 1997). "The bitter irony of this," as Heinrich Geiselberger writes, "is that in the following years all the risks of globalization that were discerned at the time actually became reality—international terrorism, climate change, financial and currency crises, and lastly, great movements of migrants—while politically no one was prepared for them. Subjectively, there is evidently an utter failure to establish a robust sense of a cosmopolitan collective identity. On the contrary, we are at present witnessing a resurgence of ethnic, national and religious us/them distinctions. The logic of a 'clash of civilizations' has replaced the friend/foe pattern of the Cold War with astonishing speed, despite the supposed 'end of history.'" Heinrich Geiselberger, ed., *The Great Regression* (Wiley, 2017), xiii.

2. Mike Davis, *The Monster at Our Door: The Global Threat of Avian Flu* (New Press, 2005); a new updated edition is available now from OR (2020); David Quammen, *Spillover: Animal Infections and the Next Human Pandemic* (Norton, 2012); Bob Wallace, *Big Farms Make Big Flu: Dispatches on Infectious Disease, Agribusiness, and the Nature of Science* (Monthly Review Press, 2016); Tedros Adhanom Ghebreyesus, *Global Influenza Strategy, 2019–2030*, World Health Organization, https://apps.who.int/iris/handle/10665/311184. See also Afelt Aneta, Frutos Roger, and Devaux Christian, "Bats, Coronaviruses, and Deforestation: Toward the Emergence of Novel Infectious Diseases?," *Frontiers in Microbiology* 9 (2018): 5. On the war in Ukraine, see John Mearsheimer, "Why the Ukraine Crisis Is the West's Fault: The Liberal Delusions That Provoked Putin," *Foreign Affairs*, September/October 2014, 1–12; Pepe Escobar, *The Empire of Chaos* (Nimble Books, 2014); on Israel, see Dan Sabbagh, "Egypt Warned Israel of Hamas Attack Days Earlier, Senior US Politician Says," *Guardian*, October 12, 2023, https://www.theguardian.com/world/2023/oct/12/israel-hamas-war-egypt-warned-foreign-affairs-gaza. "The latest strikes in Israel's 15-month war in Gaza, which has led to more than 45,500 Palestinian deaths, came as negotiations for a ceasefire-for-hostages deal appeared to have stalled again, despite pressure to

conclude an agreement before Donald Trump is sworn in as US president on 20 January." Peter Beaumont, "'Safe Zone' Among Areas Targeted as Israeli Airstrikes Kill at Least 43 in Gaza," *Guardian*, January, 2, 2025, https://www.theguardian.com/world/2025/jan/02/israeli-airstrikes-gaza-safe-zone.

3. On the state of exception, see Giorgio Agamben, *State of Exception*, trans. Kevin Attell (University of Chicago Press, 2005); on the absence of emergency as the greatest emergency, see Santiago Zabala, *Being at Large* (McGill-Queen's University Press, 2020).

4. Martin Heidegger, *Contributions to Philosophy (Of the Event)* (1989), trans. Richard Rojcewicz and Daniela Vallega-Neu (Indiana University Press, 2012), 89, 99. I have changed "plight" to "emergency" in this passage. A detailed analysis of this problem is available in Richard Polt, *The Emergency of Being* (Cornell University Press, 2006).

5. Martin Heidegger, *The Principle of Reason* (1957), trans. R. Lilly (University of Indiana Press, 1996), 119.

6. Richard Rorty, *Objectivity, Relativism, and Truth* (Cambridge University Press, 1991), 22.

7. Gianni Vattimo, *Being and Its Surroundings*, ed. Giuseppe Iannantuono, Alberto Martinengo, and Santiago Zabala, trans. Corrado Federici (McGill-Queen's University Press, 2018), 70.

8. According to Ray Brassier, speculative realism is the product of "a group of bloggers" pushing "actor-network theory spiced with panpsychist metaphysics and morsels of process philosophy ... a 'movement' whose most signal achievement thus far is to have generated an online orgy of stupidity." Ray Brassier, "I Am a Nihilist Because I Still Believe in Truth: Ray Brassier Interviewed by Marcin Rychter," *Kronos* 4 (March 2011). A more detailed analysis of this movement's global campaign is available in M. Ferraris, "A Brief History of New Realism," trans. Sarah De Sanctis, *Filozofija i drustvo* 27, no. 3 (2016): 591–609.

9. Quentin Meillassoux, *After Finitude: An Essay on the Necessity of Contingency*, trans. Ray Brassier (Continuum, 2008), 7. Simon Critchley considers it strange that just "when a certain strand of Anglo-American philosophy (think of John McDowell or Robert Brandom) is making domestic the insights of Kant, Hegel and Heidegger and even allowing philosophers to flirt with forms of idealism, the latest development in

Continental philosophy is seeking to return to a Cartesian realism that was believed to be dead and buried." Simon Critchley, "Back to the Great Outdoors," *Times Literary Supplement*, February 28, 2009, 28.

10. Graham Harman, *Object-Oriented Ontology: A New Theory of Everything* (Penguin, 2018), 43.
11. Maurizio Ferraris, "New Realism: A Short Introduction," in *Speculations VI*, ed. Fabio Gironi, Michael Austin, and Robert Jackson (Punctum, 2015), 141.
12. Maurizio Ferraris, *Manifesto of New Realism*, trans. Sarah De Sanctis, foreword by Graham Harman (SUNY Press, 2015), 19.
13. If postmodernism has not been able to deliver this emancipation, it isn't for a theoretical miscalculation of its philosophies but rather because of the return to order by the bearers of power (military, financial, technological) that have made us "all so transparent that we are unable to create confusion or Babel: search engines have been creating order in the mass of data from the beginning, and any freedom born of uncertainty and confusion now seems unthinkable." Vattimo, *Being and Its Surroundings*, 103.
14. Markus Gabriel, *Moral Progress in Dark Times: Universal Values for the Twenty-First Century*, trans. Wieland Hoban (Polity, 2022), 329, 39.
15. Markus Gabriel, "Silicon Valley y las redes sociales son unos grandes criminales," interview with Ana Carbajosa, *El Pais*, May 1, 2019, https://elpais.com/cultura/2019/04/17/actualidad/1555516749_100561.html.
16. Gabriel, *Moral Progress in Dark Times*, 359.
17. Gabriel, *Moral Progress in Dark Times*, 206.
18. These authors' arguments are principally founded on Michael Minnicino and William Lind's idea that cultural Marxism was a conspiracy by the intellectuals of the Frankfurt School to force "political correctness" and "multiculturalism" on American universities and the wider culture. As Andre Woods explains, "Whereas Minnicino proclaims that the curse of cultural Marxism has bewitched the entire American public," Lind instead wants to demonstrate not only "that there is something deeply unchristian about political correctness" but also "that political correctness is wholly un-American, because the Frankfurt School imported it into the country from Germany."

Andrew Woods, "Cultural Marxism and the Cathedral: Two Alt-Right Perspectives on Critical Theory," in *Critical Theory and the Humanities in the Age of the Alt-Right*, ed. Christine M. Battista and Melissa R. Sande (Palgrave Macmillan, 2019), 44.

19. Christina Hoff Sommers, "How to Make Feminism Great Again," *Washington Post*, December 5, 2016. See also Christina Hoff Sommers, *Who Stole Feminism? How Women Have Betrayed Women* (Simon & Schuster, 1994). Bari Weiss, "Meet the Renegades of the Intellectual Dark Web," *New York Times*, May 8, 2018, https://www.nytimes.com/2018/05/08/opinion/intellectual-dark-web.html.

20. Didier Fassin, "Are 'Woke' Academics a Threat to the French Republic? Ask Macron's Ministers," *Guardian*, March 12, 2021, https://www.theguardian.com/commentisfree/2021/mar/12/academics-french-republic-macron-islamo-leftism.

21. Pierre-Henri Tavoillot, Emmanuelle Hénin, and Xavier-Laurent Salvador, eds., *Après la déconstruction: L'université au défi des idéologies* (Odile Jacob, 2023), 1, my translation.

22. Friedrich Nietzsche, *Human, All Too Human*, trans. R. J. Hollingdale (Cambridge University Press, 1996), section 34, p. 29.

23. Gianni Vattimo, *Of Reality*, trans. Robert Valgenti (Columbia University Press, 2012), 20.

24. Vattimo, *Of Reality*, 90.

25. Gianni Vattimo and Maurizio Ferraris, "Postmoderni o realisti? L'addio al pensiero debole che divide i filosofi," *La Repubblica*, August 19, 2011.

26. Slavoj Žižek, *Sex and the Failed Absolute* (Bloomsbury, 2019), 105. In contrast to Meillassoux, Žižek writes, "I thoroughly reject the standard 'realist' approach which tries to somehow distinguish in objects the way they merely appear to us and the way they are in themselves, independently of how they relate to us. . . . This approach of trying to subtract from the object its appearance (what we, perceiving subjects, allegedly, added to it, the subjective excess) in order to arrive at or, rather, distil the object's In-itself, is to be rejected thoroughly. My point is that one should proceed in exactly the opposite way: subject is inscribed into the real, it touches the real, precisely at the point of the utmost 'subjective' excess, in what it adds to the object, in the way it

distorts the object." Slavoj Žižek, *Disparities* (Bloomsbury, 2016), 102–3.

27. Slavoj Žižek and Leonardo Caffo, "A Conversation with Slavoj Žižek," trans. Thomas Winn, *Public Seminar*, October 20, 2021, https://publicseminar.org/essays/a-conversation-with-slavoj-zizek/.
28. At a certain point in the debate—"Happiness: Capitalism vs. Marxism," on April 19, 2019 in Toronto—Žižek asks Peterson, "Where are these postmodern 'Marxists'?" The Canadian psychologist was unable to refer to a single author even though he constantly criticized them. This section of the debate is available on YouTube: https://www.youtube.com/watch?v=Wsz6ijXWS3A. See also Matt McManus, "Is Postmodernism Neo-Marxist?," *Areo*, April 11, 2022, https://areomagazine.com/2022/04/11/is-postmodernism-neo-marxist/.
29. Herbert Marcuse, *Heideggerian Marxism*, ed. R. Wolin and J. Abromeit (University of Nebraska Press, 2005), 158; Zygmunt Bauman, *Modernity and the Holocaust* (Cornell University Press, 1989), 93–94.
30. Gianni Vattimo, *A Farewell to Truth*, trans. Robert Valgenti (Columbia University Press, 2011), 77.
31. Naomi Oreskes, "We Can't Solve Our Climate Problems Without Removing Their Main Cause: Fossil-Fuel Emissions," *Scientific American*, February 1, 2023, https://www.scientificamerican.com/article/we-cant-solve-our-climate-problems-without-removing-their-main-cause-fossil-fuel-emissions/. "As philosophers going back to Plato (and perhaps before) have long recognized," Oreskes explains, "we do not have independent, unmediated access to reality and therefore have no independent, unmediated means to judge the truth content of scientific claims." Naomi Oreskes, *Why Trust Science?* (Princeton University Press, 2019), 249; Bruno Latour, *Down to Earth: Politics in the New Climate Regime*, trans. Catherine Porter (Polity, 2018), 23.
32. Among these technophiles Chris Anderson is probably the most radical believer in the power and effectiveness of transparency, that is, "dataism." When he was editor in chief of *Wired* magazine he published an article in which he called for replacing not only the humanities but every scientific method from sociology to physics with computational methods based on data. These traditional disciplines and methods have become obsolete because machines (like

AI) can reveal the patterns, trends, and relationships inherent in social, economic, political, and environmental relationships. Chris Anderson, "The End of Theory: The Data Deluge Makes the Scientific Method Obsolete," *Wired*, June 23, 2008, https://www.wired.com/2008/06/pb-theory/.

33. Stanley Fish, "'Transparency' Is the Mother of Fake News," *New York Times*, May 7, 2018, https://www.nytimes.com/2018/05/07/opinion/transparency-fake-news.html.

34. Hans-Georg Gadamer, "Authority and Critical Freedom," in *The Enigma of Health: The Art of Healing in a Scientific Age*, trans. Jason Gaiger and Nicholas Walker (Stanford University Press, 2004), 117–24. See also Hannah Arendt, "What Is Authority?," in *Between Past and Future* (Viking, 1961), 91–142; and Richard Sennett, *Authority* (Secker & Warburg, 1980).

5. I'M NOT A KEYBOARD JIHADI

1. Margaret Atwood, *The Handmaid's Tale* (1986; Harper Collins, 2023), 87; Margaret Atwood, *The Testament* (Vintage, 2019), 302, 303.
2. Atwood, *The Testament*, 34,
3. Lisa Allardice, "Margaret Atwood: For a Long Time We Were Moving Away from Gilead. Then We Started Going Back Towards It," *Guardian*, September 20, 2019, https://www.theguardian.com/books/2019/sep/20/margaret-atwood-moving-away-from-gilead-testaments; Hope Reese, "Margaret Atwood Explains How to Know If You're Living in a Totalitarian State. An Interview with the Author of *The Handmaid's Tale*," *Vox*, April 26, 2017, https://www.vox.com/conversations/2017/4/26/15435378/margaret-atwood-handmaids-tale-interview.
4. Friedrich Nietzsche, *The Will to Power* (1901), trans. Walter Kauffman and R. J. Hollingdale, ed. Walter Kauffman (Random House, 1967), 39.
5. Gilles Kepel and Antoine Jardin, *Terror in France: The Rise of Jihad* (Princeton University Press, 2017), 10, 26.
6. Olivier Roy, *Jihad and Death: The Global Appeal of Islamic State*, trans. Cynthia Schoch (Oxford University Press, 2017), 76, 32.
7. Oliver Roy, "Who Are the New Jihadis?," *Guardian*, April 13, 2017, https://www.theguardian.com/news/2017/apr/13/who-are-the-new-jihadis.

8. Roy, *Jihad and Death*, 42. Those who envision this society, according to Abdelwahab Meddeb, are those radical Islamists who preach the law, imposing its absolute application in order to abolish "all alterity and [install] a form of being that adds a new name to the catalog of totalitarian practices that have wrecked the century." This presupposes that there is a "pure Islam," a fundamentalist interpretation of which would restore the truth of Islamic civilization and custom. The faith in such an interpretation is the "malady of Islam." Abdelwahab Meddeb, *The Malady of Islam*, trans. Pierre Joris and Ann Reid (Basic Books, 2003), 226.
9. Aage Borchgrevink, *A Norwegian Tragedy: Anders Behring Breivik and the Massacre on Utoya*, trans. Guy Puzey (Polity, 2013), 176.
10. Mark Lewis and Sarah Lyall, "Norway Mass Killer Gets the Maximum: 21 Years," *New York Times*, August 24, 2012, https://www.nytimes.com/2012/08/25/world/europe/anders-behring-breivik-murder-trial.html. Sindre Bangstad explains that "Anders Behring Breivik's definition of 'cultural Marxism' in his tract is, to put it mildly, quite wide ranging. He defines the content of 'cultural Marxist/multiculturalist Alliance 100' (MA100) as the '100 political parties who indirectly or directly support the Islamization of Europe through their support for European multiculturalism.'" Sindre Bangstad, *Anders Breivik and the Rise of Islamophobia* (Zed, 2014), 88.
11. Borchgrevink, *A Norwegian Tragedy*, 3.
12. Slavoj Žižek, "A Vile Logic to Anders Breivik's Choice of Target," *Guardian*, August 8, 2011, https://www.theguardian.com/commentisfree/2011/aug/08/anders-behring-breivik-pim-fortuyn.
13. Andrew Brown, "Anders Breivik's Spider Web of Hate," *Guardian*, September 7, 2011, https://www.theguardian.com/commentisfree/2011/sep/07/anders-breivik-hate-manifesto. According to Brown, "Breivik's manifesto reveals a subculture of nationalistic and Islamophobic websites that link the European and American far right in a paranoid alliance against Islam and is also rooted in some democratically elected parties. . . . [He] referred to something he called 'the Vienna school of thought', which consists of the people who had worked out the ideology that inspired him to commit mass murder. He named three people in particular: Littman; the Norwegian Peder Jensen who wrote under the pseudonym of Fjordman; and the American Robert

Spencer, who maintains a site called Jihad Watch, and agitates against 'the Islamisation of America.'"
14. Barry Richards, "What Drove Andreas Breivik?," *Contexts* 13, no. 4 (2014): 43, 46, 47.
15. Žižek, "A Vile Logic."
16. Richards, "What Drove Andreas Breivik?"
17. Adrienne LaFrance, "The Prophecies of Q," *The Atlantic*, June 2020, https://www.theatlantic.com/magazine/archive/2020/06/qanon-nothing-can-stop-what-is-coming/610567/. According to Colin Dickey, the "term 'conspiracy theory'" first came into usage in 1945 in Karl Popper's *The Open Society and Its Enemies* and "comes from abandoning God and then asking: 'Who is in his place?' His place is then filled by various powerful men and groups—sinister pressure groups, who are to be blamed for having planned the great depression and all the evils from which we suffer." Colin Dickey, *Under the Eye of Power: How Fear of Secret Societies Shapes American Democracy* (Viking, 2023), 196. See Joanna Walters and Alvin Chang, "Far-Right Terror Poses Bigger Threat to US Than Islamist Extremism Post-9/11," *Guardian*, September 8, 2021, https://www.theguardian.com/us-news/2021/sep/08/post-911-domestic-terror.
18. Julia Carrie Wong, "QAnon Explained: The Antisemitic Conspiracy Theory Gaining Traction Around the World," *Guardian*, August 25, 2020, https://www.theguardian.com/us-news/2020/aug/25/qanon-conspiracy-theory-explained-trump-what-is; Kevin Rose, "What Is QAnon, the Viral Pro-Trump Conspiracy Theory?," *New York Times*, September 3, 2021, https://www.nytimes.com/article/what-is-qanon.html.
19. Brandy Zadrozny and Ben Collins, "How Three Conspiracy Theorists Took 'Q' and Sparked QAnon," *NBC News*, August 14, 2018, https://www.nbcnews.com/tech/tech-news/how-three-conspiracy-theorists-took-q-sparked-QAnon-n900531.
20. Using AI, two separate teams of computer scientists identified in 2022 two men as likely authors of messages that fueled the viral movement, but they both denied being Q. David D. Kirkpatrick, "Who Is Behind QAnon? Linguistic Detectives Find Fingerprints," *New York Times*, February 19, 2022, https://www.nytimes.com/2022/02/19/technology/qanon-messages-authors.html.

21. Mia Bloom and Sophie Moskalenko, *Pastels and Pedophiles: Inside the Mind of QAnon* (Red Wood, 2021), 178. In 2020, QAnon followers hijacked the hashtag #savethechildren from the charity in the same name, diverting "resources that could be used to protect vulnerable children or cause law enforcement to waste their time on fictional cases of abuse at the expense of pursuing real cases." Bloom and Moskalenko, *Pastels and Pedophiles*, 68.
22. Adam Gabbatt, "Sound of Freedom Passed the $100m Mark. Who's Really Watching the Movie?," *Guardian*, July 23, 2023, https://www.theguardian.com/us-news/2023/jul/23/sound-of-freedom-qanon-movie-conspiracy-theories. The hashtag #SaveTheChildren was hijacked by QAnon believers in July 2020, leading Facebook to temporarily disable it after it became awash with misinformation and exaggerations about trafficking statistics in order to capture more followers abroad.
23. Jude Joffe-Block, "Four years After the Capitol Riot, Why QAnon Hasn't Gone Away," NPR, December, 30, 2024, https://www.npr.org/2024/12/30/nx-s1-5230801/qanon-capitol-riot-social-media.

6. THERE IS NO RUSH TO REGULATE AI

1. "Metalhead" is the fifth episode of the fourth season of the anthology series *Black Mirror*. This episode, written by Charlie Brooker and directed by David Slade, was released on Netflix, along with the rest of series 4, on December 29, 2017.
2. Peter Guest, "Britain's Big AI Summit Is a Doom-Obsessed Mess," *Wired*, October 23, 2023, https://www.wired.com/story/britains-big-ai-summit-doom-obsessed-mess/; John Naughton, "AI Is Not the Problem, Prime Minister—the Corporations That Control It Are," *Guardian*, November 4, 2023, https://www.theguardian.com/commentisfree/2023/nov/04/ai-is-not-the-problem-prime-minister-but-the-corporations-that-control-it-are-rishi-sunak.
3. Anna Gross, "Rishi Sunak Says He Will 'Not Rush to Regulate' AI," *Financial Times*, October 23, 2023, https://www.ft.com/content/509012f9-4e08-414c-a97f-dd733b9de6ef; Kiran Stacey and Dan Milmo, "The Great Powers Signed Up to Sunak's AI Summit—While Jostling for Position," *Guardian*, November 2, 2023, https://www

.theguardian.com/technology/2023/nov/02/the-great-powers-signed-up-to-sunaks-ai-summit-while-jostling-for-position. Although a few weeks after Sunak's summit the European Union policy makers agreed on landmark legislation to regulate artificial intelligence, which EU chief Ursula von der Leyen hailed as a "global first" that will safeguard the rights of people and businesses, it is far from enough. According to Philipp Hacker—the research chair for law and ethics of the digital society at the European New School of Digital Studies, European University Viadrina Frankfurt (Oder)—the act does not address four pressing challenges in AI policy: "mandatory basic AI safety standards; the conundrum of open-source models; the environmental impact of AI; and the need to accompany the AI Act with far more substantial public investment in AI." Philipp Hacker, "What's Missing from the EU AI Act: Addressing the Four Key Challenges of Large Language Models," *VerfBlog*, December, 13, 2023, https://verfassungsblog.de/whats-missing-from-the-eu-ai-act. The bill, as the lawyer and technology specialist Petra Monlar points out, "does not sufficiently recognize the vast human rights risks of border technologies and should go much further protecting the rights of people on the move." Petra Monlar, "EU's AI Act Falls Short on Protecting Rights at Borders," *Just Security*, December, 20, 2023, https://www.justsecurity.org/90763/eus-ai-act-falls-short-on-protecting-rights-at-borders/.
4. Billi Perrigo, "Elon Musk Signs Open Letter Urging AI Labs to Pump the Brakes," *Time*, March 29, 2023, https://time.com/6266679/musk-ai-open-letter/.
5. Martin Heidegger, "Überlegungen XV," *Überlegungen XII–XV*, Gesamtausgabe 96 (Klostermann, 2014), 259.
6. Martin Heidegger, "Only a God Can Save Us: Der Spiegel's Interview" (1976), in *Martin Heidegger: Philosophical and Political Writings*, ed. Manfred Stassen (Continuum, 2003), 37.
7. James Bridle, "The Stupidity of AI," *Guardian*, March 16, 2023, https://www.theguardian.com/technology/2023/mar/16/the-stupidity-of-ai-artificial-intelligence-dall-e-chatgpt.
8. Noam Chomsky, Ian Roberts, and Jeffrey Watumull, "The False Promise of ChatGPT," *New York Times*, March 8, 2023, https://www.nytimes.com/2023/03/08/opinion/noam-chomsky-chatgpt-ai.html.

9. Geoffrey Hinton, in Scott Pelley, "'Godfather of Artificial Intelligence' Geoffrey Hinton on the Promise, Risks of Advanced AI," *60 Minutes*, October 8, 2023, https://www.cbsnews.com/news/geoffrey-hinton-ai-dangers-60-minutes-transcript/.
10. Hinton, in Pelley, "'Godfather of Artificial Intelligence.'"
11. A Goldman Sachs global economic analysis predicted that the equivalent of some 300 million full-time jobs will probably be automated with generative AI, to drive "labor cost savings and raise productivity." Joseph Briggs and Devesh Kodnani, "The Potentially Large Effects of Artificial Intelligence on Economic Growth," *Goldman Sachs Economic Research*, March, 26, 2023, https://www.gspublishing.com/content/research/en/reports/2023/03/27/d64e052b-0f6e-45d7-967b-d7be35fabd16.html. According to Jack Brewster, Zack Fishman, and Elisa Xu of the NewsGuard misinformation monitor, an increasing number of content farms now use generative AI. They define these websites as "Unreliable Artificial Intelligence–Generated News websites (UAIN)" because they "operate with little or no human oversight and publish articles written largely or entirely by bots. In just the past month [May 2023], NewsGuard analysts have updated the number of sites on its newly launched UAIN site tracker from 49 to 217." Jack Brewster, Zack Fishman, and Elisa Xu, "Funding the Next Generation of Content Farms: Some of the World's Largest Blue Chip Brands Unintentionally Support the Spread of Unreliable AI-Generated News Websites," NewsGuard's Misinformation Monitor, June 26, 2023, https://www.newsguardtech.com/misinformation-monitor/june-2023/.
12. The whole statement can be found on the Center for AI Safety, https://www.safe.ai/statement-on-ai-risk#open-letter. It is important to remember that the "experts" warning that AI could lead to extinction are generally AI stockholders indicating that only they should be trusted to safely design AI. It is important to bear in mind the financial and political agenda of AI developers. See Santiago Zabala and Claudio Gallo, "What Is the Political Agenda of Artificial Intelligence," *Al-Jazeera*, May 17, 2023, https://www.aljazeera.com/opinions/2023/5/17/what-is-the-political-agenda-of-artificial-intelligence; Garrison Lovely, "Can Humanity Survive AI?," *Jacobin*, January 22, 2024, https://jacobin.com/2024/01/can-humanity-survive-ai.

13. Cade Metz, "'The Godfather of A.I.' Leaves Google and Warns of Danger Ahead," *New York Times*, May 1, 2023, https://www.nytimes.com/2023/05/01/technology/ai-google-chatbot-engineer-quits-hinton.html.
14. Joshua Bengio, "Slowing Down Development of AI Systems Passing the Turing Test," blog, April 5, 2023, https://yoshuabengio.org/2023/04/05/slowing-down-development-of-ai-systems-passing-the-turing-test/.
15. Training a single AI model—according to Bridle—generally "emit[s] the equivalent of more than 284 tons of carbon dioxide, which is nearly five times as much as the entire lifetime of the average American car, including its manufacture. These emissions are expected to grow by nearly 50% over the next five years, all while the planet continues to heat up, acidifying the oceans, igniting wildfires, throwing up superstorms and driving species to extinction." Bridle "The Stupidity of AI." The recent launch of the Chinese AI startup DeepSeek—which shook all of Wall Street and Silicon Valley on January 27, 2025—claims to use less power and generate fewer emissions than anticipated. Justine Worland, "AI Could Reshape Everything We Know About Climate Change," *Time*, January 29, 2025, https://time.com/7210942/deepseek-ai-climate-change-reshape-what-we-know/.

7. THE "DON'T SAY GAY" LAW

1. *Orlando: My Political Biography* was written and directed by Paul B. Preciado and produced by Les Films du Poisson, 24Images, and Arte France. It premiered at the seventy-third Berlin International Film Festival on February 18, 2023. Paul B. Preciado, *Can the Monster Speak? Report to an Academy of Psychoanalysts*, trans. Frank Wynne (Fitzcarraldo, 2021), 19, 77.
2. Mary Katharine Tramontana, "Paul B. Preciado: "One Day We'll See Assigning Gender at Birth as Brutal," *i+D Magazine Vice*, March 13, 2020, https://i-d.vice.com/en/article/jgeb4b/paul-b-preciado-one-day-well-see-assigning-gender-at-birth-as-brutal.
3. Judith Butler makes the example of "intersexed infants who are born with mixed sexual characteristics. Some medical professionals seek

recourse to hormones to define their sex, whereas others take chromosomes to be the deciding factor. How that determination is made is consequential: intersexed people have become increasingly critical of the fact that medical authorities have often mis-categorized them and subjected them to cruel forms of 'correction.'" Judith Butler, "The Backlash Against 'Gender Ideology' Must Stop," *New Statesman*, April 4, 2022, https://www.newstatesman.com/culture/2019/01/judith-butler-backlash-against-gender-ideology-must-stop.

4. Dale O'Leary—an American pro-life journalist who attended the women's conference in Cairo and Beijing distributing a leaflet entitled "Gender: The Deconstruction of Women"—has seen her book translated into several languages, and it is reputed to have been read at the Vatican. Her book begins by pointing out how the word "gender has been substituted for the word sex. We used to talk about sex discrimination, but it's gender discrimination. Forms, like credit applications, used to ask for an indication of our sex, but now they ask for our gender. It certainly seems innocent enough. Sex has a secondary meaning—sexual intercourse or sexual activity. Gender sounds more delicate and refined. But, if you think the change signals a renaissance of neo-Victorian sensitivity, you could not be more wrong. This change, and a number of other things you may not have taken much notice of, are all parts of the Gender Agenda." Dale O'Leary, *The Gender Agenda: Redefining Equality* (Vital Issues, 1997), 11. Joseph Ratzinger, *Salt of the Earth: An Exclusive Interview on the State of the Church at the End of the Millennium* (Ignatius, 1997).

5. This passage can be found in Aana Marie Vigen and Patricia Beattie Jung, eds., *God, Science, Sex, Gender: An Interdisciplinary Approach to Christian Ethics* (University of Illinois Press, 2010), 127. It is important to stress that "the semantic frame 'gender ideology' reveals itself as an empty and adaptable signifier, encompassing a broad range of demands such as the right to abortion, sexual orientation and gender identity, to diverse families, education in gender and sexuality, HIV prevention and sex work, a basic basket that can be easily adjusted to the conditions of each context. Its discourses construct unusual analogies between feminism, queer theory and communism, a strategy that has echoes in contexts where this spectrum remains active, such as Brazil." Sonia Corrêa, "Gender Ideology: Tracking Its Origins and Meanings in

Current Gender Politics," *LSE Blog*, December 11, 1997, https://blogs.lse.ac.uk/gender/2017/12/11/gender-ideology-tracking-its-origins-and-meanings-in-current-gender-politics/.

6. Gavin Jones, "Pope Francis Calls for Studies Into 'Ugly' Gender Theory," Reuters, March 1, 2024, https://www.reuters.com/world/europe/pope-francis-calls-studies-into-ugly-gender-theory-2024-03-01/; Gerard O'Connell, "Pope Francis Says 'Ideology of Gender' Is 'Dangerous' and That 'Everyone' Will Vote in the Synod, in New Interview with *La Nacion*," *America: The Jesuit Review*, March, 10, 2023, https://www.americamagazine.org/faith/2023/03/10/pope-francis-ideology-gender-theory-synod-244888. If gender ideology is interpreted by Pope Francis and his colleagues as a "diabolical ideology," it's because "they see gender diversity as a historically contingent 'social construction' that is imposed on the divinely mandated natural distinction between the sexes." Butler, "The Backlash Against 'Gender Ideology' Must Stop."
7. Agnieszka Graff and Elżbieta Korolczuk, *Anti-Gender Politics in the Populist Moment* (Routledge, 2021), 164.
8. Graff and Korolczuk, *Anti-Gender Politics in the Populist Moment*, 165.
9. Martin Pengelly, "Trump Rolls Back Trans and Gender-Identity Rights and Takes Aim at DEI," *Guardian*, January, 21, 2025, https://www.theguardian.com/us-news/2025/jan/20/trump-executive-order-gender-sex; Sara Garbagnoli, "Italy as a Lighthouse: Anti-Gender Protests Between the 'Anthropological Question' and National Identity," in *Anti-Gender Campaigns in Europe: Mobilizing Against Equality*, ed. Roman Kuhar and David Paternotte (Rowman & Littlefield, 2017), 159.
10. Maya Yang, "Florida Board Approves Expansion of 'Don't Say Gay' Ban to All School Grades," *Guardian*, April, 19, 2023, https://www.theguardian.com/us-news/2023/apr/19/florida-education-board-approves-expansion-dont-say-gay-bill; Solcyre Burga, "What to Know About Florida's New 'Don't Say Gay' Rule That Bans Discussion of Gender for All Students," *Time*, April, 20, 2023, https://time.com/6273364/florida-dont-say-gay-expansion/.
11. Nathaniel Frank, "What the Science Says About 'Don't Say Gay' and Young People," *New York Times*, April 20, 2023, https://www.nytimes.com/2023/04/20/opinion/dont-say-gay-bill-florida.html.

12. The "struggle for gender equality and sexual freedom," Butler specifies, "seeks to alleviate suffering and to recognize the diverse embodied and cultural lives that we live." Butler, "The Backlash Against 'Gender Ideology' Must Stop."
13. Todd Anderson, "Florida's 'Don't Say Gay' Bill Will Hurt Teens Like Me," *New York Times*, March 12, 2022, https://www.nytimes.com/2022/03/12/opinion/florida-dont-say-gay-bill.html. This is why Nathaniel Frank believes policies of equal treatment can help also in school. "A 2017 study found that suicide attempts by young people dropped by 7 percent in states that legalized same-sex marriage. Another from 2012 found that 'policies that confer protections to same-sex couples may be effective in reducing health care use and costs among sexual minority men.'" Nathaniel Frank, "What the Science Says About 'Don't Say Gay' and Young People."

8. WE KILL PEOPLE BASED ON METADATA

1. *National Bird* was distributed by FilmRise and premiered at the Berlin International Film Festival on February 14, 2016. *Syriana* was written and directed by Stephen Gaghan and released on November 23, 2005. It is loosely based on a memoir by the CIA case officer Robert Baer, *See No Evil: The True Story of a Ground Soldier in the CIA's War Against Terrorism* (Three Rivers, 2003). "The Drone Queen" episode of *Homeland* season 4 premiered on Showtime on October 5, 2014, and was directed by Lesli Linka Glatter and written by Alex Gansa.
2. Elke Schwarz, *Death Machine: The Ethics of Violent Technologies* (Manchester University Press, 2018), 5.
3. Von Erich Follath, "The Khmer Rouge, the Nazis, and the Banality of Evil," *Der Spiegel*, December 18, 2009, https://www.spiegel.de/international/world/holocaust-as-career-the-khmer-rouge-the-nazis-and-the-banality-of-evil-a-667263.html; Juan Jesús Aznárez, "Massera no se arrepiente de los asesinatos en la dictadura argentina," *El País*, October 22, 1997, https://elpais.com/diario/1997/10/22/internacional/877471210_850215.html; Nic Robertson and Moni Basu, "Mladic Shows No Remorse as War Crimes Trial Opens," CNN, May 17, 2012, https://edition.cnn.com/2012/05/16/world/europe/netherlands-mladic-trial/index.html.

4. Roger Berkowitz, "Drones and the Question of 'The Human,'" *Ethics & International Affairs* 28, no. 2 (2014): 168.
5. David Cole, "We Kill People Based on Metadata," *New York Review of Books*, May 10, 2014, https://www.nybooks.com/online/2014/05/10/we-kill-people-based-metadata/; Susan Landau and Patricia Vargas Leon, "A Radical Proposal for Protecting Privacy: Halt Industry's Use of 'Non-Content,'" *Colorado Technology Law Journal* 21, no. 2 (2023): 276.
6. Joseph Clark, "AI Security Center to Open at National Security Agency," *US Department of Defense News*, September 28, 2023, https://www.defense.gov/News/News-Stories/Article/Article/3541838/ai-security-center-to-open-at-national-security-agency/.
7. Jeremy Scahill and Glenn Greenwald, "The NSA's Secret Role in the U.S. Assassination Program," *The Intercept*, February 10, 2014, https://theintercept.com/2014/02/10/the-nsas-secret-role/.
8. Mariella Moon, "San Francisco Approves Police Petition to Use Robots as a 'Deadly Force Option,'" *Engadget*, November 20, 2022, https://www.engadget.com/san-francisco-approves-police-robots-deadly-force-option-112647119.html; Isabelle Taft, "Police Use of Robot to Kill Dallas Suspect Unprecedented, Experts Say," *Texas Tribune*, July 8, 2016, https://www.texastribune.org/2016/07/08/use-robot-kill-dallas-suspect-first-experts-say/.
9. Tim Robinson Fraes and Stephen Bridgewater, "Highlights from the RAeS Future Combat Air & Space Capabilities Summit," *Royal Aeronautical Society News*, May 26, 2023, https://www.aerosociety.com/news/highlights-from-the-raes-future-combat-air-space-capabilities-summit/#:~:text=He%20notes%20that. The US Air Force later denied running this simulation.
10. Bonnie Docherty, "The Need for and Elements of a New Treaty on Fully Autonomous Weapons," Rio Seminar on Autonomous Weapons Systems, Fundação Alexandre de Gusmão, Brasilia, 2020, https://www.hrw.org/news/2020/06/01/need-and-elements-new-treaty-fully-autonomous-weapons; Thompson Chengeta, "Accountability Gap: Autonomous Weapon Systems and Modes of Responsibility in International Law," *Denver Journal of International Law & Policy* 1, no. 45 (January 2016): 1–50.

III. BEING WARNED

1. I use the German term *Sein* as "Being," *Seiend* as "being," and *Seiendes* as "beings." If I use the word "being" with a lowercase *b*, it is because I refer to a definite or indefinite article: e.g., "a being" = *ein Seiendes*. This difference allows me to stress the ontological import of the former term over the latter.
2. Davide Sisto, *Online Afterlives: Immortality, Memory, and Grief in Digital Culture*, trans. Bonnie McClellan-Broussard (MIT Press, 2020); Federico Vercellone, *Filosofia del tatuaggio. Il corpo tra autenticità e contaminazione* (Bollati Boringhieri, 2023); Michael Marder, *Plant-Thinking: A Philosophy of Vegetative Life*, foreword by Gianni Vattimo and Santiago Zabala (Columbia University Press, 2013); Emmanuele Coccia, *The Life of Plants: A Metaphysics of Mixture*, trans. Dylan J. Montanari (Policy, 2018).
3. Simon Critchley, Jacques Derrida, Ernesto Laclau, and Richard Rorty, *Deconstruction and Pragmatism*, ed. Chantal Mouffe (Routledge, 1995); Gianni Vattimo, *Being and Its Surroundings*, ed., Giuseppe Iannantuono, Alberto Martinengo, and Santiago Zabala, trans. Corrado Federici (McGill-Queen's University Press, 2018); Slavoj Žižek and Leonardo Caffo, "A Conversation with Slavoj Žižek," trans. Thomas Winn, *Public Seminar*, October 20, 2021, https://publicseminar.org/essays/a-conversation-with-slavoj-zizek/.

9. COMPOUND EYE

1. Graham Caldwell, *Compound Eye*, mirrors, steel, and hardware, 92 × 98 × 50 inches, Pulse Public Installation, G Fine Art, New York, 2008. Photograph by Abigail Volkmann.
2. Martin Heidegger, *Being and Time*, trans. John MacQuarrie and Edward Robinson (Harper & Row, 2008), 47–48.
3. Martin Heidegger, "The Age of the World Picture" (1936), in *Off the Beaten Track*, ed. and trans. Julian Young and Kenneth Haynes (Cambridge University Press, 2002), 67, 83.
4. Martin Heidegger, *Nietzsche*, trans. D. F. Krell (Harper & Row, 1979), 1:139. While D. F. Krell has translated *Sichtige* as "envisionment," I believe, like I. Thompson, that "lucidity" works better considering that

Heidegger is criticizing the transparent medium of aesthetics in this passage.
5. Hans-Georg Gadamer, *The Beginning of Philosophy*, trans. R. Coltman (Continuum, 2001), 123.
6. Hans-Georg Gadamer, *Truth and Method*, trans. Joel Weinsheimer and Donald G. Marshall (Continuum, 2014), 301–2.
7. M. Heidegger, *Contributions to Philosophy (of the Event)*, trans. Richard Rojcewicz and Daniela Vallega-Neu (Indiana University Press, 2012), 388.
8. Martin Heidegger, *The Concept of Time*, trans. William McNeill (Blackwell, 1992), 19e.
9. "According to Heidegger," as Ingo Farin points out, "the past is always taken up and reinscribed in the future, just as the future lives off the memory of the past. Heidegger understands 'history' as the encompassing whole of the interrelated three dimensions or 'exstases' of temporality, that is, past, present, and future. There is no past 'outside' the present and future, and vice versa. In other words, the past is never dead and 'gone.' Rather, it comes to life in the future; it does not approach the present from 'behind,' but from the 'front.'" Ingo Farin, "The Different Notions of History in Heidegger's Work," in *Hermeneutical Heidegger*, ed. Michael Bowler and Ingo Farin (Northwestern University Press, 2016), 23–24. See also David Couzens Hoy, "Heidegger on the Futural," in *The Time of Our Lives: A Critical History of Temporality* (MIT Press, 2009, 2012), 147–52.
10. Jacques Derrida, in *Derrida*, directed by Kirby Dick and Amy Ziering Kofman, produced by Jane Doe Films, distributed by Zeitgeist Films, and premiered at the 2002 Sundance Film Festival.
11. Deconstruction, as Susanne Lüdemann observes, "is both a philosophical project and a practice of reading. . . . [But] reading, in a sense requiring more detailed explication, is an altogether philosophical activity for Derrida—indeed, it may be said to represent the exemplary mode of philosophical engagement, period." Susanne Lüdemann, *Politics of Deconstruction: A New Introduction to Jacques Derrida*, trans. Erik Butler (Stanford University Press, 2014), 27. On Derrida's remainders, see S. Zabala, *The Remains of Being: Hermeneutic Ontology After Metaphysics* (Columbia University Press, 2009), 79–85.

12. Jacques Derrida, *Archive Fever: A Freudian Impression*, trans. E. Prenowitz (University of Chicago Press, 1996), 68. Jean-Paul Martinon "specifies that the expression a-venir does not refer to an act, shift, or movement strictly speaking, it does not designate the way something or someone moves or reads. A-venir is what disjoints or unhinges the movement in question. It is what provokes understanding, what allows the movement or the event to take another direction, another juncture, growth, or proportion. As such, a-venir cannot be identified as 'contemporary,' but always non-contemporary, unexpected." Jean-Paul Martinon, *On Futurity: Malabou, Nancy, and Derrida* (Palgrave, 2007), 1–2.
13. "The future speaks even now in a hundred signs, this destiny announces itself everywhere; for this music of the future all ears are cocked even now." Friedrich Nietzsche, *The Will to Power*, trans. W. Kaufmann (Random House, 1968), 3.
14. Umberto Eco, *A Theory of Semiotics* (Indiana University Press, 1979), 20, 15.
15. Eco, *A Theory of Semiotics*, 48.
16. Umberto Eco, *Semiotics and the Philosophy of Language* (Macmillan, 1984), 10.
17. Eco, *A Theory of Semiotics*, 16, 49. It is important to stress that Eco is not denying that we use signs to refer to the real world; he is simply maintaining that sign systems are grids that we impose upon reality before we put them to use. Also, as David Robey clarifies, viewing signs in this way "certainly does not entail cutting semiotics off from history. For Eco there are two vital ways in which semiotics and the historical process are integrally connected. On the one hand, viewing the structures of sign systems as methodological rather than ontological in character entails accepting our description of them not only as hypothetical and provisional, but also as the product of history, and subject to negation by history.... On the other hand, semiotics is itself an instrument of intervention in the historical process, a powerful practical tool for cultural, social, and potentially political change." David Robey, introduction to Umberto Eco, *The Open Work*, trans. Anna Cancogni (Cambridge University Press, 1989), xxiii.
18. Eco, *Semiotics and the Philosophy of Language*, 45.

19. Eco, *A Theory of Semiotics*, 15, 69. Peter Bondanella has pointed out that the "circularity of unlimited semiosis, where signs refer back to other signs which refer, yet again, still again to other signs—and not to objective referents in reality, subjective mental states, or Platonic universals—guarantees that social and historical reality will never be ignored by a semiotic perspective, since signs and their codes are directly conditioned, as Eco had already demonstrated in numerous previous essays on mass media, by the societies in which or the historical periods during which they are created." Peter Bondanella, *Umberto Eco and the Open Text: Semiotics, Fiction, Popular Culture* (Cambridge University Press, 2005), 83.

10. RADICAL LISTENING

1. Rita Charon, in Sigal Samuel, "This Doctor Is Taking Aim at Our Broken Medical System, One Story at a Time," *Vox*, March 5, 2020, https://www.vox.com/the-highlight/2020/2/27/21152916/rita-charon-narrative-medicine-health-care. The link with Hermes, which we will discuss in the following chapter, is central to understanding the ferryman of Hades. As Rebecca I. Denova explains, "Hermes Psychopompos (guider of souls) led the dead to the river Styx, which was the boundary marker for Hades. Hermes handed over the dead to Charon, the Ferryman. He ushered the dead into boats to cross the river, for which he charged a fee." Rebecca I. Denova, *Greek and Roman Religions* (Blackwell, 2019), 211.
2. Rita Charon, *Narrative Medicine: Honoring the Stories of Illness* (Oxford University Press, 2006), 25.
3. Craig Irvine and Danielle Spencer, "Dualism and Its Discontents I: Philosophy, Literature, and Medicine," in *The Principles and Practice of Narrative Medicine*, ed. Rita Charon et al. (Oxford University Press, 2017), 70.
4. Samuel, "This Doctor Is Taking Aim at Our Broken Medical System."
5. Charon, in Samuel, "This Doctor Is Taking Aim at Our Broken Medical System."
6. Graham McLeod, "Narrative Medicine: A Personal Interview with Expert Rita Charon," *University of Manitoba Journal of Medicine* 1,

no. 1 (August 2018): 17. Charon considers bioethics particularly circumscribed for its principle that patients must be protected from their doctors, since bioethics considers medicine as an adversarial enterprise where doctors often play the role of judges instead of listeners. The fact that bioethicists are often "called to assist at illnesses at particularly grave points in their courses—usually at the ends of life, especially the ends of contested lives"—is an indication that they could benefit from narrative medicine. Charon, *Narrative Medicine*, 203. On the relation of medicine, hermeneutics, and phenomenology, see Hans-Georg Gadamer, *The Enigma of Health: The Art of Healing in a Scientific Age*, trans. Jason Gaiger and Nicholas Walker (Stanford University Press, 2004); and Fredrik Svenaeus, *The Hermeneutics of Medicine and the Phenomenology of Health: Steps Towards a Philosophy of Medical Practice* (Kluwer Academic, 2000). Although Narrative Medicine (NM) and Indigenous Story Medicine both use narrative to understand and affect health, their respective conceptualizations of narrative differ. See Shane Neilson, "Contrasting Epistemologies: Biomedicine, Narrative Medicine and Indigenous Story Medicine," *Journal of Evaluation in Clinical Practice* 30 (2024): 741–48.
7. Gemma Corradi Fiumara, *The Other Side of Language: A Philosophy of Listening*, trans. Charles Lambert (Routledge, 1990), 1–3.
8. Fiumara, *The Other Side of Language*, 10, 54, 46.
9. Marcel Cobussen and Nanette Nielsen, *Music and Ethics* (Ashgate, 2012), 34.
10. Fiumara, *The Other Side of Language*, 191, 13.
11. Fiumara, *The Other Side of Language*, 191.
12. Martin Heidegger, *What Is Called Thinking?*, trans. J. Glenn Gray (Harper & Row, 1968), 55. On Heidegger's notion of hearing and listening, see David Espinet, *Phänomenologie des Hörens: Eine Untersuchung im Ausgang von Martin Heidegger* (Mohr Siebeck, 2009); and David Kleinberg-Levin, "Abyssal Tonalities: Heidegger's Language of Hearkening," in *Hermeneutical Heidegger*, ed. Michael Bowler and Ingo Farin (Northwestern University Press, 2016), 221–61. "It is such listening," as Jeff Malpas points out, "that underpins Heidegger's so frequent recourse to etymological consideration in his exploration of key terms

and concepts." Jeff Malpas, "The House of Being: Poetry, Language, Place," in *Paths in Heidegger's Later Thought*, ed. Günter Figal, et al. (Indiana University Press, 2020), 40.

13. Martin Heidegger, *Being and Time*, trans. John MacQuarrie and Edward Robinson (Harper & Row, 2008), 207.
14. Martin Heidegger, *The Principle of Reason*, trans. Reginald Lilly (Indiana University Press, 1996), 47. "Hearing, as the sensation of sounds," Heidegger clarifies, "always occurs on the basis of that hearing that is a listening to something in the sense of hearkening [*Horchens*]. Our hearkening, however, itself already hearkens in each case and in some way to what is to be heard, ready for it or not ready, [and is] somehow an obedience [*Gehorsam*]. The ear, which is necessary for correct hearing, is the obedience. That which is able to be heard—the hearkeningly perceivable—need not be anything sound-like or noise-like." Martin Heidegger, "*Logos* and Language," in *The Heidegger Reader*, ed. Günter Figal, trans. Jerome Veith (Indiana University Press, 2009), 245.
15. Martin Heidegger, *Basic Concepts of Aristotelian Philosophy*, trans. Robert D. Metcalf and Mark B. Tanzer (Indiana University Press, 2009), 76.
16. Heidegger, *The Principle of Reason*, 46.
17. Martin Heidegger, *On the Way to Language*, trans. Peter D. Hertz (Harper & Row, 1982), 124.
18. Martin Heidegger, "Letter on 'Humanism,'" trans. Frank A. Capuzzi, in *Pathmarks*, ed. William McNeill (Cambridge University Press), 239. On the failure to speak, see Markus Wild, "Heidegger and Trakl: Language Speaks in the Poet's Poem," in *Paths in Heidegger's Later Thought*, ed. Figal et al., 50.
19. Hans-Georg Gadamer, *Gadamer in Conversation*, ed. R. E. Palmer (Yale University Press, 2001), 39.
20. Hans-Georg Gadamer, *Truth and Method*, trans. Joel Weinsheimer and Donald G. Marshall (Continuum, 2014), 458.
21. Gadamer, *Truth and Method*, 458.
22. Hans-Georg Gadamer, "Hearing—Seeing—Reading," in *Ethics, Aesthetics, and the Historical Dimension of Language: The Selected Writings of Hans-Georg Gadamer*, ed. and trans. Pol Vandevelde and Arun Iyer

(Bloomsbury, 2022), 2:204. See also Hans-Georg Gadamer, "Über das Hören. Einem Phänomen auf der Spur," in *Hermeneutische Entwürfe. Der Kunstbegriff im Wandel*, ed. Thomas Vogel (Mohr Siebeck, 2000), 48–55.
23. Jean-Luc Nancy, *Listening*, trans. Charlotte Mandell (Fordham University Press, 2007), 9.
24. Nancy, *Listening*, 7.
25. Nancy, *Listening*, 6.
26. Nancy, *Listening*, 21. According to Lisabeth Lipari, regardless of "the ways these distinctions are interpreted, however, the distinction itself illustrates that 'listen' and 'hear' are not simply synonyms, but are inflected with different meanings that suggest different ways of being in the world." Lisabeth Lipari, *Listening, Thinking, Being: Towards and Ethics of Attunement* (Penn State University Press, 2014), 197.

11. THE BATTLE OF INTERPRETATION

1. Fiona Harvey, "After 30 Years of Waiting, Cop28 Deal Addresses the Elephant in the Room," *Guardian*, December 13, 2023, https://www.theguardian.com/environment/2023/dec/13/cop28-deal-significant-progress-tackle-climate-crisis; Rupert Read, "Cop28 Leaves the Highway to Climate Hell Wide Open," *Guardian*, December 15, 2023, https://www.theguardian.com/environment/2023/dec/15/cop28-leaves-the-highway-to-climate-hell-wide-open; Michael Jacobs, "A Battle for Interpretation of the Cop28 Deal on Fossil Fuel Phase-Out," *Guardian*, December 19, 2023, https://www.theguardian.com/environment/2023/dec/19/a-battle-for-interpretation-of-the-cop28-deal-on-a-fossil-fuel-phase-out ; John Foster, "The Weasel Words of Cop28 Can Be Easily Twisted," *Guardian*, December 25, 2023, https://www.theguardian.com/environment/2023/dec/25/the-weasel-words-of-cop28-can-be-easily-twisted.

2. The various origin stories of hermeneutics are evident in the following histories: George Gusdorf, *Les origines de l'herméneutique* (Payot, 1988); Gayle L. Ormiston and Alan D. Schrift, eds., *The Hermeneutic Tradition: From Ast to Ricoeur* (SUNY Press, 1990); Gayle L. Ormiston and Alan D. Schrift, eds., *Transforming the Hermeneutic Context: From Nietzsche to Nancy* (SUNY Press, 1990); Gerald L. Bruns,

II. THE BATTLE OF INTERPRETATION ⌘ 211

Hermeneutics: Ancient and Modern (Yale University Press, 1992); Jean Grondin, *Introduction to Philosophical Hermeneutics*, trans. Joel Weinsheimer (Yale University Press, 1994); Maurizio Ferraris, *History of Hermeneutics*, trans. L. Somigli (Humanities Press, 1996); Gerald L. Bruns, *Hermeneutics: Ancient and Modern* (Yale University Press, 1992); Eileen Brannan, "The History of Hermeneutics," in *The Blackwell Companion to Hermeneutics*, ed. Niall Keane and Chris Lawn (Wiley Blackwell, 2016), 11–21.

3. Bruns, *Hermeneutics: Ancient and Modern*, 215. Also see Gianni Vattimo, "The Future of Hermeneutics" and "The Consequences of Hermeneutics," in *Being and Its Surroundings*, ed. Giuseppe Iannantuono, Alberto Martinengo, and Santiago Zabala, trans. Corrado Federici (McGill-Queen's University Press, 2018), 36–45, 46–53.
4. Grondin, *Introduction to Philosophical Hermeneutics*, 22.
5. Francisco Gonzalez, "Hermeneutics in Greek Philosophy," in *The Routledge Companion to Hermeneutics*, ed. J. Malpas and Hans-Helmuth Gander (Routledge, 2015), 13. "Our very term 'hermeneutics' comes from a family of Ancient Greek terms: '*hermeneuein*' or '*hermêneusai*' and '*hermêneia*' to designate an activity, '*hermênês*' to designate the individual who carries out this activity, and '*hermêneutikê*' to designate a particular discipline associated with this activity. Given this ancient provenance of the word, it would seem not only that it makes sense to speak of an 'Ancient Hermeneutics,' but that hermeneutics is something distinctively characteristic of Ancient Greek thought" (13).
6. Jean Greisch, "Hermeneutics, Religion, and God," in *The Routledge Companion to Hermeneutics*, 439. On Hermes, see Maurizio Bettini, *The Ears of Hermes: Communication, Images, and Identity in the Classical World*, trans. Michael Short (Ohio State University Press, 2011).
7. Kathy Eden, *Hermeneutics and the Rhetorical Tradition: Chapters in the Ancient Legacy and Its Humanist Reception* (Yale University Press, 1997), 2. The anarchic vein of hermeneutics is outlined in the second part of Santiago Zabala, *Being at Large: Freedom in the Age of Alternative Facts* (McGill-Queen's University Press, 2020), 59–110.
8. Martin Heidegger, *Ontology: The Hermeneutics of Facticity*, trans. John van Buren (Indiana University Press, 1999), 10.
9. Martin Heidegger, *Being and Time*, trans. John MacQuarrie and Edward Robinson (Harper & Row, 2008), 62.

10. Heidegger's notion of *Dasein*, Being-there or human existence, it is not the world, the subject, or a property of both but the relation, the in-between, in which humanity must decide if it wants to exist as an "inauthentic" describer of objectivity or an "authentic" interpreter of Being that actually thinks. Only the latter can "be warned."
11. Heidegger, *Being and Time*, 195.
12. Heidegger, *Ontology: The Hermeneutics of Facticity*, 11.
13. Michael Bowler and Ingo Farin, introduction to *Hermeneutical Heidegger*, ed. Michael Bowler and Ingo Farin (Northwestern University Press, 2016), 4.
14. Heidegger, *Being and Time*, 188–89.
15. Heidegger, *Ontology: The Hermeneutics of Facticity*, 14.
16. Heidegger, *Ontology: The Hermeneutics of Facticity*, 14.
17. Heidegger, *Being and Time*, 272.
18. Martin Heidegger, *Logic: The Question of Truth*, trans. T. Sheehan (Indiana University Press, 2010), 113. As Christina Lafont has explained, Heidegger "intends to show that the statement cannot 'primarily disclose entities on its own.' Rather, it 'always already remains itself on the basis of being-in-the-world.' By underscoring the circular character of every understanding (or the holistic structure of language), Heidegger places into question the traditional limited way of considering the statement 'as the only clue for obtaining access to the entities which authentically are.' Here it is not a question of thematizing pre-linguistic phenomena, but of emphasizing the priority of understanding over knowing, and thus the primacy of holism in every analysis of linguistic phenomena—such as understanding." Christina Lafont, *Heidegger, Language, and World-Disclosure* (MIT Press, 2000), 54.
19. Heidegger, *Logic*, 53.

12. TRUTH IS NOT ENOUGH

1. Slavoj Žižek, *The Year of Dreaming Dangerously* (Verso, 2012), 135, 128, 133. Occupy Wall Street, the Arab Spring, and the demonstrations in Spain and Greece took place in 2010 and 2011.
2. Slavoj Žižek, *Living in the End Times* (Verso, 2011), x. "Žižek warned," as James Burgess reports from a talk delivered at the Institute of

Contemporary Arts in London, "of the dangers of 'naturalizing' nature, positing the natural world as some utopia to which we can return in balanced harmony. Nature, he says, is itself is not a balanced system, insofar as it is a set of contingent systems adapting to survive amidst various catastrophes and changing circumstances. That is not to say that we should disregard the dangers of climate change. On the contrary, despite the fact that the current global climate crisis has been caused by the structure of the particular economic system of one subset of one species, the crisis has the potential to affect the very basis of life on earth for the majority of species. Humans have become, for the first time, a geological force capable of changing the global temperatures that sustain life on Earth." James Burgess, "Everyone's Gone Green: Slavoj Žižek on the Dangers of Ecological Utopianism," *New Statesman*, November, 24, 2009, https://www.newstatesman.com/culture/2009/11/381-382-climate-crisis-global.

3. An analysis of these provocations and many debates is now available in Eliran Bar-El, *How Slavoj Became Žižek: The Digital Making of a Public Intellectual* (University of Chicago Press, 2023).

4. Macarena Ares and Silja Häusermann, "Is Europe's Left Really in Crisis? Our Research Shows It's Complex—and There Is Hope," *Guardian*, January 10, 2024, https://www.theguardian.com/commentisfree/2024/jan/10/europe-left-crisis-research-parties-progressive-politics. According to these political scientists, during the past two decades "election results in western Europe have been framed within the narrative of a crisis of the left. Think of the near-implosion of the French Socialist party as a case in point. In 2022 the Socialist presidential candidate received less than 2% of the first-round vote, the worst presidential election result in the party's history. Beyond the ups and downs of specific elections, the performance of social democratic parties has, on average, been marked by a tremendous decline across western European democracies, from a vote share of nearly 40 percent to below 20 percent."

5. kennardphillipps, an artistic duo composed of the British artists Peter Kennard and Cat Phillips, has been creating art since 2002 that responds to the invasion of Iraq and critiques the ongoing impositions of capitalism and neoliberalism. The work often consists of digital collages and is not primarily created for galleries and museums

but for the streets, the Web, and newspapers. Their work can be found at their website: https://www.kennardphillipps.com/. Until the end of 2016, Sara Ahmed was a professor of Race and Cultural Studies at Goldsmiths, University of London, having been previously based in Women's Studies at Lancaster University. She works on the intersection of feminist, queer, and race studies to analyze mechanisms of oppression and discrimination in everyday life and in institutional contexts. She coined the idea of the "feminist killjoy" to refer to someone who never tires of raising their voice against different forms of discrimination. Her books include *Complaint!* (2021), *The Feminist Killjoy Handbook* (2023), and *No Is Not a Lonely Utterance* (2025), among others. On the revelations of Julian Assange, Edward Snowden, and Christopher Wylie, see Santiago Zabala, *Being at Large: Freedom in the Age of Alternative Facts* (McGill-Queen's University Press, 2020), 149–54.

6. At the annual Intergovernmental Panel on Climate Change (IPCC), scientists no longer exclusively present the latest scientific findings; they now also call on governments to reduce greenhouse-gas emissions substantially. But governments are not the only ones called on to intervene. At scientific gatherings researchers have begun to call on the general public to agitate for political change, as it has become clear that capitalism's depletion of natural resources is indisputably the primary cause of global warning. At a recent meeting of the American Geophysical Union, the scientist Brad Werner went as far as to call on people to "adopt a certain set of dynamics that does not fit within the capitalist culture." These consist of "protests, blockades and sabotage by Indigenous peoples, workers, anarchists and other activist groups." As we can see, the scientific community is telling us to revolt because everything indicates we've reached a point of no return. Even though the IPCC was created to slow or reverse climate change, it has "not only failed to make progress over its twenty-odd years of work (and more than ninety official negotiation meetings since the agreement was adopted) [but also] overseen a process of virtually uninterrupted backsliding." Naomi Klein, *This Changes Everything: Capitalism Versus the Climate* (Simon & Schuster, 2014), 11.

7. Masha Gessen, "The Fifteen-Year-Old Climate Activist Who Is Demanding a New Kind of Politics," *New Yorker*, October 2, 2028,

https://www.newyorker.com/news/our-columnists/the-fifteen-year-old-climate-activist-who-is-demanding-a-new-kind-of-politics.
8. Naomi Klein, "Greta Thunberg on the Climate Fight: 'If We Can Save the Banks, Then We Can Save the World,'" *The Intercept*, September 13, 2019, https://theintercept.com/2019/09/13/greta-thunberg-naomi-klein-climate/.
9. "Greta Thunberg: Who Is the Climate Activist and What Has She Achieved?," BBC, February 5, 2024, https://www.bbc.com/news/world-europe-49918719.
10. Klein, "Greta Thunberg on the Climate Fight." Thunberg's call to "panic" recalls the absence of emergency I discuss in part 2.
11. "Greta Thunberg: Who Is the Climate Activist and What Has She Achieved?"
12. Slavoj Žižek, *A Left That Dares to Speak Its Name* (Polity, 2020), 82–83. Žižek is not the only philosopher of warnings who praised Thunberg. The last book by the French philosopher Bernard Stiegler—*Qu'appelle-t-on Panser?*, tome 2: *La leçon de Greta Thunberg* (Les Liens qui libèrent, 2020)—is dedicated to the Swedish activist. Thunberg, according to Stiegler, like Antigone, teaches adults how to again become responsible.
13. Hans-Georg Gadamer, *Hans-Georg Gadamer on Education, Poetry, and History: Applied Hermeneutics*, ed. Dieter Misgeld and Graeme Nicholson, trans. Lawrence Schmidt and Monica Reuss (SUNY Press, 1992), 5. Gadamer returned to the problem of education in 1999, where he emphasized the significance of educating oneself. Hans-Georg Gadamer, "Education Is Self-Education," trans. John Cleary and Padraig Hogan, *Journal of Philosophy of Education* 35, no. 4 (2001): 529–38.
14. Hans-Georg Gadamer, *Truth and Method*, trans. Joel Weinsheimer and Donald G. Marshall (Continuum, 2014), xxi.
15. Gadamer, *Truth and Method*, 290. Gadamer goes on to clarify that the "classical epitomizes a general characteristic of historical being: preservation amid the ruins of time. The general nature of tradition is such that only the part of the past that is not past offers the possibility of historical knowledge. The classical, however, as Hegel says, is 'that which is self-significant (*selbst bedeutende*) and hence also self-interpretive (*selber Deutende*).' But that ultimately means that the classical preserves itself precisely because it is significant in itself and

interprets itself; i.e., it speaks in such a way that it is not a statement about what is past—documentary evidence that still needs to be interpreted—rather, it says something to the present as if it were said specifically to it. What we call 'classical' does not first require the overcoming of historical distance, for in its own constant mediation it overcomes this distance by itself. The classical, then, is certainly 'timeless,' but this timelessness is a mode of historical being." Gadamer, *Truth and Method*, 290.

16. R. E. Palmer, ed., *Gadamer in Conversation: Reflections and Commentary* (Yale University Press, 2001), 71. In this passage I translate *Stoß* as "shock" instead of "jolts" and "knocks."

17. Gianni Vattimo, *Of Reality*, trans. Robert Valgenti (Columbia University Press, 2012), 17. Richard Rorty agrees on the insignificance of this distinction. As he explains, there "is no sharp break between natural science and social science, nor between social science and politics, nor between politics, philosophy and literature. All areas of culture are parts of the same endeavor to make life better. There is no deep split between theory and practice, because on a pragmatist view all so-called 'theory' which is not wordplay is always already practice. To treat beliefs not as representations but as habits of action, and words not as representations but as tools, is to make it pointless to ask, 'Am I discovering or inventing, making or finding?'" Richard Rorty, *Philosophy and Social Hope* (Penguin, 1999), xxv.

AFTERWORD

1. Jonathan Glazer, in David Fear, "It's Not a History Lesson, It's a Warning': Inside the Making of 'The Zone of Interest,'" *Rolling Stone*, December 26, 2023, https://www.rollingstone.com/tv-movies/tv-movie-features/the-zone-of-interest-jonathan-glazer-interview-holocaust-nazis-1234907233/; *The Zone of Interest* was directed by Jonathan Glazer, produced by James Wilson and Ewa Puszczyńska, and premiered at the seventy-sixth Cannes Film Festival on May 19, 2023; Alfredo Jaar, "Alfredo Jaar Believes in the Power of a Single Idea," *Whitewall*, Spring 2023, https://whitewall.art/art/alfredo-jaar-believes-in-the-power-of-a-single-idea/; John Pilger, "Assange Arrest

a Warning From History" (2019), *Consortium News*, January 18, 2024, https://consortiumnews.com/2024/01/18/john-pilger-assange-arrest-a-warning-from-history/; Bruno Latour, "The Pandemic Is a Warning: We Must Take Care of the Earth, Our Only Home," *Guardian*, December 24, 2021, https://www.theguardian.com/commentisfree/2021/dec/24/pandemic-earth-lockdowns-climate-crisis-environment.

2. The "trigger warning" has become a popular concept in American academia and society: It alerts students and consumers that they are about to encounter traumatic educational or media content. A historical and theoretical account can be found in the rich contributions in Emily J. M. Knox, ed., *Trigger Warnings: History, Theory, Context* (Rowman & Littlefield, 2017). After identifying "common elements and synthesizing them into a methodology," Richard A. Clarke and R. P. Eddy created the "Cassandra Coefficient," which is "a score that suggests to us the likelihood that an individual is indeed a Cassandra whose warning is likely accurate, but is at risk of being ignored." Richard A. Clarke and R. P. Eddy, *Warnings: Finding Cassandras to Stop Catastrophes* (Ecco, 2017), 6.

3. Naomi Klein, *This Changes Everything: Capitalism Versus the Climate* (Simon & Schuster, 2014). Alice Bell, *Our Biggest Experiment: An Epic History of the Climate Crisis* (Counterpoint, 2021), is an excellent account of the decades of ignored warnings. Also see David Wallace-Wells, *The Uninhabitable Earth: A Story of the Future* (Tim Duggan, 2019).

4. Gianni Vattimo, a two-time member of the European Parliament, explained that the "technocracy does not conform to the agenda of parties that support it from both the Right and the Left. It is, instead, politically neutral and therefore politically unaccountable. I do not have space here to recount this story in more detail, but most readers should already know that this is taking place elsewhere in Europe. European politics is also dominated by problems with its finance industry, banks, and the threat of government insolvency. We are all well aware that economics is neither an exact nor a neutral science. Parties of every political orientation, as well as the big media ('independent,' 'nonpartisan,' and obviously 'technical'), relentlessly impose the idea that these special circumstances require a sort of *union sacrée* (sacred union): the suspension of political confrontation in order to fix the economy

(ultimately to shore up international financial power)." Gianni Vattimo, *Being and Its Surroundings*, ed. Giuseppe Iannantuono, Alberto Martinengo, and Santiago Zabala, trans. Corrado Federici (McGill-Queen's University Press, 2018), 79.
5. Timothy Snyder, *Black Earth: The Holocaust as History and Warning* (Penguin, 2015), xv.
6. Katherine Richardson et al., "Earth Beyond Six of Nine Planetary Boundaries," *Science Advances*, September 13, 2023, https://www.science.org/doi/epdf/10.1126/sciadv.adh2458. See also Ian Angus, "The Earth System Has Passed Six of Nine Planetary Boundaries," *Resilience*, September 23, 2023, https://www.resilience.org/stories/2023-09-18/the-earth-system-has-passed-six-of-nine-planetary-boundaries/.
7. Kyle Whyte, "Time as Kinship," in *The Cambridge Companion to Environmental Humanities*, ed. Jeffrey Cohen and Stephanie Foote (Cambridge University Press, 2021), 4.
8. Josep Ramoneda, *La izquierda necesaria. Contra el autoritarismo posdemocrático* (RBA, 2012); Ramoneda, "Autoritarismo o democracia," *El País*, November 4, 2022, https://elpais.com/opinion/2022-11-04/autoritarismo-o-democracia.html. In a recent editorial Ramoneda listed a number of warnings that take into account this new axis of politics: Josep Ramoneda, "Advertències," *Ara*, April 11, 2023, https://www.ara.cat/opinio/advertencies-josep-ramoneda_129_4673459.html.
9. "Why am I so sure that we have to look to religion to find the origin of this curious form of indifference to warnings about the current state of nature? Because of the resurgence, or even the omnipresence, of the term apocalypse. As soon as you speak with some degree of seriousness about ecological mutations, without even raising your voice, you are immediately accused of 'apocalyptic discourse' or, in a somewhat attenuated version, 'catastrophist discourse.'" Bruno Latour, *Facing Gaia: Eight Lectures on the New Climatic Regime*, trans. Catherine Porter (Polity, 2017), 193–94. Marcel Danesi, *Warning Signs: A Semiotics of Danger* (Bloomsbury, 2022), instead believes that indifference toward warnings "may be found, arguably, in a radical shift in culture, starting in the late nineteenth century, when conspiratorial thinking and false narratives became widespread to explain world events, most of which were fabricated for self-serving political or ideological reasons."

Marcel Danesi, "Ignoring Pandemics: The Effects of Conspiratorial Culture," *La Maleta de Portbou* 66 (September/October 2024): 118.

10. Cornelius Castoriadis, *A Society Adrift: Interviews and Debates, 1974–1997*, ed. Enrique Escobar, Myrto Gondicas, and Pascal Vernay, trans. Helen Arnold (Fordham University Press, 2010), 122.
11. Viktor Orban, Hungary's prime minister, has been accused of turning his country back into an autocracy by passing laws against universities' autonomy. As Felix Schlagwein reports, they "will no longer be state owned, but will become foundations instead, according to a new law passed by Orban's Fidesz party. In the process, they will also be endowed billions of euros in assets from the state budget, as well as real estate and shares in large companies." Felix Schlagwein, "Hungary: Orban Seeks to Control Universities," *DW*, June 5, 2022, https://www.dw.com/en/hungarys-viktor-orban-seeks-to-control-universities/a-57444869. Giorgia Meloni is attempting to rewrite Italy's postfascist constitution to undermine parliamentary authority, concentrate power in the hands of a single individual, and undermine the delicate checks and balances that despite their shortcomings are vital for the autonomy of the country's public institutions. Amy Kazmin, "Meloni's Radical Plan: Rewriting Italy's Post-Fascist Constitution," *Irish Times*, April 14, 2024, https://www.irishtimes.com/world/europe/2024/04/14/melonis-radical-plan-rewriting-italys-post-fascist-constitution/. Among the Argentinean president's plans to dismantle "useless" institutions, he is taking aim at the country's main science agency, the National Scientific and Technical Research Council (CONICET). Martín De Ambrosio and Fermín Koop, "'Despair': Argentinian Researchers Protest as President Begins Dismantling Science," *Nature*, March 7, 2024, https://www.nature.com/articles/d41586-024-00628-1. See also Santiago Zabala and Claudio Gallo, "The Neoliberal Populism of Meloni and Milei," *Al-Jazeera*, May 21, 2024, https://www.aljazeera.com/opinions/2024/5/21/the-neoliberal-populism-of-milei-and-meloni.
12. Patrick Wingrove and Jennifer Rigby, "Trump Orders US Exit from the World Health Organization," Reuters, January 21, 2025, https://www.reuters.com/world/us/trump-signs-executive-withdrawing-world-health-organization-2025-01-21/. David Smith, "Trump Halts

World Health Organization Funding Over Coronavirus 'Failure,'" *Guardian*, April 15, 2020, https://www.theguardian.com/world/2020/apr/14/coronavirus-trump-halts-funding-to-world-health-organization. In 2024, the World Health Organization accused Nigel Farage of diffusing misinformation after he launched a campaign to block an international treaty designed to improve global pandemic preparedness and cooperation. The British populist politician, according to Ben Quinn, "is fronting the campaign group Action on World Health (AWH)," which claims that "the WHO treaty will 'strip away' the UK's decision-making powers." Ben Quinn, "WHO Accuses Nigel Farage of Spreading Misinformation About Pandemic Treaty," *Guardian*, May 16, 2024, https://www.theguardian.com/politics/article/2024/may/16/who-accuses-nigel-farage-of-spreading-misinformation-about-pandemic-treaty.

BIBLIOGRAPHY

Agamben, Giorgio. *A che punto siamo? L'epidemia come politica.* Quodlibet, 2021; 2nd updated ed., 2021.
———. *State of Exception.* Translated by Kevin Attell. University of Chicago Press, 2005.
———. *Where Are We Now: The Epidemic as Politics.* Trans. Valeria Dani. Rowman & Littlefield, 2021. 2nd updated ed., ERIS, 2021.
Angus, Ian. "The Earth System Has Passed Six of Nine Planetary Boundaries." *Resilience*, September 2023, https://www.resilience.org/stories/2023-09-18/the-earth-system-has-passed-six-of-nine-planetary-boundaries/.
Arendt, Hannah. *Eichmann in Jerusalem.* Penguin, 2022.
———. *Essays in Understanding, 1930–1954.* Ed. Jerome Kohn. Harcourt, 1994.
———. *The Life of the Mind: The Groundbreaking Investigation on How We Think.* Harcourt Brace Jovanovich, 1978.
———. "Personal Responsibility Under Dictatorship." *The Listener*, August 6, 1964, 185–87, 205.
———. *Thinking Without a Banister.* Ed. Jerome Kohn. Knopf Doubleday, 2018.
———. "Understanding and Politics." *Partisan Review* 20, no. 4 (July–August 1953): 377–92.
———. "What Is Authority?" In *Between Past and Future*, 91–142. Viking, 1961.
Arendt, Hannah, and Martin Heidegger, *Letters, 1925–1975.* Ed. Ursula Ludz. Trans. Andrew Shields. Harcourt, 2004.
Atwood, Margaret. *The Handmaid's Tale.* Harper Collins, 1986, 2023.

———. *The Testament*. Vintage, 2019.
Bachelard, Gaston. *Le rationalisme appliqué*. PUF, 1949.
Bacon, Francis. *The New Organon and Related Writings*. Bobbs-Merrill. 1960.
Baer, Robert. *See No Evil: The True Story of a Ground Soldier in the CIA's War Against Terrorism*. Three Rivers, 2003.
Bangstad, Sindre. *Anders Breivik and the Rise of Islamophobia*. Zed, 2014.
Bar-El, Eliran. *How Slavoj Became Žižek: The Digital Making of a Public Intellectual*. University of Chicago Press, 2023.
Barrett, William. *Irrational Man: A Study in Existential Philosophy*. Anchor, 1958, 1990.
Bauman, Zygmunt. *Modernity and the Holocaust*. Polity, 1989.
Beauvoir, Simone de. *The Prime of Life*. Trans. Peter Green. World, 1962.
———. *The Second Sex*. Trans. E. M. Parshley. Vintage, 1973.
———. *The Second Sex*. Trans. Constance Borde and Sheila Malovany-Chevallier. Knopf, 2000.
Bell, While Alice. *Our Biggest Experiment: An Epic History of the Climate Crisis*. Counterpoint, 2021.
Benjamin, Walter. "Theses on the Philosophy of History." In *Illuminations*, trans. Harry Zohn. Schocken, 1969.
Bernstein, Richard J. "Arendt on Thinking." In *The Cambridge Companion to Hannah Arendt*, ed. Dana Vila, 277–92. Cambridge University Press, 2006.
Bettini, Maurizio. *The Ears of Hermes: Communication, Images, and Identity in the Classical World*. Trans. Michael Short. Ohio State University Press, 2011.
Bloom, Mia, and Sophie Moskalenko. *Pastels and Pedophiles: Inside the Mind of QAnon*. Red Wood, 2021.
Boetzkes, Amanda. "Realism Without Authority." *La Furia Umana: International and Multilanguage Journal of the History and Theory of Cinema* 39 (2020), https://web.archive.org/web/20220706192658/http://www.lafuriaumana.it/index.php/73-archive/lfu-39/946-amanda-boetzkes-realism-without-authority-the-performance-of-viewership.
Bondanella, Peter. *Umberto Eco and the Open Text: Semiotics, Fiction, Popular Culture*. Cambridge University Press, 2005.
Borchgrevink, Aage. *A Norwegian Tragedy: Anders Behring Breivik and the Massacre on Utoya*. Trans. Guy Puzey. Polity, 2013.

Brannan, Eileen. "The History of Hermeneutics." In *The Blackwell Companion to Hermeneutics*, ed. Niall Keane and Chris Lawn, 11–21. Wiley Blackwell, 2016.
Bruns, Gerald L. *Hermeneutics: Ancient and Modern*. Yale University Press, 1992.
Butler, *Gender Trouble: Feminism and the Subversion of Identity*. Routledge, 1990.
———. "Sex and Gender in Simone De Beauvoir's *Second Sex*." *Yale French Studies* 72 (1986): 35–49.
Castoriadis, Cornelius. *A Society Adrift: Interviews and Debates, 1974–1997*. Ed. Enrique Escobar, Myrto Gondicas, and Pascal Vernay. Trans. Helen Arnold. Fordham University Press, 2010.
Charon, Rita. *Narrative Medicine: Honoring the Stories of Illness*. Oxford University Press, 2006.
Clarke, Richard A., and R. P. Eddy. *Warnings: Finding Cassandras to Stop Catastrophes*. Ecco, 2017.
Cobussen, Marcel, and Nanette Nielsen. *Music and Ethics*. Ashgate, 2012.
Coccia, Emmanuele. *The Life of Plants: A Metaphysics of Mixture*. Trans. Dylan J. Montanari. Policy, 2018.
Corradi Fiumara, Gemma. *The Other Side of Language: A Philosophy of Listening*. Trans. Charles Lambert. Routledge, 1990.
Critchley, Simon, Jacques Derrida, Ernesto Laclau, and Richard Rorty. *Deconstruction and Pragmatism*. Ed. Chantal Mouffe. Routledge, 1995.
Danesi, Marcel. *Warning Signs: A Semiotics of Danger*. Bloomsbury, 2022.
Davis, Mike. *The Monster at Our Door: The Global Threat of Avian Flu*. New Press, 2005, 2020.
d'Eaubonne, Francoise. *Feminism or Death: How the Women's Movement Can Save the Planet*. Trans. Ruth Hottell. Verso, 2022.
Denova, Rebecca I. *Greek and Roman Religions*. Blackwell, 2019.
Depoortere, Frederiek. *The Death of God: An Investigation Into the History of the Western Concept of God*. T&T Clark, 2007.
Derrida, *Archive Fever: A Freudian Impression*. Trans. E. Prenowitz. University of Chicago Press, 1996.
Dewey, John. *Democracy and Education*. Macmillan, 1916.
Dickey, Colin. *Under the Eye of Power: How Fear of Secret Societies Shapes American Democracy*. Viking, 2023.

Drouin, Jean-Marc. *A Philosophy of the Insect*. Trans. Anne Trager. Columbia University Press, 2019.

Eco, Umberto. *Semiotics and the Philosophy of Language*. Macmillan, 1984.

———. *A Theory of Semiotics*. Indiana University Press, 1979.

Eden, Kathy. *Hermeneutics and the Rhetorical Tradition: Chapters in the Ancient Legacy and Its Humanist Reception*. Yale University Press, 1997.

Escobar, Pepe. *The Empire of Chaos*. Nimble, 2014.

Espinet, David. *Phänomenologie des Hörens: Eine Untersuchung im Ausgang von Martin Heidegger*. Mohr Siebeck, 2009.

Farin, Ingo. "The Different Notions of History in Heidegger's Work." In *Hermeneutical Heidegger*, ed. Michael Bowler and Ingo Farin, 23–63. Northwestern University Press, 2016.

Farrell Krell, David. *Ecstasy, Catastrophe: Heidegger from 'Being and Time' to the 'Black Notebooks.'* SUNY Press, 2015.

Ferraris, Maurizio. *History of Hermeneutics*. Trans. L. Somigli. Humanities, 1988.

———. *Manifesto of New Realism*. Trans. Sarah De Sanctis. Foreword by Graham Harman. SUNY Press, 2015.

Fish, Stanley. *The First: How to Think About Hate Speech, Campus Speech, Religious Speech, Fake News, Post-Truth, and Donald Trump*. Atria/One Signal, 2019.

Foucault, Michel. *Discipline and Punish: The Birth of the Prison*. Trans. Alan Sheridan. Penguin, 2020.

———. *Ethics: Subjectivity and Truth*. Vol. 1 of *The Essential Works of Michel Foucault, 1954–1984*. Ed. Paul Rabinow. Trans. Robert Hurley et al. Penguin, 2020.

Gabriel, Markus. *Moral Progress in Dark Times: Universal Values for the 21st Century*. Trans. Wieland Hoban. Polity, 2022.

Gadamer, Hans-Georg. "Authority and Critical Freedom." In *The Enigma of Health: The Art of Healing in a Scientific Age*, trans. Jason Gaiger and Nicholas Walker, 117–24. Stanford University Press, 2004.

———. *The Beginning of Philosophy*. Trans. R. Coltman. Continuum, 2001.

———. "Education Is Self-Education." Trans. John Cleary and Padraig Hogan. *Journal of Philosophy of Education* 35, no. 4 (2001): 529–38.

———. *Gadamer in Conversation*. Ed. R. E. Palmer. Yale University Press, 2001.

———. *Hans-Georg Gadamer on Education, Poetry, and History: Applied Hermeneutics.* Ed. Dieter Misgeld and Graeme Nicholson. Trans. Lawrence Schmidt and Monica Reuss. SUNY Press, 1992.

———. "Hearing—Seeing—Reading." In *Ethics, Aesthetics, and the Historical Dimension of Language: The Selected Writings of Hans-Georg Gadamer*, ed. and trans. Pol Vandevelde and Arun Iyer, 2:203–10. Bloomsbury, 2022.

———. *Truth and Method.* Trans. Joel Weinsheimer and Donald G. Marshall. Continuum, 2014.

———. "Über das Hören. Einem Phänomen auf der Spur." In *Hermeneutische Entwürfe. Der Kunstbegriff im Wandel*, ed. Thomas Vogel, 48–55. Mohr Siebeck, 2000.

Garbagnoli, Sara. "Italy as a Lighthouse: Anti-Gender Protests Between the 'Anthropological Question' and National Identity." In *Anti-Gender Campaigns in Europe: Mobilizing Against Equality*, ed. Roman Kuhar and David Paternotte. Rowman & Littlefield, 2017.

Geiselberger, Heinrich, ed. *The Great Regression.* Wiley, 2017.

Gonzalez, F. "Hermeneutics in Greek Philosophy." In *The Routledge Companion to Hermeneutics*, ed. J. Malpas and Hans-Helmuth Gander, 13–22. Routledge, 2015.

Gordon, Jane Anna, and Lewis R. Gordon. *Of Divine Warning: Reading Disaster in the Modern Age.* Routledge, 2016.

Gothlin, Eva. "Reading Simone de Beauvoir with Martin Heidegger." In *The Cambridge Companion to Simone de Beauvoir*, ed. Claudia Card, 45–65. Cambridge University Press, 2003.

Graff, Agnieszka, and Elżbieta Korolczuk. *Anti-Gender Politics in the Populist Moment.* Routledge, 2021.

Greisch, Jean. "Hermeneutics, Religion, and God." In *The Routledge Companion to Hermeneutics*, ed. J. Malpas and Hans-Helmuth Gander, 439–50. Routledge, 2015.

Grondin, Jean. *Introduction to Philosophical Hermeneutics.* Trans. Joel Weinsheimer. Yale University Press, 1994.

Gusdorf, George. *Les origines de l'herméneutique.* Payot, 1988.

Haraway, Donna. *Simians, Cyborgs, and Women: The Reinvention of Nature.* Routledge, 1991.

Harman, Graham. *Object-Oriented Ontology: A New Theory of Everything.* Penguin, 2018.

Heidegger, Martin. "The Age of the World Picture." In *Off the Beaten Track*, ed. and trans. Julian Young and Kenneth Haynes, 57–85. Cambridge University Press, 2002.

——. *Basic Concepts of Aristotelian Philosophy*. Trans. Robert D. Metcalf and Mark B. Tanzer. Indiana University Press, 2009.

——. *Being and Time*. Trans. John MacQuarrie and Edward Robinson. Harper & Row, 2008.

——. *The Concept of Time*. Trans. William McNeill. Blackwell, 1992.

——. *Contributions to Philosophy (of the Event)*. Trans. Richard Rojcewicz and Daniela Vallega-Neu. Indiana University Press, 2012.

——. *Heraclitus: The Inception of Occidental Thinking; and, Logic: Heraclitus's Doctrine of the Logos*. Trans. Julia Goesser Assaiante and S. Montgomery Ewegen. Bloomsbury, 2018.

——. *Introduction to Metaphysics*. Trans. F. Fried and R. Polt. Yale University Press, 2000.

——. "Letter on 'Humanism.'" Trans. Frank A. Capuzzi. In *Pathmarks*, ed. William McNeill, 239–76. Cambridge University Press, 2002.

——. *Logic: The Question of Truth*. Trans. T. Sheehan. University of Indiana Press, 2010.

——. "*Logos* and Language." In *The Heidegger Reader*, ed. Günter Figal, trans. Jerome Veith, 239–52. Indiana University Press, 2009.

——. *Nietzsche*. Trans. D. F. Krell. Harper & Row, 1979.

——. "Nietzsche's Word: 'God Is Dead.'" In *Off the Beaten Track*, ed. and trans. Julian Young and Kenneth Haynes. Cambridge University Press, 2002.

——. *On the Way to Language*. Trans. Peter D. Hertz. Harper & Row, 1982.

——. *Ontology: The Hermeneutics of Facticity*. Trans. John van Buren. Indiana University Press, 1999.

——. "Only a God Can Save Us: *Der Spiegel*'s Interview." In *Philosophical and Political Writings*, ed. Manfred Stassen, trans. Maria P. Alter and John D. Caputo, 24–48. Continuum, 2003.

——. *The Principle of Reason*. Trans. Reginald Lilly. University of Indiana Press, 1996.

——. *The Question Concerning Technology and Other Essays*. Trans. William Lovitt. Garland, 1977.

——. "Überlegungen XV." In *Überlegungen XII–XV*. Gesamtausgabe 96. Klostermann, 2014.

———. *What Is a Thing?* Trans. W. B. Banon Jr. and Vera Deutsch. Gateway, 1967.

———. *What Is Called Thinking?* Trans. J. Glenn Gray. Harper & Row, 1968.

Hobbes, Thomas. *Leviathan*. Ed. Richard Tuck. Cambridge University Press, 1991.

Hoff Sommers, Christina. *Who Stole Feminism? How Women Have Betrayed Women*. Simon & Schuster, 1994.

Hoy, David Couzens. *The Time of Our Lives: A Critical History of Temporality*. MIT Press, 2009, 2012.

Irvine, Craig, and Danielle Spencer. "Dualism and Its Discontents I: Philosophy, Literature, and Medicine." In *The Principles and Practice of Narrative Medicine*, ed. Rita Charon et al. Oxford University Press, 2017.

Kant, Immanuel. *Reflexionen zur Metaphysik*. In *Gesammelte Schriften, herausgegeben von der Preussischen Akademie der Wissenschaften zu Berlin*, vol. 18. Walter de Gruyter, 1928.

Kepel, Gilles, and Antoine Jardin. *Terror in France: The Rise of Jihad*. Princeton University Press, 2017.

Klein, Naomi. *No Logo*. Picador, 1999.

———. *This Changes Everything: Capitalism Versus the Climate*. Simon & Schuster, 2014.

Kleinberg-Levin, David. "Abyssal Tonalities: Heidegger's Language of Hearkening." In *Hermeneutical Heidegger*, ed. Michael Bowler and Ingo Farin, 222–61. Northwestern University Press, 2016.

Knox, Emily J. M., ed. *Trigger Warnings: History, Theory, Context*. Rowan & Littlefield, 2017.

Lafont, Cristina. *Heidegger, Language, and World-Disclosure*. MIT Press, 2000.

Latour, Bruno. *Down to Earth: Politics in the New Climate Regime*. Trans. Catherine Porter. Polity, 2018.

———. *Facing Gaia. Eight Lectures on the New Climatic Regime*. Trans. Catherine Porter. Polity, 2017.

Leboeuf, Céline. "'One Is Not Born, but Rather Becomes, a Woman': The Sex-Gender Distinction and Simone de Beauvoir's Account of Woman: The Second Sex." In *Feminist Moments: Reading Feminist Texts*, ed. Katherine Smits and Susan Bruce. Bloomsbury Academic, 2016.

Lipari, Lisabeth. *Listening, Thinking, Being: Towards an Ethics of Attunement*. Penn State University Press, 2014.

Lüdemann, Susanne. *Politics of Deconstruction: A New Introduction to Jacques Derrida*. Trans. Erik Butler. Stanford University Press, 2014.

Malpas, Jeff. "The House of Being: Poetry, Language, Place." In *Paths in Heidegger's Later Thought*, ed. Günter Figal, Diego D'Angelo, Tobias Keiling, and Guang Yang, 15–44. Indiana University Press, 2020.

Mann, Bonnie. Introduction to *'On ne naît pas femme: on le devient': The Life of a Sentence*, ed. Bonnie Mann and Martina Ferrari, 1–6. Oxford University Press, 2017.

Marcuse, Herbert. *Heideggerian Marxism*. Ed. R. Wolin and J. Abromeit. University of Nebraska Press, 2005.

——. *One-Dimensional Man: Studies in the Ideology of Advanced Industrial Society*. Trans. Douglas Kellner. Routledge, 2007.

Marder, Michael. *Plant-Thinking: A Philosophy of Vegetative Life*. Foreword by Gianni Vattimo and Santiago Zabala. Columbia University Press, 2013.

Marieke, Borren. "Arendt's Phenomenologically Informed Political Thinking." In *Hannah Arendt and the History of Thought*, ed. Daniel Brennan and Marguerite La Caze, 181–204. Lexington, 2022.

Martinon, Jean-Paul. *On Futurity: Malabou, Nancy, and Derrida*. Palgrave, 2007.

McLeod, Graham. "Narrative Medicine: A Personal Interview with Expert Rita Charon." *University of Manitoba Journal of Medicine* 1, no. 1 (August 2018): 17–19.

Mearsheimer, John. "Why the Ukraine Crisis Is the West's Fault: The Liberal Delusions That Provoked Putin." *Foreign Affairs*, September/October 2014, 1–12.

Meddeb, Abdelwahab. *The Malady of Islam*. Trans. Pierre Joris and Ann Reid. Basic Books, 2003.

Meillassoux, Quentin. *After Finitude: An Essay on the Necessity of Contingency*. Trans. Ray Brassier. Continuum, 2008.

Mendieta, Eduardo. *The Philosophical Animal: On Zoopoetics and Interspecies Cosmopolitanism*. SUNY Press, 2024.

Nancy, Jean-Luc, *Listening*. Trans. Charlotte Mandell. Fordham University Press, 2007.

Nietzsche, Friedrich. *Beyond Good and Evil: Prelude to a Philosophy of the Future*. Trans. Walter Kauffman. Knopf, 2010.

———. *The Gay Science: With a Prelude in German Rhymes and an Appendix of Songs*. Ed. Bernard Williams. Trans. Josefine Nauckhoff. Cambridge University Press, 2001.

———. *Human, All Too Human*. Trans. R. J. Hollingdale. Cambridge University Press, 1996.

———. *Thus Spoke Zarathustra*. Ed. Adrian del Caro and Robert Pippin. Trans. A. Del Caro. Cambridge University Press, 2006.

———. *The Will to Power*. Trans. Walter Kauffman and R. J. Hollingdale. Ed. Walter Kauffman. Random House, 1967.

O'Leary, Dale. *The Gender Agenda: Redefining Equality*. Vital Issues, 1997.

Ormiston, Gayle L., and Alan D. Schrift, eds. *The Hermeneutic Tradition: From Ast to Ricoeur*. SUNY Press, 1990.

———, eds. *Transforming the Hermeneutic Context: From Nietzsche to Nancy*. SUNY Press, 1990.

Oreskes, Naomi. *Why Trust Science?* Princeton University Press, 2019.

Palmer, R. E., ed. *Gadamer in Conversation: Reflections and Commentary*. Yale University Press, 2001.

Pallante, Francesco. "Direct Democracy." In *Outspoken: A Manifesto for the Twenty-First Century*, ed. Adrian Parr and Santiago Zabala, 58–67. McGill-Queen's University Press, 2023.

Parr, Adrian. *Earthlings: Imaginative Encounters with the Natural World*. Columbia University Press, 2022.

Piketty, Thomas. *Capital in the Twenty-First Century*. Trans. Arthur Goldhammer. Belknap, 2014.

Polt, Richard. *The Emergency of Being*. Cornell University Press, 2006.

Popper, Karl. *The Open Society and Its Enemies*. Foreword by George Soros. Princeton University Press, 2020.

Preciado, Paul B. *Can the Monster Speak? Report to an Academy of Psychoanalysts*. Trans. Frank Wynne. Fitzcarraldo, 2021.

Quammen, David. *Spillover: Animal Infections and the Next Human Pandemic*. Norton, 2012.

Ramoneda, Josep. *La Izquierda Necesaria. Contra el autoritarismo posdemocrático*. RBA, 2012.

Rentmeester, Casey. *Heidegger and the Environment*. Rowman & Littlefield, 2016.

Richardson, Katherine, et al. "Earth Beyond Six of Nine Planetary Boundaries." *Science Advances* 37, no. 9 (September 2023): https://www.science.org/doi/epdf/10.1126/sciadv.adh2458.
Robey, David. Introduction to *The Open Work*, by Umberto Eco, trans. Anna Cancogni, vii–xxxii. Cambridge University Press, 1989.
Rorty, Richard. *Achieving Our Country*. Harvard University Press, 1997.
———. *Essays on Heidegger and Others*. Cambridge University Press, 1991.
———. *Objectivity, Relativism, and Truth*. Cambridge University Press, 1991.
———. *Philosophy and Social Hope*. Penguin, 1999.
Roy, Olivier. *Jihad and Death: The Global Appeal of the Islamic State*. Trans. Cynthia Schoch. Oxford University Press, 2017.
Sandford, Stella. *How to Read Beauvoir*. Granta, 2006.
———. *Vegetal Sex: Philosophy of Plants*. Bloomsbury, 2022.
Schwarz, Elke. *Death Machine: The Ethics of Violent Technologies*. Manchester University Press, 2018.
Sennett, Richard. *Authority*. Secker & Warburg, 1980.
Sisto, Davide. *Online Afterlives: Immortality, Memory, and Grief in Digital Culture*. Trans. Bonnie McClellan-Broussard. MIT Press, 2020.
Smith, Justin E. H. *The Internet Is Not What You Think It Is: A History, a Philosophy, a Warning*. Princeton University Press, 2022.
Snyder, Timothy. *Black Earth: The Holocaust as History and Warning*. Penguin, 2015.
Stanley, Manfred. *The Technological Conscience: Survival and Dignity in an Age of Expertise*. Free Press, 1979.
Stiegler, Bernard. *The Age of Disruption*. Trans. Daniel Ross. Polity, 2019.
———. *Qu'appelle-t-on Panser?* Tome 2: *La leçon de Greta Thunberg*. Les Liens qui libèrent, 2020.
Stiglitz, Joseph. *Globalization and Its Discontents*. Norton, 2002.
Svenaeus, Fredrik. *The Hermeneutics of Medicine and the Phenomenology of Health: Steps Towards a Philosophy of Medical Practice*. Kluwer Academic, 2000.
Taminiaux, Jacques. *La fille de Thrace et le penseur professionnel: Arendt et Heidegger*. Éditions Payot, 1992.
Tavoillot, Pierre-Henri, Emmanuelle Hénin, and Xavier-Laurent Salvador, eds. *Après la déconstruction. L'université au défi des idéologies*. Odile Jacob, 2023.

Vasterling, Veronica. "Political Hermeneutics: Hannah Arendt's Contribution to Hermeneutic Philosophy." In *Gadamer's Hermeneutics and the Art of Conversation*, ed. A. Wiercinski, 571–82. LIT Verlag, 2011.

Vigen, Aana Marie, and Patricia Beattie Jung, eds. *God, Science, Sex, Gender: An Interdisciplinary Approach to Christian Ethics*. University of Illinois Press, 2010.

Villa, Dana R. *Arendt and Heidegger: The Fate of the Political*. Princeton University Press, 1996.

Vattimo, Gianni. *Being and Its Surroundings*. Ed. Giuseppe Iannantuono, Alberto Martinengo, and Santiago Zabala. Trans. Corrado Federici. McGill-Queen's University Press, 2018.

———. *Dialogue with Nietzsche*. Trans. William McCuaig. Columbia University Press, 2006.

———. *A Farewell to Truth*. Trans. Robert Valgenti. Columbia University Press, 2011.

———. *Scritti filosofici e politici*. La nave di Teseo, 2021.

———. *Of Reality*. Trans. Robert Valgenti. Columbia University Press, 2012.

Vercellone, Federico. *Filosofia del tatuaggio. Il corpo tra autenticità e contaminazione*. Bollati Boringhieri, 2023.

Wallace, Bob. *Big Farms Make Big Flu: Dispatches on Infectious Disease, Agribusiness, and the Nature of Science*. Monthly Review Press, 2016.

Wallace-Wells, David. *The Uninhabitable Earth: A Story of the Future*. Tim Duggan, 2019.

Weber, Max. *Economy and Society: An Outline of Interpretive Sociology*. Vol. 2. University of California Press, 1978.

Whyte, Kyle. "Time as Kinship." In *The Cambridge Companion to Environmental Humanities*, ed. Jeffrey Cohen and Stephanie Foote, 39–55. Cambridge University Press, 2021.

Wild, Markus. "Heidegger and Trakl: Language Speaks in the Poet's Poem." In *Paths in Heidegger's Later Thought*, ed. Günter Figal, Diego D'Angelo, Tobias Keiling, and Guang Yang, 45–63. Indiana University Press, 2020.

Woods, Andrew. "Cultural Marxism and the Cathedral: Two Alt-Right Perspectives on Critical Theory." In *Critical Theory and the Humanities in the Age of the Alt-Right*, ed. Christine M. Battista and Melissa R. Sande, 39–59. Palgrave Macmillan, 2019.

Zabala, Santiago. *Being at Large: Freedom in the Age of Alternative Facts.* McGill-Queen's University Press, 2017.

———. "Imagining a Philosophy of Warnings for Our Greatest Emergency." *Philosophy Today* 64, no. 4 (Fall 2020): 1–5.

———. "The Philosophy of Warnings. Facing Up to the Emergencies Surrounding Us." *Institute of Art and Ideas News*, October 7, 2020, https://iai.tv/articles/the-philosophy-of-warnings-auid-1646.

———. *The Remains of Being: Hermeneutic Ontology After Metaphysics.* Columbia University Press, 2009.

———. *Why Only Art Can Save Us: Aesthetics and the Absence of Emergency.* Columbia University Press, 2017.

Žižek, Slavoj. *Disparities.* Bloomsbury, 2016.

———. *Hegel in a Wired Brain.* Bloomsbury, 2020.

———. *A Left That Dares to Speak Its Name.* Polity, 2020.

———. *Like a Thief in Broad Daylight: Power in the Era of Post-Humanity.* Penguin, 2018.

———. *Living in the End Times.* Verso, 2011.

———. *Pandemic 2. Chronicles of a Time Lost.* OR, 2020.

———. *The Parallax View.* MIT Press, 2006.

———. *Sex and the Failed Absolute.* Bloomsbury, 2019.

———. *The Year of Dreaming Dangerously.* Verso, 2012.

INDEX

absence of emergency, 9, 12; Heidegger on, 35, 65, 189n3, 215n10; pandemic as, 9; and state of emergency, 65; as warning, viii, 174; world events as, 61, 63–64

Adorno, Theodore, 4, 79, 81

Agamben, Giorgio, 6–7, 126, 162, 181n10; theory of exception, 64

"Age of the World Picture, The" (Heidegger), 128

Agrippa (Henri-Corneille Agrippa de Nettesheim), 40

Ahmed, Sara, 163, 213n5

Allen, Woody, 29

Altman, Sam, 102

Amis, Martin, 171

Anderson Todd, 111, 192n32

Apollo, 4

Arendt, Hannah, 8, 16, 18, 30, 114, 116, 123, 175; on Eichmann, 56–59; and Gadamer, 54–55; and Heidegger, 52–53; and hermeneutics, 55–56; on imagination, 55–56; rationalization of the world, 79; on scientific knowledge, 53–54; on thinking, 59; warning of, 51–52, 56–59, 81, 144, 119, 175. *See also* banality of evil; inability to think

Ares, Macarena, 162, 213n4

Aristotle, 48, 52, 127, 154

artificial intelligence, 98–103, 116, 118, 196n3; Bridle on, 103, 199n15; Chomsky on, 100, 103; DeepSeek, 199n15; Heidegger and, 99–100; unemployment, 198n11

Assange, Julian, 163, 171

Atwood, Margaret, 85–86

Augustine, Saint, 4, 156, 158

Bacon, Francis, 4

Bachelard, Gaston, 4

Badiou, Alain, 5

banality of evil, 51, 56; Arendt on, 114, 175; as a warning, 57

Baker, Stewart, 116
Banksy, 12
Barrett, Willian, 29
Bauman, Zygmunt, 5, 79–80
Beauvoir, Simone De, 8, 16, 18, 51–52, 123, 175; and the "don't say gay" law, 111; on freedom, 42–43, 46, 107; and gender, 40; influence of Heidegger, 43–44, 46–47; ontological difference, 47; and Sartre, 42–43, 46; and *The Second Sex*, 39–40; and sex difference, 45–46; warnings, 40–42, 44–45, 48, 106, 111; on women as "other," 45–47. See also Eichmann, Adolf; "one is not born, but rather becomes a woman"; *Second Sex, The*
Being and Time (Heidegger), 30, 47, 52–53, 127, 132, 146
Being warned, Being, and being, 121–22, 126, 129, 172182n18; and facts; thinking and, viii; truth, 12, 122, 169; living past, 133; future, 135, 163; signs, 137; requires listening, 142, 149; and interpretation, 154
Bengio, Joshua, 102
Benjamin, Walter, 5, 125
Bernstein, Richard, 52
Biden, Joseph, 93
Black Earth (Snyder), 173
Blanquer, Jean-Michel, 75
Boetzkes, Amanda, 10
Bolsonaro, Jair, 65, 92
Borde, Constance, 41

Bridle, James, 103, 199n15
Breivik, Anders: on cultural Marxism, 194n10; manifesto, 90, 194n13; murderous act of, 89–92, 95
Bruns Gerald L. 154
Buddha, 25
Bush, George W., 64,
Butler, Judith, 3, 11, 162; on Arendt, 60; on Beauvoir, 40, 185n9; on gender, 106; and gender ideology, 199n3, 201n6, 202n12; and gender studies, 111

Cable, Vince, 165
Caldwell, Graham. vii, 7; visual example of warnings, 125–126, 129, 131
Can the Monster Speak? (Preciado), 105
Cassandra, 4, 161, 217n2; coefficient, 172, 217n2
Castoriadis, Cornelius, 17, 176
Caviezel, Jim, 94
Charon, Rita, 166, 207n1, 207n6; and limits of bioethics, 142; as patient, 141; and radical listening, 139–41, 149
Chung-shu, Tung, 4
Chomsky, Noam, 100, 103
Clavis scripturae sacrae (Flacius), 154
climate change, 1, 5, 9; as greatest emergency, 64, 65, 121, 151–152, 164, 167, 173–175, 188n1, 213n2, 214n6
Clinton, Hillary, 92

Collins, Ben, 93
Coming of Age, The (Beauvoir), 40
Compound Eye (Caldwell), vii, 125, 131
Corbyn, Jeremy, 165
COVID-19 pandemic, 2–3, 61, 63, 181n10; and emergency, 61, 63–65; as a warning, 171–72; and *Where Are We Now: The Epidemic as Politics*, 6–7
crisis, 1, 5, 9, 179n1, 212n2, 213n4; 2008 financial, 61, 63; Latour on, 171; pandemic as, 7, 61, 64; and science, 61, 63; and Thunberg, 164–66, 169, 174; as warning, 121, 149, 162–63, 174
Critique of Pure Reason (Kant), 20

Dalai Lama, 93
Dannhauer, Johann, 154
Danto, Arthur C., 125
d'Eaubonne Françoise, 5
Decline of the West, The (Spengler), 79
Derrida, Jacques, 66, 75, 79, 123, 131, 148; on avenir, vii, 15, 131, 133; and deconstruction, 205n11; on the future, 133–35, 137, 206n12; and truth, 133–35, 206n12
DeSantis Ron, 109–11
Descartes, 17, 32, 66, 70
de Scudéry, Madeleine, 40
Dewey, John, 6
Dialectic of Enlightenment (Adorno and Horkheimer), 79
Dilthey, Wilhelm, 53, 156, 169

Docherty Bonnie, 118
Don't Look Up (McKay), 1, 179n1
Dussel, Enrique, 173

Eco, Umberto, 2, 131; and the difference between signs and signals, 135–36; and the real, 136–37; and semiotics, 136; and signs, 206n17, 207n19
Eden, Kathy, 155
education, 88, 110; Gadamer and, 167–68, 215n13; medical, 142; and warning, 6; Thunberg and, 166
Eichmann, Adolf, 51, 56–59, 187n15
Eichmann in Jerusalem: The Banality of Evil (Arendt), 56, 114
emergency, 2; Heidegger's notion of, 65, 167; and pandemic, 3, 9, 11–12, 61; translation of, 184n9, 189n4. *See also* absence of emergency
Escobar, Pepe, 63

facts, 67, 77; alternative, 62; for Arendt 54; for Beauvoir, 45; and Fish, 83; and history, 132–33, 137; as insufficient, 10, 164, 167; for Latour, 82; moral, 72–73; and Nietzsche, 20, 22; and philosophy, 69; and politics of warning, 172; for Žižek 78
"Faith and Knowledge" (Hegel), 20
Fanon, Frantz, 5
Fassin, Didier, 74

Ferraris, Maurizio, 70–72; and Vattimo 76–77, 81
Feuerbach, Ludwig, 17
Fish, Stanley, 10; and facts, 83
Fiumara, Corradi Gemma, 141; and listening, 145, 166; and logos, 143–44
Flacius, 154
Fortuyn, Pim, 91,
Fosse, Jon, 30
Foster, John, 153
Foucault, Michel, 3; and warning, 5
Francis (pope), 93, 108
Frank, Nathaniel, 110, 202n13
Frege, Gottlob, 29
Freud, Sigmund, 21
future, vii, 4, 131, 153, 172; and AI, 103; and Arendt, 114; as avenir, 18, 123, 135, 162–63; of democracy, 73; and Derrida, 133–35, 137, 206n12; difference from avenir, vii, 15, 131, 133; and events, 61; and Heidegger, 65, 205n9; and history, 132; Nietzsche, 206n13; and predictions, 58; as signs, 161–62; and warning, 59, 121, 123, 126, 133, 172; Žižek, 123, 166

Gabriel, Markus, 70, 78, 81; and moral facts, 72–73
Gadamer, Hans-Georg, 54–55, 83, 145, 123; classical, 215n15; and dialogue, 147; on education, 167–68, 215n13; on Heidegger, 129; and horizon, 130; on listening, 147–49
Gates, Bill, 102
Gay Science, The (Nietzsche), 25
Geiselberger, Heinrich, 62, 188n1
gender ideology, 201n6, 200n5; and DeSantis, 109, 199n3; meaning of, 200n5; and Trump, 109
Glazer, Jonathan, 172–73; and warning, 171
global return to order through realism, 2, 9, 175; and AI, 103; believers and, 95; politics of warning and, 172; as symptom of gender crusade, 107; Vattimo and, 77, 82; and warnings, 61, 62, 163; weapons and, 119; Žižek against, 123, 191n26. See also realism
God, vii, 20; and Nietzsche, 23–24; objectivity of, 25; and truth, 23
"God is dead," 19, 76; Hegel and, 20; Nietzsche and, 25–26; roots of, 20; and the *Übermensch*, 27; as a warning, 19, 24–26
Goethe, 78
Gordon, Jane Anna and Lewis R., 8, and warning, 121–22
Gothlin, Eva, 43
Graff, Agnieszka, 108
Greenwald, Glenn, 117,
Grondin, Jean, 154
Grumach, Ernst, 52

Habermas, Jürgen, 29
Hamilton, Tucker "Cinco," 118

INDEX ❦ 237

Handmaid's Tale, The
  (Atwood), 85
Hansen, Stanley, 12
Haraway, Donna, 3
Harris, Kamala, 99
Harris, Sam, 74
Harman, Graham, 70
Harvey, Fiona, 152,
Hassan, Ihab, 79–80
Häusermann, Silja, 162, 213n4
Hayden, Michael, 116
Hegel, Georg Wilhelm Friedrich, 16, 19; and the classical, 215n15; the future, 4; and "God is dead," 20, 29, 47
Heidegger, Martin, 8, 15–18, 40, 42, 51, 55, 123; absence of emergency, 35, 65, 189n3, 215n10; and Arendt, 52–54, 56, and Beauvoir, 43–44; and Dasein, 43, 53, 127, 157–58, 212n10; and destruction, 126, 143; on hearing and listening, 145–47, 149, 208n12, 209n14; history and past, 131–33, 135, 137, 205n9; interpretation and hermeneutics, 37, 53, 155–59; Klee and, 125; modern representation, 66–67, 99, 128; notion of Dasein, 212n10; notion of emergency, 35, 65, 167; notion of truth, 212n18; and ontological difference, 129, 148; politics, 29–30; the question of Being, 30, 37, 46, 127–28; and Sartre, 47; and science's inability to think, 36, 38, 100; the technological in, 34–35, 184n9, 102; thinking in, 32–33; warning, 3, 15, 30–31, 35–36, 53, 99, 122, 129, 175. *See also* Arendt, Hannah; Beauvoir, Simone de; inability to think
Heine, Heinrich, 20
Heraclitus, 30, 132
hermeneutics, 8, 37, 70, 77, 153–54, 156; and Arendt, 54–55, 59; and Gadamer, 54–55, 59; Heidegger's, 35, 37, 156–59, 211n5; and Hermes, 154–55; origins of, 211n5; and Schleiermacher, 156; of suspicion, 21; and Vattimo 82; and Žižek 78, 81
Herodotus, 154
Hitler, Adolf, 26, 29–30, 60
Hinton, Geoffrey, 101–102
Histories (Herodotus), 154
Hobbes, Thomas, 4
Homeland (Glatter), 113, 119
Human, All Too Human (Nietzsche), 22
Hume, David, 29
Husserl, Edmund, 47, 130; warning, 5

inability to think, 118; Arendt on, 51, 56, 114, 118; Heidegger on, 35, 38, 99–100
intensity, 11; and Thunberg's activism, 169; and truth, 124, 162–63, 168; and warning, 12, 163, 173

interpretation, 153–54, 156, 159; anarchy of, 155; Arendt snf, 54, 59; battle of, 153–55, 157–59; battle for, 153, 151–55, 157–59; Beauvoir and, 48; and demythification, 21; Gadamer and, 130; Heidegger and, 127, 155–58; Kant and, 4; Nietzsche and, 20; rejection of, 10–11; and truth, 10; Vattimo and, 76–77; and warnings, 17, 27, 126, 154, 160
Irrational Man (Allen), 29

Jaar, Alfredo, 171–72
Jaber, Sultan al-, 151
Jacobs Michael, 153
John Paul II (pope), 107
Jonas, Hans, 51
Jones, Owen, 64

Kaing Guek Eav (Comrade Duch), 114, 119
Kant, Immanuel, 10, 17, 70; and God's death, 20; warning 4; and women, 29, 48
Karadžić, Radovan, 115
kennardphillipps, 163, 213n5
Kennebeck, Sonia, 113
Kepel, Gilles, 87
Kierkegaard, Søren, 16
Klee, Paul, 125
Klein, Naomi, 12, 62; activism, 214n6; and scientists, 172–73; and Thunberg, 164–65
Korolczuk, Elżbieta, 108
Kuhn, Thomas, 130

Lady Gaga, 93
Latour, Bruno, 10, 175; facts, 82; warning, 7, 171, 218n9
Leibniz, 66, 70
Lévi-Strauss Claude, 80, 136–37
Lévy, Henry-Bernard, 82; and role of intellectual, 68–69
Lind, William, 91
listening, 1, 9, 11–12, 210n26, 144; and Charon, 139–42, 166, 207n1, 207n6; dialogue and, 144–45; difference from hearing, 142, 146–48, 208n12, 209n14, 210n26; Fiumara and, 142–43, 166; and Gadamer, 147–49; and Heidegger, 145–46, 149, 208n12, 209n14; interpretation and, 82, 122, 126, 172; logos and, 142–143; and Nancy, 147–49; radical, 139–41, 145, 149, 163; to warnings, 27, 133, 142, 172
Löwith, Karl, 52
Lucas, Caroline, 165
Luther, 53, 126, 156, 158; and "God is dead," 19–20
Lyotard, Jean-François, 79–81

Machiavelli, 102
Malabou, Catherine, 17, 126
Mallick, Terrence, 30
Malovany-Chevallier, Sheila, 41
Mann, Bonnie, 42
Marcuse, Herbert, 17; warning, 5, 79–80

Marx, Karl, 21
Massera, Emilio, 114, 119
Mearsheimer, John, 63
Meddeb, Abdelwahab, 194n8
Meillassoux, Quentin, 70
Meloni, Giorgia, 92, 175–76, 219n11
Merleau-Ponty, Maurice, 42–43
Milei, Javier, 65, 92, 175–76
Mladić, Ratko, 114, 119
Morozov, Evgeny, 82
Morris, Errol, 113
Musk, Ellon, 82
Mussolini, Benito, 30
Myrdal, Gunnar, 46

Nancy, Jean-Luc, 126, 145; pandemic and, 7; and listening, 147–49
narrative medicine, 207n6; and Charon, 139–141, 173, 207n6
National Bird (Kennback), 113
Naughton, John, 98
Nietzsche, Friedrich, 8, 16, 19, 66, 76, 130; and Arendt, 52; and Beauvoir, 39, 40; and demythification, 21–22; facts, 20, 22; future and, 206n13; and God, 19–20, 23–24; and "God is dead," 19–20, 25–26; and Heidegger, 30, 36, 40; and interpretation, 20, 27; and *The Sinner*, 19; and *The Sopranos*, 19; and truth, 22–23, 135, 206n13; and *Übermensch*, 26–27; and

Vattimo, 27; warning, 4, 8, 16, 18–19, 23, 30, 86–87, 123, 175
Notebooks (Heidegger), 35
Novák, Novák, 109

Oakley, Anne, 40
Obama, Barack, 93, 114
Of Reality: The Purpose of Philosophy (Vattimo), 76
O'Leary, Dale, 107, 200n4
Oreskes, Naomi, 10; and realism, 82, 192n31
Origins of Totalitarianism, The (Arendt), 56, 79
Orlando: My Political Biography (Preciado), 105
"one is not born, but rather becomes a woman," 39; translation of, 41–42, 44–45; as a warning, 44–45, 48, 51, 106
On the Genealogy of Morals (Nietzsche), 22

Parmenides, 4, 127
Parshley, Howard Madison, 41
Pascal, 20
Peabody, Francis, 140
Peirce, Charles S., 136–37
Pensées (Pascal), 20
Peri hermeneias (De interpretatione) (Aristotle), 154
Peterson, Jordan, 74, 82; and Žižek, 79, 192n28
Phenomenology of Sprit (Hegel), 20
philosophy of animals, 2–3, 180n4
philosophy of insects, 2–3, 180n4

philosophy of plants, 2–3, 122, 180n4
philosophy of tattoos, 122
philosophy of warnings, vii–viii, 2–3, 11, 21, 123; and Being warned, 122; and *Compound Eye*, 125; philosophers of, 19, 40, 162, 215n12; and preventing emergencies, 12
Phoenix, Joaquin, 29
Pilger, John, 171–72
Plato, 3, 20, 52, 59, 192n31; and Being, 31; and Gadamer, 167; and Hermes, 154–155
Plutarch, 20
Piketty, Thomas, 6,
Podesta, John, 92
politics of warning, 13, 172–73, 175
Pol Pot, 115
Popper, Karl, 79, 81, 195n17
Postmodern Condition, The (Lyotard), 80
Preciado, Paul, B., 111, 162, 199n1; *Can the Monster Speak?* 105; *Orlando: My Political Biography*, 105; the nonbinary revolution, 105–6
predictions, 2, 4, 94; and AI, 100, 116; difference from warnings, 8, 12, 16, 17, 44–45, 83, 129, 163, 174; future and, 15–16; Žižek, 61
pressure, 11–12, 63; and *Compound Eye*, vii; political, 172–73; and Thunberg's activism, 169; and truth, 163, 168, 173; and warning 12, 121–22, 124, 131, 162–63, 173

prophets, 3, 16
Putin, Vladimir, 102

Quammen, David, 63
QAnon, 92–95, 195n20, 196n21, 196n22
Quine, W. V. O., 67

Ramoneda, Josep, 175, 218n8
Ratzinger, Joseph, 107
Read, Rupert, 152, 154
realism, 17, 42, 67, 70, 75, 80, 83, 175; without authority, 10, 62, 82, 176; and Beauvoir, 44–45; and contemporary philosophy, 67, 70, 11n8, 189n8, 189n9; moral, 72–73; Heidegger and, 36; Oreskes and, 82; transparent, 10–11, 62, 82; Vattimo and, 76–77, 82; Žižek and, 78, 191n26. *See also* global return to order through realism
Richard Barry, 91
Ricoeur, Paul, 21, 53
Roberts, Ian, 100
Rorty, Richard, 3, 123; and metaphysics, 68, 216n17; and warning, 34, 62
Rothschild, Mike, 95
Rousseau, Jean-Jacques, 40
Roy, Oliver, 87–89

Said, Edward, 5,
Sartre, Jean-Paul, 42–43, 47
Saussure, Ferdinand de, 135
Scahill, Jeremy, 117

INDEX ᖇ 241

Schleiermacher, Friedrich, 155
Schmitt, Carl, 64
Schwarz, Elke, 114
science, vii, 3, 10, 16–17, 21, 100, 136, 173, 176; Arendt and, 53, 54; Gadamer and, 168; Heidegger and, 30, 32, 34–37, 53, 131; listening to, 1, 166; Nietzsche and, 22, 25; and realism, 67–68; Rorty and, 2026n17; Searle and, 68–69; Vattimo and, 217n4
"science does not think," 36–37; as a warning, 34, 36; Heidegger and, 30, 32–37, 53
Searle, John, 73; and realism, 76, 78; and role of intellectual, 68–69
Second Sex, The (Beauvoir), 39, 40–41, 44, 46–48, 185n12
sign, 2, 12, 172; and Being warned, 121; difference from signal, 126, 131, 135; Eco and, 2, 135–37, 206n17; from the future, 11, 121, 162, 165; Nietzsche and, 206n13; Žižek and, 161–62
Simons, Margaret, 41
Smith, Justin E. H., 6
Snowden, Edward, 63, 163
Snyder, Timothy, 173
social media, 94, 122; Butler and, 11; Fish and, 10; philosophy of, 122
Sound of Freedom, The (Monteverde), 94
Spencer, Robert, 91
Spengler, 79
Spivak, Gayatri, 75
Socrates, 49, 59; and warning, 4

Sommers, Christina Hoff, 78; and factual feminism, 74
Stanley, Manfred, 5
state of exception, 7, 64; Agamben and 6, 7
Stiegler, Bernard, 12, 215n12
Stiglitz, Joseph, 62,
Sunak, Rishi, 98–99
Syriana (Gaghan), 113, 119

Tarski, Alfred, 77
Testaments, The (Atwood), 85–86
Thomas, Saint, 48
Thunberg, Greta, 1–2, 11–12, 164–65; and absent emergency, 215n10; and crisis, 164–66, 169, 174; Stiegler and, 215n12; and warning, 164, 165–66, 169, 172; Žižek and, 61
Thus Spoke Zarathustra (Nietzsche), 26
trigger warnings, viii, 172, 217n2
Trotta, Margarethe von, 50
Trump, Donald, 61, 64–65, 176; and gender ideology, 85, 109; and QAnon, 92–95
truth, 3,5, 88–89, 124–25, 136; and culture of description, 68; Gadame andr, 54, 148, 167–68; Heidegger and, 3, 31–32, 36, 53, 67, 128, 159, 212n18; and interpretation, 10, 158–59; Nietzsche and, 22–23; Oreskes and, 192n31; Vattimo and, 81; and warning, 11–12, 16, 162–63, 166, 169, 173; Žižek and, 78

Truth About Muhammad: Founder of the World's Most Intolerant Religion, The (Spencer), 91
Truth and Method (Gadamer), 54, 147
Twilight of the Idols (Nietzsche), 22

Uspiz, Ada, 51
Übermensch, 86, 95; Nietzsche and, 26–27

Van Gogh, Vincent, 125
Vattimo, Gianni, 79, 173; and global return to order through realism, 69, 82, 76–77; and hermeneutics, 154; and Nietzsche, 27; and politics, 217n4; and postmodernity, 81, 190n13
Vercellone, Federico, 122
Videla. Jorge, 115
Villa, Dana, 56

Warhol, Andy, 125
warning, 2–4, 8, 11, 86, 101, 121, 137, 163, 171–73, 176, 180n1; as absent emergency, 9, 174; Agamben and, 6–7, 126, 162, 181n10; Arendt and, 51–52, 56–59, 144, 119, 175; Beauvoir and, 40–42, 44–45, 48, 106, 111; and compound eye, vii, 126; and crisis, 7, 122, 149; difference from predictions, 2, 7–9, 16, 83, 129, 131; in documentary, 51–52, 106, 113, 186n2, 202n1; and facts, 82, 122; in films, 113, 119, 171–73, 179n1; future and, 11, 15–16, 45, 59, 121, 123, 126, 133, 172; Danesi and, 218n9; Heidegger and, 3, 15, 30–31, 35–36, 53, 99, 122, 129, 175; and inability to listen, 2–3, 7–9, 61, 62, 64; Latour and, 7, 218n9; Nietzsche and, 4, 8, 16, 18–19, 23, 30, 86–87, 95, 123, 175; as a pandemic, 7, 173; philosophers of, 19, 40, 162, 215n12; prevention of, 220n12; Ramoneda and, 175, 218n8; and series, 19, 97, 103; Thunberg and, 164, 165–66, 169, 172; trigger, viii; weakness of, 17, 24, 27, 163, 174; Žižek, 61, 162–63, 212n2. *See also* interpretation; philosophy of warnings; politics of warnings; pressure; truth
Watumull, Jeffrey, 100
Weber, Max, 6
Weiss, Bari, 74
Wenders, Win, 113
What Is Called Thinking (Heidegger), 15, 33, 53
Where Are We Now? The Epidemic as Politics (Agamben), 6–7, 181n10
Whyte, Kyle, 5, 174
Wilde, Oscar, 171
Winfrey, Oprah, 93
Wittgenstein Ludwig, 145, 169
Wolf, Brandon, 110
Woolf, Virginia, 105
Wylie, Christopher, 163

Year of Dreaming Dangerously, The (Žižek), 160
Ye'or Bat, 91

Zadrozny, Brandy, 93
Žižek, Slavoj, 1–2, 7, 61, 82, 91, 161–62; and facts, 78; and future, 8, 123; and Heidegger, 184n9; hermeneutics, 81, 123–24; and Peterson, 79, 191n28; and realism, 78, 123, 191n26; and Thunberg, 1, 165–66, 215n12; and warning, 162–63, 212n2
Zone of Interest, The (Glazner), 171
Zuckerberg, Mark, 82

GPSR Authorized Representative: Easy Access System Europe, Mustamäe tee 50, 10621 Tallinn, Estonia, gpsr.requests@easproject.com

www.ingramcontent.com/pod-product-compliance
Lightning Source LLC
Chambersburg PA
CBHW022048290426
44109CB00014B/1026